Programming C#
With Visual Studio .NET 2005

By Jeffery Suddeth

Programming C# With Visual Studio .NET 2005
Copyright © 2006 by Jeffery Suddeth

For more information contact

Jeffery Suddeth
PO Box 4182
Wheaton, IL 60189-4182

jeff@jefferysuddeth.com
http://www.jefferysuddeth.com

ISBN: 1-4116-6447-7

Printed in the USA. Lulu Press, Napa, California,
http://www.Lulu.com.

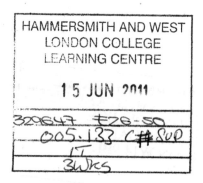
Microsoft product screen shots reprinted with permission from Microsoft Corporation
Microsoft, Excel, Access, and Visual C# are Trademarks of Microsoft Corporation
The Google logo is a Trademark of Google Inc

For Rachel, Katy, Evy, and Ben.

Acknowledgements

Creating this book required help and support from a number of individuals and I would like to thank them all.

- My editor, Francha Menhard, for helping me make this book better than I ever thought it could be
- Eric Wolfe for being my technical editor and giving me his support and encouragement when I needed it
- The cover was created by John Scaletta at Digital Studio Inc in Lagrange, IL. Thanks for the great cover, John
- The people in Microsoft's Support and PR departments for helping me get the information I needed quickly
- A big shout out to the people in the Support department at lulu.com for helping me realize a lifelong dream. Also to the people in the lulu.com forums
- And of course this never would have happened without the support of my loving wife and kids who tolerated my long hours.

Table of Contents

Preface

The computing industry is consistently coming up with new innovations to make software development easier than ever. One of the latest innovations is .NET, a platform for application development that includes a vast programming library for many common tasks. Several programming languages exist that can target the .NET platform, with C# being one of the most popular.

A quick search for programming jobs on the Internet will show you that C# programmers are in high demand. The language is favored by many programmers because it offers features that C++ and Java programmers have come to love over the years.

Who is this book for?

This book is for beginning and intermediate programmers who want to learn software development with C#. The beginning of the book teaches the fundamentals of the C# language, using programs that are short and to the point, yet complete, so that a beginning programmer can see how it all fits together. Later, the programs are more complex and involve more advanced concepts.

How This Book Is Organized

The purpose of this book is to teach how to create software using the C# programming language. First we teach the fundamentals of the C# language and basic programming techniques like Object Oriented Programming, arrays, and event driven programming. Each chapter builds on the previous, beginning with simple input and output and then moving on to logic, object oriented programming, arrays and collections, delegates, events, and Exception handling.

After covering the fundamentals, we look at the Visual Studio environment to learn about solutions and projects, debugging, and using the designer to create a Windows application. In the remaining chapters you will apply all your knowledge from the previous chapters to learn how to create windows programs, database applications, multithreaded programs, and network programs.

The Curly Braces

Like other C-style languages, C# uses curly braces to denote blocks of code. This section briefly explains placement of braces so that beginning programmers will not be confused when the see different styles in the book.

When I begin and end a block of source code I typically put the curly braces on their own line because it is easier on my eyes when I read the later.

```
public void Demo()
{
        // function body here
}
```

In some cases, however, I moved the opening brace to the end of the previous line so that the program would take fewer lines and fit within a smaller space. This style is often used by Java programmers.

```
public void Demo(){
        // function body here
}
```

Either technique is perfectly valid, but the second technique was used in some places to avoid spilling the last line or two of code over to the next page. As you type the programs in this book, you should use the style that you are more comfortable with.

What Software You Need

To get the most out of this book, you will need Visual Studio 2005. Many of the features shown in this book are new to Visual Studio 2005 and .NET version 2.0. If you are using earlier versions, some of the programs in this book will not compile.

All the programs from this book can be compiled with the .NET SDK, which you can download for free from Microsoft. However, the setup program for the .NET SDK is a large file to download. Readers who do not have a fast Internet connection, may want to order it on a CD.

Chapter 15 is about database access and some of the examples require a database server, such as Microsoft Access or SQL Server.

Downloading the Example Programs

The source code for all the examples can be downloaded from my website, http://www.jefferysuddeth.com. That page also has a link where you can email me with any questions. I will try to answer as many as I can.

Chapter 1 - .NET and the C# Language

This is an exciting time for the world of software development. Over the years, programmers have seen technology go from machine languages, to assembly languages, to high level languages like BASIC and C. Then Object oriented programming changed the way software was written, and languages like C++ and Java dominated the market place, and for good reason. These modern programming languages where more than just mere syntax. They offered extensive programming libraries, as well as support for object oriented programming and structured error handling, both of which promised to speed up development times and reduce the number of bugs in software.

Then Microsoft released .NET, a program execution environment that can be targeted by many programming languages and platforms.

Business logic written for the .NET platform can be integrated seamlessly by other .NET programs, whether they are web based, desktop based, or even written in a different language. Programmers have never been able to write software faster, nor get more usability out of their applications. One language that targets the .NET platform is C# - the topic of this book.

The .NET Platform

The software development world is in constant change. One of the most recent and largest changes was the unleashing of .NET, a platform that provides a common runtime environment that can be targeted by any programming language. Programmers can use any of several languages that support .NET, making application logic easier to reuse in other environments. For example, logic from a .NET application that manages inventory could be seamlessly integrated into other applications, including web based applications or programs written in other languages.

Intermediate Language and the Common Language Runtime

.NET programs execute within a managed environment called the *Common Language Runtime (CLR)*. Programs written for the .NET platform do not compile directly to machine code, as with programs written in other languages. Instead they compile to numeric instructions that get translated at runtime by the CLR into machine instructions, and then executed. These numeric instructions are part of a language called *Microsoft Intermediate Language (MSIL)*. All .NET languages understand how to work with MSIL, making it easy for programs written in other .NET languages such as Visual Basic.NET to use functionality written in C#.

The Common Type System

Another way the .NET platform makes it easy to use functionality from other languages is by defining a set of data types that all .NET languages can implement. These data types are defined in the *Common Type System (CTS)*, a specification that includes integers, characters, Booleans, and other data types. Thanks to the CTS, a string can be passed from one .NET language to another without having to convert to other formats. This is because behind the scenes both languages are using the same data format. Anyone who has had to pass strings between C++ and Visual Basic before .NET will appreciate the CTS.

The Framework Class Library

There exists a large library of classes within .NET that your programs can use. This library is called the *Framework Class Library (FCL)*. The FCL provides thousands of classes for most of the common programming logic on Windows. Now that you have been overloaded with acronyms, look to the following list for a quick summary.

.NET Acronyms
- CLR – Common Language Runtime
- MSIL – Microsoft Intermediate Language
- CTS – Common Type System
- FCL – The Framework Class Library

The C# Language

C# (pronounced like the music key, *C Sharp*) is a programming language developed by Microsoft. Because it uses the .NET platform, it has an extensive set of software components, making it a highly productive programming tool. With C#, you can quickly create Windows based applications, web based applications, Console applications, network programs, database applications, or programming libraries that can be used by other applications.

C# is an object oriented language, which means that a C# program consists of a set of objects that communicate with each other at runtime. These objects are described by classes that you define when you write your program. C# also has exceptional error handling features and automated memory management (a feature called *garbage collection*) to make application development easier.

Introduction to Object Oriented Programming

Object oriented programming has grown in popularity over the years. When done properly, it makes the functionality of your programs easier to reuse in other applications. It also allows you to extend the functionality of your existing applications without changing existing source code. The net affect is shorter development times and fewer bugs. This is all possible because object oriented programming minimizes the dependencies between systems by hiding the implementation details.

This section will briefly introduce you to the object oriented concepts of Encapsulation and Inheritance, which are the main topic of chapter 7. Encapsulation refers to the way a class contains data, objects, and the methods that operate on them. Inheritance refers to the ability of one class to inherit the characteristics of another. Both concepts are central to object oriented programming because they describe the relationships between the classes.

Encapsulation

In object oriented programming a class provides an abstraction for data and functionality so that we do not have to worry about all the minute details of the implementation of the class. One way of abstracting those details is encapsulate them. That is, to contain them within, so that the user of the class does not have to deal with them. For example, a class that provides a method to download a web page needs a TCP socket, an Internet address, and information about the HTTP protocol. All those details can be encapsulated within the class so you do not have to worry about them. Then you can download the web page by calling a single method exposed by the class. The WebBrowser class used in Chapter 13 is one example of this.

Another example is a car. When you drive a car, you only worry about the gas pedal, brake pedal, and steering wheel. Those provide the interface for driving the car. The parts of the engine and how they work together are the details encapsulated inside the car; hidden from the user. You don't have to understand those details to drive the car.

Inheritance

Inheritance allows programmers to create a class that inherits the characteristics of another class. The inherited class is called the base class. The class that inherits the base is the subclass. Any public method or data contained in the base class will also be accessible through a subclass.

Inherited relationships exist all over in the physical world. A human inherits from mammal. A hammer is a type of tool. We can classify any type of object into a more general category and claim that the object inherits characteristics from that category.

In software we can take a class that has useful functionality and use it as the base class for another. Consider a Timer class that can trigger an alarm at set intervals. If you are creating a class that draws circles and you want those circles to be drawn at specific intervals, you might inherit the Timer class into your CircleDrawer class. Doing so would give you the timer functionality for free.

A subclass is essentially a specialized version of its base class. The C# compiler understands and enforces this relationship, allowing us to use a subclass object any place in the program where a base class object is expected. Since the CircleDrawer class inherits the Timer class, any block of code in the program that expects a Timer object can also accept a CircleDrawer object. Stated another way, a CircleDrawer *is a* Timer.

One reason it is so important to understand inheritance is because it is omnipresent within the .NET library. Every data type in .NET, including primitive types like int, char, float, bool and any classes you define, inherit from a base class named *object*. The object class has a number of public methods, such as GetType, GetHashCode, and ToString. Since all types inherit from object, all types have those methods. Furthermore, every data type in .NET, including any that you define, is essentially a specialized type of object. Therefore, if a block of code is expecting an object type, that block will accept any data type.

Writing C# Programs

In order to write software in any language, you need two things; a text editor and a compiler for the language that you want to program in. Any text editor will work for writing programs, but you will find that some text editors are far superior to others. The next two sections describe two ways to write C# programs; Visual Studio.NET and the .NET SDK, which can be downloaded for free from Microsoft.

Visual Studio .NET

The most productive way to write programs in C# is with Visual Studio.NET, a product from Microsoft. Visual Studio.NET has many features that make writing software a snap, such as an intelligent programming editor that color codes your source code to make it easier to read. There is a feature called Intellisense that gives you a list of member variables for an object as you are typing so you don't have to remember how all those members are spelled. Visual Studio also includes a visual designer environment that simplifies many of the tasks for creating Windows and Web based programs. The cost of Visual Studio.NET can range from $99 to over $1000 depending on the edition of the product you buy. If you are a college student, you can probably get the student edition of Visual Studio.NET for next to nothing from your school's book store.

The .NET SDK

If you find even the cheapest edition of Visual Studio.NET to be cost prohibitive, you can still write C# applications using the .NET Software Development Kit. The .NET SDK can be downloaded from Microsoft for free. It includes the Common Language Runtime, the

Framework Class Library, and command line tools for compiling .NET applications, including the C# compiler.

Any C# program that can be compiled in the Visual Studio environment can also be compiled from the command line with the SDK. The disadvantage to using the SDK is that you do not have access to the great features that Visual Studio provides to make programming so much easier. There are advantages too. For instance, you can use any text editor that you want to write your C# programs. So if you already have an editor that you are attached to, you can continue to use it. There are many free programming editors, and many will integrate with the SDK, saving you the trouble of having to type the command lines for compiling programs.

To compile programs with the SDK you will need to have your PATH environment variable set correctly so that the command line tools can be found. A normal DOS console probably will not have those environment variables set by default, so you will need to run a batch file that ships with the SDK to set up your environment. This batch file is named sdkvars.bat and on my system is located at

C:\Program Files\Microsoft Visual Studio 8\SDK\v2.0\Bin\sdkvars.bat

The location of your sdkvars.bat file may be different on your system depending on your version of the SDK. Furthermore, the SDK installer may have added a shortcut to your Start menu that launches a DOS console and sets up the environment for you. Either way, once you have your environment set up correctly, you will be ready to compile programs.

The command to compile a C# program is *csc*. The command takes one or more arguments, depending on what kind of program you are compiling.

For the beginning of this book, the programs are less complex because they are designed to show basic concepts. Therefore, compiling programs from the command line might be easier in the beginning. Later, the programs start getting more complex and involve tools like the menu designer, so the features of the Visual Studio editor will come in handy.

Your First C# Program

Our first C# program is a real classic. It does nothing more than print a welcome message to the screen. Yet, this simple program still has much to teach about the basic structure of all C# programs.

```
// Example1_1.cs
// This program sends a simple greeting to the console
//

using System;

namespace csbook.ch1
{
   class Example1_1
   {
        static void Main(String [] args)
        {
             Console.WriteLine("Welcome to C# Programming.");
        }
   }
}
```

Listing 1.1

After typing the code for the previous listing into your favorite text editor, save the file as Example1_1.cs. I find it helpful to name a source file after the class that it contains, but C# does not require this. The command to compile Example1_1.cs is

csc Example1_1.cs

When you execute that command in a Dos window, you should get few lines of output from the command and if all goes well you should have a new file in your directory named Example1_1.exe. If you run that file you should see your welcome message print to the screen.

```
Welcome to C# Programming.
```

Figure 1.1

If you have a typo in your source code then you will see one or more error messages from the compiler. Usually the error messages are pretty good about telling you the line number where the compiler detected the error, giving you a clue about where your problem is. If you have any errors, then you need to correct them before your program will compile. In that case, carefully compare the code you typed to the code in the listing and recompile.

Comments

The first three lines in the program are comments. There are two types of comments, single line comments and multiple line comments. Example1_1.cs uses single line comments, which begin with //.

```
// Example1_1.cs
// This program sends a simple greeting to the console
//
```

Single line comments can occur anywhere in the program. Everything after the // characters is ignored by the compiler. Comments are used to provide extra information about your program, making your programs easier to read and understand. Since comments do not get compiled into your program, they do not affect the size or performance of your application. Use comments liberally.

Multiple line comments begin with the /* character sequence and end with */. The compiler ignores everything in between so the comments can span over multiple lines.

```
/* this is a
   multiple line
   comment
*/
```

Which style of comments you use is largely a matter of preference. You will notice in my code that I have a strong preference for the single line comments.

Using Namespaces

Large programs tend to have many classes, making it likely that two classes might end up with the same name. When these name clashes occur, the compiler becomes confused and will not know which class you are talking about. For example, if you created a class named *Point,* that represented a pair of latitude and longitude coordinates on a map, without namespaces when you tried to declare an instance of Point, the compiler would not know if you were trying to use your Point class or the Point class already defined by the .NET Framework.

To keep things straight for the compiler, we organize our classes into namespaces. The name of each class is appended to the name of the namespace containing it to form the class' official name. So if your namespace is *csbook.ch1* then your Point class would be officially named csbook.ch1.Point, making it distinct from the Point in the .NET Framework, which is in the *System.Drawing* namespace and officially named System.Drawing.Point.

Listing 1.1 uses the *Console* class, which is in the *System* namespace. By default, we need to access Console by its complete name, *System.Console*. However, it grows tiresome typing System-dot all over the place. As a shortcut we can announce to the compiler that we are using the System namespace in our program. This allows us to directly use any classes declared within the System namespace without having to specify the complete formal name. The first uncommented line of the program makes this announcement for us.

```
using System;
```

The *using* statements always go at the top of your program before any other declarations or statements. You can include as many namespaces in your program as you want to, but keep in mind that the more namespaces you include in your file, the more likely it is that you will have name clashes.

Creating Namespaces

In addition to using the .NET namespaces, you can also define namespaces of your own. You define a namespace with the *namespace* keyword followed by the name of the namespace, and a pair of curly braces. Any classes defined within the curly braces belong to that namespace. Our program uses a namespace called csbook.ch1. Notice that the rest of the program is contained within the namespace.

```
namespace csbook.chapter1
{
        // define classes here
}
```

Creating your own namespace is not required because .NET provides a default namespace. However, since namespaces are so helpful at organizing your programs, it is a good habit to get into.

Classes

Every C# program must contain at least one class. Our program defines a class named Example1_1. You can see in the listing that a class definition begins by declaring the class and then providing the body of the class. The body of the class is contained within the opening and closing curly braces

```
class Example1_1
{
        // class implementation
}
```

Although we did not explicitly declare it, the Example1_1 class inherits from the object class. This inheritance is implied because all types inherit from object.

The Main Method

Every program has a Main method that serves as its starting point. The Main method is special because the CLR calls it after loading your program into memory. Once the CLR calls Main, your program takes over. Then when Main returns, the program ends.

```
static void Main(string [] args)
{
        Console.WriteLine("Welcome to C# Programming.");
}
```

The Main method is the block of code that the CLR knows to call when it starts your program. Because the CLR has to call it, you have to declare the Main method in a way that the CLR will be able to find it. The Main method must be static and it must be named *Main* with a capital M, not *main*. C# is case sensitive.

Since methods can return data, every method must specify the type of the data that it will return. If the method does not return data, it must specify a return type of void. Since the Main method of Listing 1.1 does not return data, its return type is void.

The body of our Main method contains a single line of code that invokes a method on the Console class. This method, WriteLine, takes a string of characters and prints it to the console. Use of the WriteLine method and other methods of the Console class are covered in the next chapter.

The Visual Studio Environment

Most applications are written with more than one source code file and often contain references to other programming libraries. Managing all those files and references can be difficult when compiling from the command line. This section shows how to use the Visual Studio .NET environment to create your C# programs, so that you can focus on programming problems and let the development environment manage your files and references.

Visual Studio .NET is much more than an editor. It is a software development environment that helps you to write, compile, debug, and even package your software. Some of its features include syntax highlighting, automatic outlining, and Intellisense, a feature that lets you choose members from a list and completes variable names for you so that you don't have to worry about spelling. Programming is much easier with Visual Studio .NET because you can let the environment handle some of the more tedious tasks while you focus on the logic of your program.

Projects and Solutions

Visual Studio .NET manages your program's files and references by organizing them into a *project*. A project is a collection of files that are compiled to make an application. Some applications are so complex that they may contain more than one project. For instance, you might have a programming library in one project and a program that uses the library in a separate project. Visual Studio.NET will group these related projects for you into something called a *solution*. When you open a solution in Visual Studio.NET, all the projects within that solution are listed in your Solution Explorer, making it very easy to move between them.

Creating a Project

To create a project, start Visual Studio .NET and click on the *File* menu. Then click on the *New* menu item and select *Project*. You should see the following dialog box prompting you for information about your project.

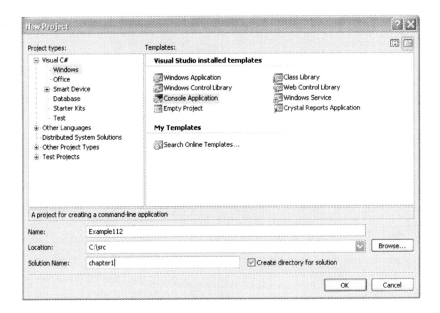

Figure 1.2

There are several different types of projects that you can create. Select the Console Application project. Then look towards the bottom of the dialog to find the Name, Location, and Solution fields. They will have some default values that will differ from the picture shown.

The Name field will name your application. This name will be used as the namespace for your program and it will also be used as the name of your executable file. The location is the directory where you solution will be created.

Enter "Example1_2" for the Name field. Then type "c:\src" for the location. For the Solution Name type "chapter1". There is also a check box asking if you want Visual Studio .NET to create a directory for the solution. Go ahead and check it if it is not checked by default. Then click the OK button. After the project is created you should see the following window.

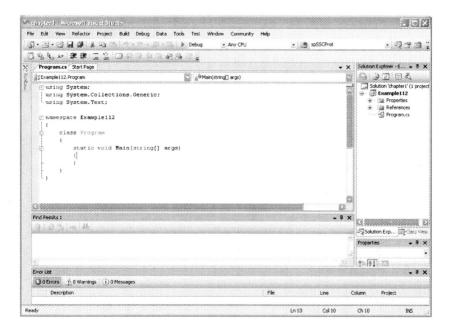

Figure 1.3

The center of the window contains tabs. When you open a file in the project a new editor tab will appear with the contents of that file. To the right of the window you see the Solution Explorer. This is a Tree View that has nodes for all projects in the current solution. Each project node can be expanded to see all the files in that project. If you double click file node, that file will open in an editor tab.

The project has been created with a single source file named Program.cs. If you're like me then you probably won't want to stick with the default names. You can change the name of the source file by right clicking it in the Solution Explorer and choosing "Rename" from the popup menu. Then type Example1_2.cs for the new file name. To keep your code consistent with the examples you can also change the namespace to "csbook.ch1" and the class name to "Example1_2". Finally, you can remove the using statements for the System.Text and System.Collections.Generic namespaces since we won't be using any classes from those namespaces in this program.

The source code should now look something like Listing 1.2.

```
// Example1_2.cs
using System;

namespace csbook.ch1
{
    class Example1_2
    {
        static void Main(string[] args)
        {
        }
    }
}
```

Listing 1.2

Add the following line to your Main method, which displays the user name of the user currently logged into your computer.

```
Console.WriteLine(Environment.UserName);
```

As you type that line you will notice the Intellisense feature mentioned earlier. When you type the period after the word "Console" you will see a list of members of the Console class. This list will zoom in on the method you are typing as you type. You can also scroll through that list and press the tab key when the WriteLine method is selected. Then Intellisense will type in the method call for you.

Compiling and Running

You are now ready to compile and test your program. To compile your program you use the Build menu. Click on Build and then choose "Build Example1_12". The compiler will build your program for you.

If there were any errors they will turn up in the Error List at the bottom of the window. Double clicking on an error in that list will bring you directly to the line of code that had the error. If there were no errors then the status bar at the lower left corner of your window will say "Build succeeded".

Now you can run the program. There are two modes to run in. You can run with the debugger or without. Later we will learn about debugging. For now, from the Debug menu click on "Start Without Debugging" or just press Control-F5. You should see a console window appear with the output of your program.

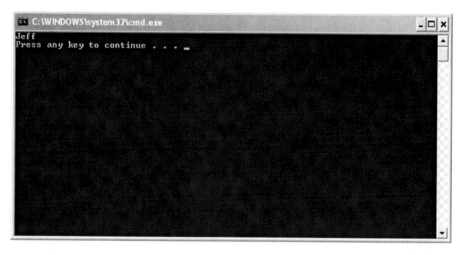

Figure 1.4

When you are finished looking at your output, press a key and the console window goes away

Chapter 2 – Input and Output

Programs would not be very useful if they could not interact with the user. There needs to be a way to read input from the user and display output. We also need to format the output, using field widths and formatting codes that can display data as currency or other formats for a more attractive user interface.

The examples from Chapter 1 used the WriteLine method of the Console class to write a line of text to the screen. You probably noticed, after the characters were written to the screen that a new line was created and the cursor repositioned to the beginning of that line. The WriteLine method always begins a new line before it returns. However, sometimes you might not want to begin a new line. Sometimes you might want the cursor to stay right where you left it. The next section shows another way to write output that does not begin a new line.

The Write Method

It is often useful to print text to the screen without advancing to the next line. This is done with another method of the Console class named *Write*.

```
// Example2_1.cs
// using Write
using System;

namespace csbook.ch2
{
    class Example2_1
    {
        static void Main(string[] args)
        {
            Console.Write("This is ");
            Console.Write("all on one line");
        }
    }
}
```

Listing 2.1

To compile this program save it as Example2_1.cs and use the command

csc Example2_1.cs

Listing 2.1 writes a single line of text to the screen even though it uses two lines of code to do it. The Write method prints text but leaves the cursor in the last position after the text.

```
This is all on one line
```

Figure 2.1

You can make the Write method behave like the WriteLine method by inserting a newline character at the end of the string. The newline character is a special character recognized by the system to mean "go to the beginning of the next line". The newline character is a backslash followed by the letter 'n'.

```
// Example2_2.cs
// using control characters
using System;

namespace csbook.ch2
{
    class Example2_2
    {
        static void Main(string[] args)
        {
            Console.Write("This is on \n");
            Console.Write("Two lines!");
        }
    }
}
```

Listing 2.2

The output from listing 2.2 is shown below.

```
This is on
Two lines!
```

Figure 2.2

Control Characters

In Listing 2.2 the string in the first Write statement ends with the \n, telling the Console class to go to the next line. The \n character is a special type of character called a control character. The backslash before the character is an escape character that tells the compiler to treat the next character as a control character instead of a normal 'n'. Other control characters exist as well, such as the tab and form feed characters. The following table shows some common control characters.

Table 2.1 – Commonly Used Control Characters

Control Character	Purpose
\t	Tab
\f	Form Feed
\r	Carriage Return
\b	Backspace
\'	Single Quote
\"	Double Quote
\\	Backslash

Not only does the escape character tell the compiler to treat normal characters as control characters, but you can also use the escape character to tell the compiler to treat special characters as normal ones.

We can take quotation marks as an example. Quotation marks are used to begin and end a literal string, such as "Hello". But what if you want the quotation mark to be apart of the string?

If you put a backslash in front of a quotation mark then the compiler will treat it as a normal character to be printed to the screen, instead of the string termination character. The following two variable declarations demonstrate.

```
string s1 = "This string has no quotes";
string s2 = "This string contains a quote: \".";
```

When those two strings are printed out they look like this:

```
This string has no quotes
This string contains a quote: ".
```

Figure 2.3

In the declaration of the s2 string there are three sets of quotation marks. The first and last will begin and end the literal string as usual, but the middle one is actually part of the string. Therefore, we must tell the compiler to treat the middle string as a normal character by putting a backslash in front of it.

When a Backslash is Really Just a Backslash

Since the compiler uses the backslash as the escape character we need a way to tell the compiler to treat it as a normal character in the cases when we actually want the backslash to be part of the string. This happens a lot when we store file names as strings because file names contain backslashes to separate the directory names. We inform the compiler that a backslash is really just a backslash by using a double backslash. Look at the next two strings that are initialized with the names of a text file.

```
string s1 = "c:\\test.txt";
string s2 = "c:\test.txt";
```

When those file names are printed out they look like this.

```
c:\test.txt
c:        est.txt
```

Figure 2.4

The problem with the second file name is that the compiler treats the backslash as an escape character so the 't' that follows it is converted into a tab character. If we want the backslash to be a part of the string instead of being used as an escape character then we have to put another backslash in front of it as we did in the first string.

So whenever you store a file name in a string variable you have to use double backslashes after the directory names or the compiler will think you are trying to use a control character. All those double backslashes in file names must have bothered somebody at Microsoft because they decided to use the @ symbol as a signal to the compiler that says the literal string contains no control characters. So s2 could be initialized with the literal value @"c:\test.txt" instead of using the double backslash. The following two statements produce the same result.

```
string s1 = "c:\\test.txt";
string s2 = @"c:\test.txt";
```

The @ in front of a literal string tells the compiler that there are no control characters in the string, so backslashes are treated as part of the string instead of as escape characters.

Formatted Output

The Write and WriteLine statements have a handy feature that allows you to pass variables as extra arguments that can be formatted into the output. The example below shows how the call is made.

```
// Example2_3.cs
using System;

namespace csbook.ch2{
    public class Example2_3{
        public static void Main(String [] args)
        {
            string name = "Jeff Suddeth";
            double accountBalance = 25.99;

            Console.WriteLine("Name {0} Account Balance {1}",
                        name, accountBalance);
        }
    }
}
```

Listing 2.3

In the listing we declare a string to store the name. Then we declare a double value named accountBalance and assign its initial value 25.99. In the WriteLine statement we include two place holders in the string. The first place holder is {0} and it will be filled in with the first variable that follows the string. The second place holder is {1} and it will be filled in with the second variable that follows the string. The output will display a string showing the name and account balance.

```
Name Jeff Suddeth Account Balance 25.99
```

Figure 2.5

The place holders can also contain field widths and formatting codes to specify how variables are to be displayed. The field width goes within the curly braces and is separated from the first number with a comma. Listing 2.4 shows how to specify a field width for output.

```
// Example2_4.cs
using System;

namespace csbook.ch2
{
    public class Example2_4
    {
        public static void Main(String [] args)
        {
            int x = 10;
            int y = 5;

            Console.WriteLine("(X, Y) is ({0,2}, {1,2})", x, y);
        }
    }
}
```

Listing 2.4

In output from listing 1.5 you can see that the variables x and y are printed and each has a field width of 2 characters.

```
(X, Y) is (10,    5)
```

Figure 2.6

You can also use a formatting code to tell the WriteLine method to print the value as currency or to use some other special formatting. Listing 2.5 uses the formatting code for currency.

```
// Example2_5.cs
using System;
namespace csbook.ch2{
    public class Example2_5 {
        public static void Main(String [] args){
            int x = 10;
            int y = 5;

            Console.WriteLine("X is {0,7:C}\nY " + "is {1,7:C}", x, y);
        }
    }
}
```

Listing 2.5

The output from this code will print the values as currency with a precision of 2 decimal values. The entire field width will be 7 characters.

```
X is   $10.00
Y is    $5.00
```

Figure 2.7

Table 2.2 shows several formatting codes supported by .NET.

Table 2.2 – Formatting Codes

Code	Description	Usage	Output
C	Currency	{0,7:C}	$100.00
P	Percent	{0:P}	100.00%
E	Exponential	{0:E1}	1E+2
F	Fixed Point	{0:F1}	22.1
D	Decimal	{0:D5}	00022
G	General	{0:G4}	8.375E+06
X	Hex	{0:X}	7FCA41

To see these formatting codes in action have a look at listing 2.6. The listing declares 2 variables, a double value and a long value and prints them out using the different formatting codes.

```
// Example2_6.cs
using System;

namespace csbook.ch2
{
    public class Example2_6
    {
        public static void Main(string [] args)
        {
                double d = 22.0557;
                long l = 8374849;

                Console.WriteLine("Decimal formats for "+ d);
                Console.WriteLine("Currency {0:C2}", d);
                Console.WriteLine("Exponential {0:E1}", d);
                Console.WriteLine("Fixed Point {0:F1}", d);
                Console.WriteLine("Number {0:N}", d);
                Console.WriteLine("Percent {0:P}", d);
                Console.WriteLine("Integer formats for " + l);
                Console.WriteLine("Decimal {0:D10}", l);
                Console.WriteLine("General {0:G4}", l);
                Console.WriteLine("Hex {0:X}", l);
        }
    }
}
```

Listing 2.6

```
Decimal formats for 22.0557
Currency $22.06
Exponential 2.2E+001
Fixed Point 22.1
Number 22.06
Percent 2,205.57 %
Integer formats for 8374849
Decimal 0008374849
General 8.375E+06
Hex 7FCA41
```

Figure 2.8

The final printing example uses the decimal data type. Instead of typing the field width you can use one or more # characters to specify as place holders that will contain a digit if necessary. If the digit is not necessary it will be padded with a space. The value will be left-justified. You can also use 0 as a place holder if you want your number to be padded with 0's such as 007.

```
// Example2_7.cs
using System;
namespace csbook.ch2
{
    public class Example2_8
    {
        public static void Main(String [] args)
        {
            decimal Pi = 3.14159M;

            Console.WriteLine("Pi is {0:00.00000000000}", Pi);
            Console.WriteLine("Pi is {0:#0.###########}", Pi);
        }
    }
}
```

Listing 2.7

Here we declared a single decimal value and print it out using 2 different formatting strings. The output is shown below.

```
Pi is 03.14159000000
Pi is 3.14159
```

Figure 2.9

Reading Input

Input may come from the user typing it on a keyboard, from a file, socket, serial port, or some other device. When we cover Windows programming we will build a graphical user interface (GUI) to gather input from the user. For now we will use the command line so that we can focus on programming concepts. The Console class has a method named ReadLine that reads a line of text from the standard input stream, which is normally the keyboard.

The next example uses ReadLine to allow users to type in their name. Then the program builds a customized message for that user and displays it with the WriteLine method.

```
// Example2_8.cs
using System;

namespace csbook.ch2
{
    public class Example2_8
    {
        public static void Main(string [] args)
        {
            string input= "";
            Console.Write("Enter your name:");

            input = Console.ReadLine();
            Console.WriteLine("Hello, " + input
                        + " and welcome to C# programming!");
        }
    }
}
```

Listing 2.8

Listing 2.8 is very similar to what we have seen before but this time we declare a string variable and set its value to the line of text that is read from the keyboard. Then we concatenate that string with others to build a message and write it to the console.

```
Enter your name:Jeff
Hello, Jeff and welcome to C# programming!
```

Figure 2.10

Notice that the call to WriteLine is broken into 2 lines of code. Spaces, tabs, and line breaks in source code are considered white space and they are ignored by the compiler. So splitting the statement into multiple lines is fine (and it's even a good idea if your statements become so long that they scroll off of the screen). Make sure that you don't split the statement in the middle of a variable name or literal string. Otherwise the compiler will get confused.

Chapter 3 – Variables and Operators

Every program works with variables in some way. For example, in a windows program the data representing every characteristic of the window; its color, size, position, and text in the title bar are all stored in variables. Variables are placeholders in memory that store the data used by your programs. There are different types of variables defined by .NET and you can even define variable types of your own.

Each variable type has certain operators defined for it. Those operators perform actions on the variable, such as modifying the variable, comparing it to other variables of the same type, or performing mathematical operations on it. This chapter looks at different variable types and operators. By the end of the chapter, you will be able to write programs that perform calculations and even make decisions.

Declaring and Using Variables

Before you use a variable, you must declare it. This is so the compiler knows what the valid operations are on that variable and so that it calls the proper operators to perform those operations. Variables are declared by specifying the data type of the variable and an identifier used to access it from your program. The syntax for declaring a variable is

variable_type identifier;

where *variable_type* is the data type of variable, such as *int* or *string*. We will explore the different data types later.

The *identifier* is the name that you want to use in your program to access that variable. It is a good idea to choose a name that describes what the variable is used for. The following line declares a variable that could be used to store the balance of an account.

```
double accountBalance;
```

All variable declarations are terminated by a semicolon. When the compiler encounters a declaration, it claims a space in memory that is large enough to store a double value. The figure 3.1 shows what this would look like in memory.

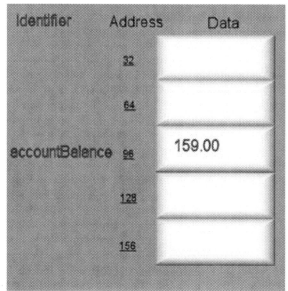

Figure 3.1

In figure 3.1, you see that the identifier accountBalance is used to identify a place in memory that contains the value 159.00, a double value.

Variable Identifiers

Keep in mind that C# identifiers are cases sensitive. As a convention, programmers often begin variable names with a lower case letter and capitalize the first letter of each word after that. You can use just about any variable name that you want as long as you follow a few rules.

Rules for Identifiers

1   Identifiers can only contain letters, digits, or underscores
2   Identifiers cannot begin with a digit
3   Identifiers must be unique within their scope
4   None of the C# key words can be used as identifiers
5   Identifiers cannot contain spaces

The following identifiers are *valid*.
userName, UserName, user_name, _userName, userName99

The following identifiers are *not valid*.
99_userName, user Name, user+Name

The next listing uses two variables to perform a calculation. Then it prints out the result.

```
// Example3_1.cs
// Declaring and using variables

using System;

namespace csbook.ch3
{
    public class Example3_1
    {
        public static void Main(String [] args)
        {
            int x = 10;
            int y = 5;
            int z = x + y;
            Console.WriteLine(z);
        }
    }
}
```

Listing 3.1

The first two lines of the Main method declare variables *x* and *y* as integers. Then we create a variable named *z* that stores the sum of *x* and *y*. The final line prints out the value of *z*. The output of the program is shown below.

15

Figure 3.2

Variable Initialization

In C#, you cannot use a variable until you have given it an initial value. This rule prevents a lot of programming errors that are common in other languages.

You can either initialize a variable at the time you declare it or you can initialize it later, but you must give it an initial value before you try to access it. To initialize a variable you use the assignment operator with the value that you want to initialize the variable with.

```
int x = 7;  // initialize
int y;  // delay initialization
int z;  // delay initialization

Console.WriteLine(x);  // okay!

y=10;  // initialize
Console.WriteLine(y); // okay!
Console.WriteLine(z); // bad!  Unitialized!
```

In the code segment above, the first two WriteLine statements are legal because both use variables that have been initialized. The first uses *x*, which was initialized at the time it was declared. The *y* variable was not initialized until later but as long as it is initialized before WriteLine tries to access it the compiler will be happy. The third WriteLine statement violates the rule, causing a compiler error.

Data Types

The Type of the variable is important for a few reasons. First, the compiler needs to ask the system to create a memory space to store the variable and it will not know how much space to ask for without knowing the variable's type. The compiler also needs to know what operations are valid for a particular variable so it can enforce the rules when you try to use the variable. Without knowing the type it has know way of knowing which rules to enforce.

There are several primitive types built into the C# language. There are numeric types to represent integers and floating point numbers. There is a *char* type designed to represent a single character such as 'a' or '9'. There is also a *bool* type, representing a Boolean value of true or false. The *string* type represents a sequence of characters. The following table lists some common types used in C# programs and shows how they are declared.

Table 3.1 - Datatypes Defined in the Common Type System

Type	Description	Example
int	Signed 32 bit integer	int x = 10;
long	Signed 64 bit integer	long population = 1000000L;
float	Single precision	float percent = .34F;
double	Double precision	double circumference = 5.1345;
char	16 bit Unicode character	char middleInitial = 'C';
string	Reference to a string	string firstName = "Jeff";
bool	true or false	bool isTrue = true;
byte	Unsigned 8 bit integer	byte n = 255;
short	Signed 16 bit integer	short n = 10;
ushort	Unsigned 16 bit integer	ushort n = 10;
ulong	Unsigned long integer	ulong n = 10;
uint	Unsigned 32 bit integer	uint x = 100;
decimal	Floating point with 28 significant figures	decimal PI = 3.14159;

The int, long, short, ushort, ulong, and uint types all represent types of integers. The int, long, and short types can have positive and negative values but the ushort, uint, and ulong types are unsigned, meaning that they can only have positive values.

The float and double types are both for floating point numbers but the double has twice the precision of a float. For even greater precision you can use the decimal type, which has 28 significant figures.

The next listing illustrates the use of several of the primitive variable types.

```
// Example3_2.cs
using System;

namespace csbook.ch3
{
        public class Example3_2
        {
            public static void Main(String [] args)
            {
                // declare some numeric types
                ushort x1 = 50;
                int x2 = 100;
                long x3 = 200;

                // declare a boolean type
                bool isValid = true;

                // calculate the average
                double average = (x1 + x2 + x3) / 3.0;

                // print the results
                Console.WriteLine("x1 is {0}, x2 is {1},"
                     + " x3 is {2} and the average is {3}",
                     x1, x2, x3, average);

                Console.WriteLine("isValid is " + isValid);

            }
        }
}
```

Listing 3.2

```
x1 is 50, x2 is 100, x3 is 200 and the average is
116.666666666667
isValid is True
```

Figure 3.3

The program starts out by declaring 3 different kinds of integers, an unsigned short, an int, and a long with the names *x1*, *x2*, and *x3*. A bool named *isValid* is also declared and assigned the initial value of true. All variables are initialized at the time they are declared. We then calculate the average and store it in a variable accurately named *average*. Finally, we print our values.

Constant Variables

Consider an order entry application where the business rules dictate that an order must have a minimum of 10 units. You could have a statement that tests the quantity to make sure it is greater than 10 like in the following segment.

```
if (qty < 10)
{
        Console.WriteLine("Orders must be greater than 10");
}
else
{
        ProcessOrder();
}
```

This enforces the rule but there is a problem with comparing against the literal value 10. If the business rule ever changes so that the minimum order quantity must be 25 then you have to go through your thousands of lines of code finding all the places where you test for a quantity less than 10.

A better solution is to use a constant variable. This way when the business rule changes, you only need to change the value of the constant and recompile the program. To use a constant variable you use the const modifier when you declare the variable. A constant variable must be initialized at the time you declare it. Once it has been initialized, it can never be changed.

```
const int MINIMUM_QUANTITY = 10;
if (qty < MINIMUM_QUANTITY)
{
        Console.WriteLine("Orders must be greater than 10");
}
else
{
        ProcessOrder();
}
```

In the example, we declare a constant int variable named MINIMUM_QUANTITY and assign it the value of 10. Then any place in the program that has to test against the minimum quantity can use this variable instead of the literal value 10.

As a convention, programmers often use all upper case letters in my constant variable identifiers, such as

```
const double PI = 3.14159;
```

Operators

Once you declare and initialize a variable, you can use one of its defined operators. There are several operators defined by C#. It is helpful to categorize them as mathematical operators, logical operators, or assignment operators.

Math Operators

The math operators include those that perform basic arithmetic operations like addition and subtraction. These operators take two arguments perform the operation and return the result. The Math operators are shown in Table 3.2. You will probably be familiar with most of these from grade school math.

Table 3.2 - Binary Math Operators

Operator	Name
+	Addition
-	Subtraction
*	Multiplication
/	Division
%	Modulus – returns the remainder

Integer Division

Beginning programmers are often confused about integer division on computers when they discover that *three divided by four is zero*! This is because when the compiler sees that both variables passed to the division operator are integers it calls the *integer division* operator. The integer division operator only returns the integer portion of the quotient. Since 3 / 4 = 0.75, its integer portion is 0.

```
// Example3_3.cs
using System;

namespace csbook.ch2
{
        public class Example3_3
        {
                public static void Main(string [] args)
                {
                        float answer = 3 / 4;
                        Console.WriteLine("3 / 4 is " + answer);

                }
        }
}
```

Listing 3.3

In listing 3.3, the first statement in the Main method divides the integer 3 by the integer 4. Since the numerator and denominator are both integers, the return value will be the integer part of 0.75, which is 0. The output of this program is shown in figure 3.4

```
3 / 4 is 0
```

Figure 3.4

Integer division is handy when used in conjunction with the modulus operator because between the two operators you can get the quotient and the remainder.

```
// Example3_4.cs
using System;

namespace csbook.ch3
{
    public class Example3_4
    {
        public static void Main(string [] args)
        {
            int quotient = 43 / 10;
            int remainder = 43 % 10;

            Console.WriteLine("43 / 10 is "
                    + quotient + " remainder " + remainder);
        }
    }
}
```

Listing 3.4

In Listing 3.4, we use integer division in the first line of Main to get the integer part of the quotient when dividing 43 by 10, which is the integer value 4. Then we use the modulus operator to get the remainder. Finally, we write a line of text to the screen showing the solution.

43 / 10 is 4 remainder 3

Figure 3.5

Unary Math Operators

The unary math operators only take one argument. They perform an operation on that argument and return the result. Table 3.3 shows the increment and decrement operators and their use.

Table 3.3 – Unary Math Operators

Operator	Description	Example
++	Pre or post increment	++x; x++;
--	Pre or post decrement	--x; x--;

The increment and decrement operators can be used to increment and decrement numbers. The difference between the pre and post variations is that the pre increment operator (used when the ++ is in front of the variable) will increment the variable and then return the new value but the post increment operator will increment the value while returning the value from before the increment. Listing 3.5 demonstrates the use of pre and post increment operators.

```
// Example3_5.cs
using System;

namespace csbook.ch3
{
    public class Example3_5
    {
        public static void Main(string [] args)
        {
            int x = 0;
            int y = 0;

            Console.WriteLine("Pre increment x " +
                    "where current value is " + x);

            Console.WriteLine(++x);
            Console.WriteLine("Now x is " + x);

            Console.WriteLine("Post increment of y " +
                    " where current value is " + y);

            Console.WriteLine(y++);
            Console.WriteLine("Now y is " + y);
        }
    }
}
```

Listing 3.5

The x variable was incremented with the pre-increment operator. The output shows that x was incremented before it was printed. The y value was incremented with the post-increment operator. The output shows that y's original value was printed even though it was incremented, as the last line in the output confirms.

```
Pre increment x where current value is 0
1
Now x is 1
Post increment of y where current value is 0
0
Now y is 1
```

Figure 3.6

Logical Operators

The logical operators are used to test a condition and return true or false. They can be used in decision making for if statements and conditional loops, as you will read about later. The logical operators are listed in Table 3.4.

Table 3.4 – Logical Operators

Operator	Name	Usage
<	Less than	(x < y)
<=	Less than or equal to	(x <= y)
>	Greater than	(x > y)
>=	Greater than or equal to	(x >= y)
==	Equal to	(x == y)
!	Negates a condition	!(x==y)
!=	Not equal to	(x != y)

The next code segment shows how the logical operators can be used to evaluate a Boolean condition. The isGreater variable is a bool that will hold the result of the evaluation of (1 > 2). Since 1 is not greater than 2, the condition returns false. Next we use the == operator to test for equality. If isGreater is equal to the value true then we print the top message. Since 1 will never be greater than 2 the condition will be false. So we print the bottom message.

```
bool isGreater = (1 > 2);

if (isGreater == true)
        Console.WriteLine("isGreater is true");
else
      Console.WriteLine("isGreater is false");
```

Assignment Operators

The assignment operators are used to assign a value to a variable. You can use the plain old = assignment operator or you can use one of several assignment operators that combine a math operation with assignment. Table 3.5 lists the assignment operators.

Table 3.5 – Assignment Operators

Operator	Name	Usage
+=	Addition assignment	X += 2;
-=	Subtraction assignment	X -= 2;
*=	Multiplication assignment	X *= 2;
/=	Division assignment	X /= 2;

These assignment operators are a shorthand for writing statements of the form x = x + y. The code below shows some of the assignment operators in use.

```
int x = 0;
int y = 10;
int z = 2;

x += 10;   // increment x by 10
y /= 2;    // cut y in half with integer division
z *= z;    // multiply z by itself
```

Operator Precedence

Because multiple operators can exist within the same statement, it is necessary to define the order in which operators will be executed. For instance, multiplication and division have higher precedence than addition and subtraction. Consider the statement

A = 1 + 3 * 10;

After that statement is executed, the value of A would be 31 because the multiplication is carried out before the addition. If you want to force the compiler to perform the addition first, you must enclose the addition operator and its two arguments in parentheses.

A = (1 + 3) * 10;

Now the addition will be performed first to get the result 4. Then the multiplication of 4 times 10 would yield the result 40. Finally, the assignment operator would be executed, assigning the value 40 into the variable A. Table 3.6 lists the operators ordered by their precedence.

Table 3.6 – Operator Precedence

Descriptions	Operators
Unary	++, --, !, -
Multiplication and division	*, /
Addition and subtraction	+, -
Logical	<, >, <=, >=
Equal to	==, !=
Assignment	=, *=, +=, /=

Listing 3.6 calculates an average twice incorrectly before finally calculating it the correct way on the third try.

```
// Example3_6.cs
using System;
namespace csbook.ch3
{
    public class Example3_6
    {
        public static void Main(string [] args)
        {
            int x = 2;
            int y = 5;
            int z = 3;

            double avg1 = x + y + z / 3.0;  // bad!

            double avg2 = (x + y + z) / 3; // still bad!

            double avg3 = (x + y + z) / 3.0;  // good!

            Console.WriteLine("{0}\t{1}\t{2}", avg1,
                    avg2, avg3);
        }
    }
}
```

Listing 3.6

Listing 3.6 declares three integer variables and initializes them to the values 2, 5, and 3. The first attempt to calculate the average is incorrect because the division has operation has higher precedence than the additions, resulting in z / 3.0 being evaluated before the addition operations.

The second calculation is incorrect because the sum of the three integer types will always produce an integer type. When that integer is divided by another integer, the compiler will use integer division, which drops the fractional part of the answer and gives an incorrect result.

The final attempt to calculate the average is correct. The parenthesis forces the addition operations to happen before the division. The addition operations result in an integer value, which is implicitly up-cast to a double when we divide by 3.0, producing a double value for the answer.

Overflow Errors and Implicit Type Casts

An *overflow error* will occur when you assign a value to an integer that is too large to fit in its memory space. Consider the case when you have two integer values being added together. Because both arguments of the addition operator are of type int, the return value will be an int, even if you try to store it in a long variable. However a 32 bit integer can only hold a value up to $2 \wedge 31$ -1, which is 2147483647. So if the sum of your addition operation is greater than that value an overflow error will occur.

```
int x = 2147483647;
long y = x + 1;

Console.WriteLine(y);
```

When you execute those statements, do not be surprised when you see a negative value printed to the screen.

```
-2147483648
```

Figure 3.7

One way to protect against the overflow problem is to tell the .NET runtime to check for overflow errors and throw an OverflowException when they occur. You can turn overflow checking on by enclosing your code in a block labeled as *checked,* as demonstrated in listing 3.7.

```
// Example3_7.cs
using System;
namespace csbook.ch3
{
    public class Example3_7
    {
        public static void Main(string [] args)
        {
            try
            {
                checked
                {
                    int x = 2147483647;
                    long y = x + 1;
                    Console.WriteLine(y);
                }
            }
            catch(OverflowException)
            {
                Console.WriteLine("overflow");
            }
        }
    }
}
```

Listing 3.7

Another solution is to force the addition operator to use the *long* addition operator instead of the *int* addition operator. You do this by changing one of the arguments to be a long variable. When the compiler sees that one of the variables is a long type, it will implicitly cast the other to a long as well and perform long addition. The returned value will be a long type.

```
int x = 2147483647;
long y = x + 1L;

Console.WriteLine(y);
```

The code segment above shows that the literal value 1 is being forced as a long value. The 'L' on the back of the 1 tells the compiler to make it a long. Adding a long to an int forces the compiler to implicitly cast the x integer up to a long type so that no overflow error occurs.

```
2147483648
```

Figure 3.8

Since the compiler implicitly casts the variable for you there is no reason to do an explicit cast. However if you want to do it anyway for clarity then the line would be changed to look like the following.

```
long y = (long)x + 1L;
```

The pair of parentheses when used with a type name inside is the cast operator. The statement above explicitly casts the variable *x* to a long type.

As the previous example showed, whenever necessary the compiler will implicitly cast an int up to a long. This is allowed because the long type is larger than an int so the cast can occur without data loss. However, the compiler will never implicitly cast a long down to an int because the int is smaller and data would be lost.

The following 2 lines each result in a compiler error because it tries to store the value of a long variable in an int variable.

```
int x = (long)1;
int y = 1L;
```

Chapter 4 – User Defined Types

The variables that you create in programs represent something real to the program. Sometimes using one of the primitive types is good enough, but it is often better to create your type to get a more accurate model of the system you are trying to program. This section explores three different ways to create your own data types. We will look at enumerations, structures, and classes.

Enumerations

An enumeration defines a named constant that represents a *state* rather than an ordinal value. For instance, we could represent colors as an enumeration by declaring the Color enum.

```
enum Color
{
        Blue,
        Red,
        Yellow
}
```

The enum uses an integer as the underlying type. The integer value of each item in the enum will be unique. If you do not specify a value then the first one will be 0 and each item will get a value of one higher than the previous.

To use one of the enum values you have to specify the name of the enum type followed by a period and then the item in the enum that you want to use.

```
Color col = Color.Blue
```

You can define an enum within a namespace or within a class. However you cannot define an enum within a method.

Listing 4.1 shows how you can use an enum to represent colors. The program declares some Color enums and prints them out first by printing their names and then by printing the integer values.

```
// Example4_1.cs
using System;

namespace csbook.ch4
{
    class Example4_1
    {
        enum Color
        {
            Blue,
            Red,
            Yellow
        }

        public static void Main(string[] args)
        {
            // print the enum value names
            Console.WriteLine(Color.Blue);
            Console.WriteLine(Color.Red);
            Console.WriteLine(Color.Yellow);
```

```
// print the numeric values
Console.WriteLine((int)Color.Blue);
Console.WriteLine((int)Color.Red);
Console.WriteLine((int)Color.Yellow);
    }
  }
}
```

Listing 4.1

In the output of the program, you can see that the first three lines printed are the names of the enum values. The second set of three lines displays the integer values of the Color enums by type casting them to (int).

```
Blue
Red
Yellow
0
1
2
```

Figure 4.1

The output in Figure 4.1 shows that the enums can be displayed as strings or as integers. You can also take strings and integers and convert them into Enum values. Converting an integer to an enum is can be done with a type cast.

```
Color myFavoriteColor = (Color)1;
```

To convert a string to an enum you must parse the string name to find the appropriate enum value. The Enum class (notice the capital E) contains a Parse method that accepts the Type for the enum and the string that you want to parse into the value. The result is returned as an object type so you must cast it to the appropriate enum type.

```
Color myFavoriteColor =
        (Color)Enum.Parse(typeof(Color), "Blue");
```

In the following example, the program prompts the user to enter her favorite color. The program will then convert the input string to the appropriate Color enum value.

```csharp
// Example4_2.cs
using System;

namespace csbook.ch4
{
    class Example4_2
    {
        enum Color
        {
            Blue,
            Red,
            Yellow
        }

        public static void Main(string[] args)
        {
            Color myFavorite = Color.Blue;

            // prompt for favorite
            Console.Write("What is your favorite color: " +
                        "Blue, Red, Yellow? ");
            string fav = Console.ReadLine();

            // convert to a Color enum
            try
            {
                Color yourFavorite =
                (Color)Enum.Parse(typeof(Color), fav);

                if (yourFavorite == myFavorite)
                {
                    Console.WriteLine("That's my " + favorite too!");
                }
                else
                {
                    Console.WriteLine("That is a " + nice color");
                }
```

```
        }
        catch
        {
            Console.WriteLine("I don't know that color");
        }

        }
    }
}
```

Listing 4.2

Using Structures

Any data can be represented in a program using the variable types that we have seen so far. However, it is often more convenient to group related data into your own custom type. Defining your own types provides an abstraction for the data, making it easier to work with.

As an example, think of how you might represent a customer in your program. A customer could be described by a first and last name, account number, and a balance.

```
string firstName = "Jeff";
string lastName = "Suddeth";
string accountNumber = "12345";
double balance = 5.25;
```

It would be very cumbersome to have to manage all that data for even a single customer. The situation becomes much worse if we had to declare multiple customers.

Structures can be used to group data into a single type so that you only have to create one variable instead of many.

```
struct Customer
{
    public string firstName;
    public string lastName;
    public string accountNumber;
    public double balance;
}
```

You define a structure using the *struct* keyword followed by the name of the type you are creating. Then you group the members of the struct between the curly braces. For this example, we create a Customer struct that contains strings representing the first name, last name, and account number. There is also a double value to hold the customer's balance. You can define methods within the struct as well.

In the Customer declaration, you also notice the *public* keyword in front of each variable declaration. By default the members are considered private and not accessible to any methods accept those that are defined within the struct.

You can create a Customer variable by declaring one, just as you declare variables of the other types. Once you have a Customer variable you can use the dot operator to access its members.

```
Customer cust;
cust.balance = 225.5;
```

For a complete example using this Customer structure, see Example4_3.cs.

```
// Example4_3.cs
using System;

namespace csbook.ch4
{
    class Example4_3
    {
        struct Customer
        {
                public string firstName;
                public string lastName;
                public string accountNumber;
                public double balance;
        }
```

```
public static void Main(string[] args)
{
        // declare a customer and read their data
        Customer cust;
        cust.balance = 225.5;

        Console.Write("Enter the first name:");
        cust.firstName = Console.ReadLine();

        Console.Write("Enter the last name:");
        cust.lastName = Console.ReadLine();

        Console.Write("Enter account number:");
        cust.accountNumber = Console.ReadLine();
        Console.Write("Enter the balance:");

        try
        {
                cust.balance =
                        double.Parse(Console.ReadLine());
        }
        catch
        {
                Console.WriteLine("Bad format."
                                + "  Defaulting to $0.00");
                cust.balance = 0.0;
        }

        // print the customer's data. First print a
        // header
        Console.WriteLine("\n\n\n{0,8} {1,10} "
                        + "{2,15} {3,10}\n",
                        "Acct No", "First", "Last", "Balance");

        // next print the only line in the report
        Console.WriteLine("{0,8} {1,10} {2,15}"
                        + " {3,10:C}",
                cust.accountNumber, cust.firstName,
                cust.lastName, cust.balance);

    }
  }
}
```

Listing 4.3

```
Enter the first name:Jeff
Enter the last name:Suddeth
Enter account number:12345
Enter the balance:125.55



 Acct No        First          Last      Balance

    12345        Jeff         Suddeth    $125.55
```

Figure 4.2

Using Classes

You learned in Chapter 3 that when you declare a variable you get a chunk of memory set aside to store the contents of that variable. For the types that you have worked with so far, that is true. They are called *value* types because the memory identified by the variable name contains the value of the variable. However, classes are different.

When you declare an int variable, the compiler knows how much memory the variable will use because all int variables in .NET are 32 bits. Since the compiler has this information, it can claim that space at compile time. Now consider a string variable. When you declare a string, you might initialize it with an empty string "", taking up the minimal amount of memory for a string. However, during the life of your program, you might change that string's value to "This is a much longer string". Now we have a problem. How much memory should the compiler set aside for your string variable if it doesn't know how long the string will be?

The way this problem is handled in .NET is that the memory for the string is not reserved at compile time, but instead at runtime when the value of the string will be known. The string variable does not really store the contents of the string, but instead stores a pointer to a position in memory. At runtime when the memory for the string is finally allocated, the string's pointer will be pointed at that memory. This type of variable is called a *reference* variable because the contents of the variable refer to data that is stored elsewhere.

In C#, a string is implemented as a class and all classes are reference types. Understanding the difference between reference types and value types will help you avoid making mistakes in your programs.

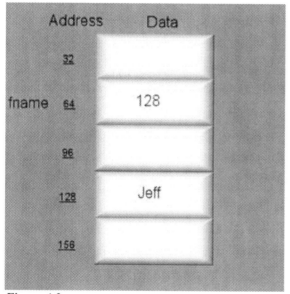

Figure 4.3

Figure 4.3 shows how a reference variable is stored in memory. You can see that the string variable *fname* is located at memory location 64. The value stored in that address is not the string, but the address of a different memory location where the string data is actually stored.

Listing 4.4 uses another reference type, the Random class. Objects of the Random class are used to generate random numbers.

```
// Example4_4.cs
using System;

namespace csbook.ch4
{
    class Example4_4
    {
        // simulate a turn in a role playing game
        public static void Main(string[] args)
        {
            Random r = new Random();

            // simulate the roll of a 6 sided die
            int roll = r.Next(6) + 1;

            Console.WriteLine("Your roll was {0}", roll);
        }
    }
}
```

Listing 4.4

Listing 4.4 uses a Random object to simulate the roll of a six-sided die. Notice that there are two steps in creating a variable of a class. First we must declare the variable. Then we must create the object that the variable refers to.

In the listing, we declare an object of the Random class and give it the variable name *r*. Then we initialize the variable by pointing it at an instance of the Random class. We create the instance using the *new* operator. This is all accomplished in one line of code.

```
Random r = new Random();
```

The new operator does more than create a place in memory for the object. It also calls a *constructor* method to initialize the object's state. Sometimes you will need to pass parameters to control how the object is initialized. If you need to pass parameters to the constructor call, then you place them within the parenthesis.

Once we create instance of Random we can access its public data and members through the *r* variable that refers to it. Then we call the *Next* method, which generates a random integer from 0 up to (but not including) the parameter passed. Since we want to roll a six-sided die, we generate a number from 0 through 5 and then add 1 to it, giving us a random value between 1 and 6 inclusively.

```
int roll = r.Next(6) + 1;
```

Creating Your own Classes

You define a class in C# using the *class* keyword. We have already created many classes. Recall that every C# program contains at least one class with a Main method. However, the class with the Main method does not have to be instantiated since it is being called from the .NET framework. Creating and using classes is covered in chapter 6.

The next example defines a class named OrderTaker, which exposes two methods. The first displays its product list to the screen and the second accepts an order. In addition, we define the Example4_5 class, which contains the Main method for our application.

```
// Example4_5.cs
using System;

namespace csbook.ch4
{
    class OrderTaker
    {
        public void DisplayProducts()
        {
            Console.WriteLine("Product List");
            Console.WriteLine("1) Large Coffee");
            Console.WriteLine("2) Bagel");
            Console.WriteLine("3) Scone");
        }

        public void TakeOrder(int prodId, int qty)
        {
            if (prodId == 1)
                Console.WriteLine("{0} Large Coffee coming "
                        + "right up!", qty);
            else if (prodId == 2)
                Console.WriteLine("{0} Bagel coming right up!", qty);
            else if (prodId == 3)
                Console.WriteLine("{0} Scone coming right up!", qty);
            else
                Console.WriteLine("I don't have that product.");
        }
    }

    class Example4_5
    {
        static void Main(string[] args)
        {
            OrderTaker orderTaker = new OrderTaker();
            orderTaker.DisplayProducts();

            Console.Write("\nEnter the integer product code>");
            string prodAsString = Console.ReadLine();

            Console.Write("\nHow many would you like?");
            string qtyAsString = Console.ReadLine();

            try
            {
                int prodAsInt = int.Parse(prodAsString);
                int qtyAsInt = int.Parse(qtyAsString);

                orderTaker.TakeOrder(prodAsInt, qtyAsInt);
            }
```

```
catch (FormatException)
{
    Console.WriteLine("Product code and Qty "
        + "must be integer!");
}
    }
  }
}
```

Listing 4.5

The listing for Example4_5.cs defines a class named OrderTaker that exposes two pieces of functionality. It can display its product list and it can accept an order. The class is defined when we use the *class* keyword followed by the name of the class. The body of the class is enclosed in the curly braces. It contains only the two methods previously mentioned.

Both of the OrderTaker's methods are declared as public so that they can be called from other classes. The DisplayProducts method writes several lines to the screen to display a product list. The TakeOrder method accepts a product code and quantity as method parameters and prints a different message depending on the product code. An *if* statement is used to figure out which product code has been passed. Chapter 5 covers *if* statements.

The Main method creates an instance of the OrderTaker object. Once again, the new operator must be used to instantiate the OrderTaker because all classes are reference types. Then Main invokes the DisplayProducts method and prompts the user for a product code and quantity.

The try and catch blocks make the code safer because we don't know if the user will type their input correctly or not. The try block uses the int.Parse method to create integer types for the product code and quantity and then passes them to the OrderTaker's TakeOrder method.

```
Product List
1) Large Coffee
2) Bagel
3) Scone
Enter the integer product code>1
How many would you like?3
3 Large Coffee coming right up!
```

Figure 4.4

Chapter 5 – Logic and Loops

So far, the programs you have seen in previous chapters have been very straightforward. Most have consisted of a set of statements that execute in the order in which they were written. Real programs however, are not so simple. They require logic for making decisions about which statements to execute, and sometimes whether a block of statements should be repeated.

In this chapter, you will learn how to use *if* statements and loops to provide the logic that will control the flow of execution through your programs. You will also learn more about writing class methods.

The Single Case If Statement

The basic structure of an *if* statement uses the *if* keyword followed by a logical test. If the logical test evaluates to true then the statement or block of statements that immediately follows the condition will execute. If the condition evaluates to false then the statement or block of statements will be skipped.

The syntax for an if statement is as follows.

if (*Condition*)   or   if (*Condition*)
    Statement   {
                                         Statement Block

                                               }

The condition within the parentheses must be an expression that evaluates to true or false. The expression can be a logical operator such as ==, method call that returns a bool, or a single variable of type bool.

The following if statement will print to the console only if the x variable has a greater value than y.

```
if (x > y)
    Console.WriteLine("X is bigger");
```

If x is not greater than y then the expression x > y will return false and the WriteLine statement will be skipped.

When there is more than one statement that must be conditionally executed then you must use the block syntax.

```
if (x > y)
{
    Console.WriteLine("X is bigger");
    Console.WriteLine("Y is smaller or equal");
}
```

The first example of this chapter demonstrates an if statement using a random number. The example will take a random number from 1 to 100 and test if it is odd or even.

```
// Example5_1.cs
using System;

namespace csbook.ch5
{
        public class Example5_1
        {
                public static void Main(string [] args)
                {
                        Random r = new Random();

                        int val = r.Next(100) + 1;
                        if (val % 2 == 0)
                        {
                                Console.WriteLine("The value "
                                    + val + " is even");
                        }
                }
        }
}
```

Listing 5.1

The first line of the Main method creates a new Random object that will be used to generate a random number. The next line reads a random number from 1 to 100 from the *Next* method on the object. Recall from Chapter 4 that the Next method returns a random integer that can be from 0 up to, but not including, the value passed as argument.

Once we have the random number we have to decide if it is even or odd so that we know if we should display the message. The example uses an *if* statement to determine if the number is even. If the value is even then the modulus return value in the condition will be equal to 0 and the == operator will return true. When the == operator returns true the block of statements guarded by the condition will execute. If the number is odd then the return value of the modulus operation will be 1 and == will return false, causing the block of statements to be skipped.

Compound Conditions

The logical operators such as <, >, and == return a bool value of true or false. The value returned by those logical operators can be used as part of another logical expression. This chaining of logical operators allows us to build some very complicated logic with multiple conditions. A condition that is composed of other logical operations is called a *Compound Condition*.

The Logical AND Operator

One way to create a compound condition is with the AND operator, &&. The && operator will return true if and only if the expressions on both sides of it evaluate to true.

The syntax for the && operator is

if (*Condition1* && *Condition2*)
{
      Statements
}

The statement block will only be executed if *Condition1* and *Condition2* both evaluate to true.

```
// Example5_2.cs
using System;
namespace csbook.ch5
{
    public class Example5_2
    {
        public static void Main(string [] args)
        {
            Random rand = new Random();

            // role a pair of dice
            int die1 = rand.Next(5) + 1;
            int die2 = rand.Next(5) + 1;
            Console.WriteLine(die1.ToString() + " and "
                            + die2.ToString());
            if (die1 == 1 && die2 == 1)
            {
                Console.WriteLine("Snake Eyes! " +
                                    "You Win!");
            }

            Console.WriteLine("done.");
        }
    }
}
```

Listing 5.2

In Listing 5.2, we simulate the rolling of a pair of dice. Since the valid values of a die roll can be 1 through 6 we ask for a number in the range 0 to 5 and add 1.

In this game, the user wins if they roll a pair of 1's. It may be a silly game but it does demonstrate the use of a compound && condition. The if statement tests to see if each die is equal to 1. If the first die is equal to one, then that part of the condition evaluates to true. The second part will then be evaluated. If the second value is 1 as well then the entire condition is evaluated as true and the WriteLine statement in the block will be executed.

If the first die roll was not equal to 1 then the first part of the condition will evaluate to false. Since both sides must be true for the whole condition to be true and the first one is already known to be false, we already have enough information to know that the whole condition is false. Therefore, the second part of the condition will not be evaluated and the block containing the WriteLine statement will be skipped.

The Logical OR Operator and Exclusive OR

Another way to combine logical expressions into a compound condition is to use the OR operator, ||. The OR Operator will return true if one or both of the expressions at its sides evaluates to true.

The syntax for the || operator is

if (*Condition1* || *Condition2*)
{
        Statement Block
}

The next example uses a logical OR operator in a compound condition to test for a valid product code entered by a user.

```
// Example5_3.cs
using System;

namespace csbook.ch5
{
    class Example5_3{
        static void Main(string[] args){
            Console.WriteLine("Inventory Management System");
            Console.Write("Enter Product Code >");

            string prodCode = Console.ReadLine();

            if (prodCode == null || prodCode.Length == 0)
            {
                Console.WriteLine("Invalid Product Code");
                return;
            }
            Console.WriteLine("Yeah, we have that.");
        }
    }
}
```

Listing 5.3

In Listing 5.3, we ask the user to enter a product code so that we can pretend to look the product up in an inventory database. Since it is possible that prodCode could contain a null value or an empty string, we need to screen for invalid product codes. If either of those conditions is true, we should display an error message. The example uses an if statement with a logical OR to test both conditions. If the prodCode is null or if its length is zero then we enter the block guarded by the if statement to process the error.

There may be times when we want to know if either one of the conditions is true but not both. The Exclusive OR operator is the ^ symbol. If either one of the conditions is true then ^ will return true. If both or neither are true then it returns false.

Truth Tables

A truth table can be used to show the resulting value of an expression using the logical operations. The truth table for &&, ||, and ^ are all shown below in tables 5.1, 5.2, and 5.3.

The first column and row represent the possible values of the conditions that are combined into a compound if statement. You can use the intersection of the row and column to find out the final value of the expression.

For example, in the AND truth table, the *true* row intersects the *true* column with a value of *true*. This means that true and true produce a true value for the AND operator. The *true* row intersects the *false* column with a value of *false*, meaning that (true && false) produces a value of false.

Table 5.1 - AND Truth Table

	true	false
true	true	false
false	false	false

Table 5.2 - OR Truth Table

	true	false
true	true	true
false	true	false

Table 5.3 - Exclusive OR Truth Table

	true	false
true	false	true
false	true	false

The Double Case If Statement

The single case if statement is often too limited because it only offers a single case that can either be executed or skipped. Sometimes you might want to execute one block of statements when a condition is true and a different block of statements when a condition is false. For these double case situations we can use the *else* clause.

The else clause is placed immediately following the statement or block of statements for the true condition. The double case if statement uses the following syntax.

if (*Condition*)   or   if (*Condition*)
         Statement1   {
else   *Block1*
         Statement2   }
                                                              else
                                                              {
                                                                      Block2
                                                              }

The next statement shows a double case if statement.

```
if (x > y)
    Console.WriteLine("X is bigger");
else
    Console.WriteLine("X is not bigger");
```

In the code fragment if x has a greater value than y then the > operator will return true and the first case will be executed. However, if > returns false, then we know that x is not greater than y and the second case will be executed.

The next example builds onto Example 5.1 by providing an else case.

```
// Example5_4.cs
using System;

namespace csbook.ch5
{
    public class Example5_4
    {
        public static void Main(string [] args)
        {
            Random r = new Random();

            int val = (r.Next() % 100) + 1;
            if (val % 2 == 0)
            {
                Console.WriteLine("The value " + val + " is even");
            }
            else
            {
                Console.WriteLine("The value " + val + " is odd");
            }
        }
    }
}
```

Listing 5.4

In Example 5.4 we see that an else clause has been added to the if statement from the Example5_1.cs. Other than that, the program is identical. The else clause provides a case that will be executed when the condition in the if statement evaluates to false (i.e., when the random value is odd).

```
>Example5_4
The value 24 is even

>Example5_4
The value 7 is odd

>Example5_4
The value 65 is odd

>Example5_4
The value 40 is even
```

Figure 5.2

The Multiple Case If Statement

The double case if statement gives us a way to execute one block of statements when the condition is true and another block when the condition is false. However, there are also times when we have more than two possible outcomes.

Consider a range of numbers that might represent a score on a student's exam. Each letter grade represents a range of numbers in the grading scale.

Table 5.4 – A Grading Scale

Score	Letter Grade
90 – 100	A
80 – 89	B
70 – 79	C
60 – 69	D
< 60	F

If we are to write a program to assign a letter grade, we could do so with a multiple case if statement and compare the test score against each range of numbers to assign the correct letter grade. One way to do this is to have a bunch of if statements comparing against the ranges.

```
if (grade >= 90)
    letterGrade = 'A';

if (grade >= 80 && grade <= 89)
    letterGrade = 'B';

if (grade >= 70 && grade <= 79)
    letterGrade = 'C';

...
```

But this solution is wasteful. Once we know that the grade is greater than 90, we already know the letter grade. There is no reason to perform the other comparisons. Instead, we can use the *else if* clause to test multiple conditions. The syntax for using the *else if* clause follows.

if (*Condition1*)
        Statement1
else if (*Condition2*)
        Statement2
else
        Statement3

The multiple case if statement begins like any other if statement. If *Condition1* evaluates to true, the statement or block at *Statement1* will be executed. Then control will jump to the next position after the *else* case and *Condition2* will not be evaluated.

But if *Condition1* is false then *Condition2* will be evaluated. If *Condition2* is true then *Statement2* will be executed. Otherwise control will jump into the *else* block (if it exists) and begin execution from there. The *else* case is optional.

We can now assign a letter grade using the following if statement.

```
if (grade >= 90)
    letterGrade = 'A';
else if (grade >= 80)
    letterGrade = 'B';
else if (grade >= 70)
    letterGrade = 'C';
else if (grade >= 60)
    letterGrade = 'D';
else
    letterGrade = 'F';
```

Each condition here is now simpler. By the time we get to the test to see if grade >= 70 we don't have to worry about the upper limit test because if the grader were higher than 79 it would have been handled in a previous case.

The next example uses a multiple condition if statement to test the values of strings. The program simulates the Welcome screen for a travel planner. The user will type in the city that they plan to travel to and the program will respond by printing a message.

```
// Example5_5.cs
using System;

namespace csbook.ch5
{
    class Example5_5
    {
        static void Main(string[] args)
        {
            Console.WriteLine("Jeff's Travel "
                    + "Agency Main Menu");

            Console.Write("Which city are you "
                    + " going to? >");

            string city = Console.ReadLine();

            string output = "";
            if (city == "Chicago")
                output = "Enjoy your trip to "
                        + city + ", IL";
            else if (city == "New York")
                output = "Enjoy your trip to "
                        + city + ", NY";
            else if (city == "Las Vegas")
                output = "Enjoy your trip to "
                        + city + ", NV";
            else
                output = "Enjoy your trip to "
                        + city;

            Console.WriteLine(output);
        }
    }
}
```

Listing 5.5

```
Jeff's Travel Agency Main Menu
Which city are you going to? >Chicago
Enjoy your trip to Chicago, IL
```

Figure 5.3

The Switch Statement

Another way to evaluate multiple conditions is to use a switch statement. A switch statement will test a condition and jump to a case with a label for the condition's value. Unlike the conditions of an if statement, the condition of a switch statement does not have to evaluate to a bool.

The syntax for the switch statement is

```
switch(Condition)
{
case CASE1:

        break;

case CASE2:

        break;

case CASE3:

        break;

default:
        break;
}
```

The *Condition* must be a valid C# expression or variable. The *case* labels must be possible values of the same data type that the condition evaluates to in the switch expression. For instance, if the *Condition* expression is x+1 and x is an integer then the *case* labels should be integers.

The default case is optional. It will be executed if none of the other cases were valid.

Each case must end with a break or return statement. If you forget to put a break or return statement at the end of a case, the compiler will generate an error because it is illegal to fall from one case into the next.

The following example is a computerized interface for a reptile pet shop. It uses a command line interface to display a menu and prompt the user for a request. After the user issues their request, the appropriate price listing will be displayed.

```csharp
// Example5_6.cs
using System;

namespace csbook.ch5
{
    public class Example5_6
    {
        public static void Main(string [] args)
        {
            string housingPrices =
                "Large Tank - $300\n" +
                "Basking Rock - $15\n" +
                "Food Bowl - $8";

            string feedPrices =
                "Crickets - $5\n" +
                "Meal Worms - $4\n" +
                "Wax Worms - $3.75";

            string reptilePrices =
                "Bearded Dragon - $45\n" +
                "Green Iguana - $100\n" +
                "Red Eared Slider - $15\n" +
                "Ball Python - $90";
```

```
Console.WriteLine("Jeff's Reptile Emporium");
Console.WriteLine("Enter Department Code - "
                + "(R) Reptiles, (F) Feeders"
                + ", (H) Housing");

string input = Console.ReadLine();

switch(input.ToUpper()[0])
{
   case 'R':
           Console.WriteLine(reptilePrices);
           break;

   case 'F':
           Console.WriteLine(feedPrices);
           break;

   case 'H':
           Console.WriteLine(housingPrices);
           break;

   default:
           Console.WriteLine("Invalid"
                  + " Department Code");
           break;
}


         }
      }
}
```

Listing 5.6

```
Jeff's Reptile Emporium
Enter Department Code - (R) Reptiles, (F) Feeders, (H) Housing
R
Bearded Dragon - $45
Green Iguana - $100
Red Eared Slider - $15
Ball Python - $90
```

Figure 5.5

Listing 5.6 first builds 3 strings that contain the pricing information of 3 different departments. Then we display the menu, which tells the user the 3 valid department codes that they can use to view prices. Next, we read a line of input and use the first character of that input as the department code. Finally, we process the request by testing the department code in a switch statement.

The expression within the switch test converts the string to upper case and tests the first character. We have a case statement for each of the valid department codes. If the first character of the input was not one of the valid department codes then the program falls into the default case, which informs the user that they entered an invalid department code.

Loops

Programs often require more than a single pass through a set of statements. In fact, being able to execute a block of statements in a loop is what makes programs so useful. Consider listing 5.6, the computer interface for a reptile pet shop. That program only handles one customer and then exits. It would be much more useful if it ran in a loop so that other customers could use it too.

The two basic types of loops are conditional loops and counter loops. Conditional loops will repeat a block of statements until a condition is no longer true. The counter loops are useful when you know exactly how many times you want a loop to execute.

Loops can also be top tested or bottom-tested. Top tested loops will test the condition before entering the body of the loop. If the condition is false on the first test then the body of the loop will never be executed. Bottom tested loops will execute the body of the loop once and then test to see if the loop should be executed again. Top tested loops are implemented in C# with the *while* loop, shown in the next section.

The While Loop

You can use the while loop to write a top tested loop. With a while loop, the condition is tested before the block of statements is executed. If the condition evaluates to false the first time it is tested then the block of statements will never execute. A while loop may execute 0 or more times.

The syntax for a while loop is

```
while(Condition)
{
    Statement Block
}
```

where the *Condition* is a valid C# expression that returns a bool value, just like with an *if* statement. The block of statements will execute repeatedly until the condition evaluates to false.

Listing 5.7 demonstrates use of the while loop. The program manages an account balance and allows the user to deposit or withdraw money from the account. Because the program is executed in a loop, the user is allowed to enter many transactions before exiting the program.

```
// Example5_7.cs
using System;

namespace csbook.ch5
{
  public class Example5_7
  {
    public static void Main(string [] args)
    {
        double balance = 0;
        double transAmt = 0;
        string input = "";

        while (input.ToUpper() != "QUIT")
        {
                Console.Write("Enter Command "
                       + "[DEP, WD, VIEW, or QUIT]>");
                input = Console.ReadLine();

                if (input.ToUpper() == "DEP"){
                     Console.Write("Amount of Deposit:");

                     transAmt =
                         double.Parse(Console.ReadLine());

                     balance += transAmt;

                     Console.WriteLine("The balance is now "
                                    + "{0:C2}", balance);
                }
                else if (input.ToUpper() == "WD"){
                     Console.Write("Amount of Withdrawal:");

                     transAmt =
                         double.Parse(Console.ReadLine());

                     balance -= transAmt;

                     Console.WriteLine("The balance is now"
                                    + "{0:C2}", balance);
                }
                else if (input.ToUpper() == "VIEW"){
                     Console.WriteLine("The balance is "
                                    + "{0:C2}", balance);
                }

        }
    }
  }
}
```

Listing 5.7

The program starts by initializing the input value as an empty string and initializing two double values to 0. The balance variable is used to track the running balance of the account. The transAmt variable is the amount of a single transaction. Depending on the type of transaction, the transAmt value will be either added to or subtracted from the balance.

After entering the loop, we give the user a menu with a list of commands. Then we read the input and execute the command. If the command was DEP then we execute a deposit command by prompting the user for the amount of the deposit. Then we add that amount our balance and display the new balance.

If the command was WD then we execute a withdrawal. We prompt the user for the amount of the withdrawal and subtract that amount from the balance. Then we display the new balance.

If the command was VIEW then we display the current balance.

What is important to see in this program is that we continue prompting the user for a new command until the command they type is "QUIT". When that happens the expression (input != "QUIT") will evaluate to false and the body of the loop will not be executed again, allowing the program to exit.

The Do Loop

Example5_7.cs used a loop that evaluated an expression first and executed the body of the loop only if that expression was true. It is possible that a top tested loop might never be executed. Imagine if I had initialized the value of input as "QUIT."

Often you know that you want the loop to execute at least one time. For those occasions, we can use a bottom-tested loop. A bottom-tested loop will execute the body of the loop and then test an expression to see if the loop should execute again. A bottom-tested loop guarantees that the body of the loop will be executed at least one time.

The syntax for the bottom-tested loop is

do
{
    Statement Block
} while (*Condition*);

The *do* keyword begins the bottom-tested loop. The statements in the body of the loop will be executed once before the condition will be evaluated. If the expression evaluates to true then the body of the loop will be executed again. The statements in the body of the loop will continue to repeat until the condition is no longer true. Notice that the *while* condition on a bottom-tested loop is terminated with a semicolon but the *while* condition on the top tested loop is not.

The following listing creates a text file using a bottom-tested loop.

```
// Example5_8.cs
using System;
using System.IO;

namespace csbook.ch5
{
    class Example5_8
    {
        static void Main(string[] args)
        {
            // make sure they specified a filename
            if (args.Length == 0)
            {
                Console.WriteLine(
                    "Usage: Example5_8 outfile");
                return;
            }
```

```
    try
    {
            // open the text file for output
            StreamWriter writer = new StreamWriter(args[0]);

            string input = null;
            do
            {
                    input = Console.ReadLine();
                    if (input != null)
                            writer.WriteLine(input);

            }while(input != null);


            writer.Flush();
    }
    catch(IOException ex)
    {
            Console.WriteLine("Error: {0}\n{1}",
                    ex.Message,
                    ex.StackTrace);
    }
            }
        }
    }
```

Listing 5.8

The listing uses a bottom-tested loop to create a text file. It uses the StreamWriter class from the System.IO namespace to create the text file.

In the listing, we take the first command line argument and use it as the name of the file that we want to create. We pass that file name to the constructor of the StreamWriter.

```
// open the text file for output
StreamWriter writer = new StreamWriter(args[0]);
```

We then enter a bottom-tested loop that reads a string from the command line. If the string object returned from ReadLine is not null it will be written to the StreamWriter with its WriteLine method. If the user enters the end-of-file character by hitting Control-Z then the input stream will return null, causing our bottom test to fail and the loop to exit.

```
string input = null;
do
{
        input = Console.ReadLine();

        if (input != null)
                writer.WriteLine(input);

}while(input != null);
```

The StreamWriter class does not immediately write the text to file but instead buffers the text in memory. To flush the text to the file we must call the Flush method.

```
writer.Flush();
```

If the StreamWriter detects any problems, such as failing to create the file, it may throw an IOException. Therefore I contain the use of the StreamWriter object within a try block and handle any IOExceptions that may be thrown within the catch block.

Counter Controlled Loops

The previous two examples continued to loop until a condition was true. Example5_8.cs for example, continues to loop until the user enters Control-Z as the input. In that example, we do not know how many times the loop will execute because we have no way of knowing when the user will hit Control-Z. However, sometimes we know exactly how many times the loop. For those situations we can use a counter variable to control how many times the loop executes.

One way to create a counter controlled loop is to use either the top tested or bottom-tested loops we have seen already and use a counter as the condition.

```
int x = 0;
while (x < 10)
{
    Console.WriteLine(x++);
}
```

The previous segment will execute the body of the loop 10 times, as the value of x, initialized at 0, is incremented to 10. When the value of x is 10, the condition x < 10 will no longer be true and the loop will exit.

Counter controlled loops are so common that we have a special syntax for them, the *for* loop.

for(*Initialization*; *Condition*; *Modification*)
{

    Statements

}

The header of a for loop begins with the *for* keyword, followed by a set of parentheses. The interesting part is inside those parentheses. There are three parts, separated by semicolons. The first part is the control variable initialization. In this part, we declare a counter variable and give it an initial value.

The second part is the condition that we are testing for with each pass through the loop. The condition must evaluate to a *bool*, i.e. true or false. If the value is true then the loop is executed. If it is false then we break out of the loop.

The final part of the header is the control variable modification. This is where the control variable is changed, typically by incrementing it by one. A for loop that prints out the even numbers between 1 and 10 inclusively, looks like

```
for (int i = 1; i <= 10; i++)
{
        if (i % 2 == 0)
                Console.WriteLine(i);
}
```

The control variable in the code segment is an integer named i. It is initialized to 1. In the condition we test to see if i is less than or equal to 10. Since it is, the program enters body of the loop. After the body of the loop is executed, we run the control variable modification part, which increments the counter by 1, giving it the value 2. Then we run the test again and continue executing the body and incrementing by one until the condition is no longer true.

Listing 5.9 is a complete example using a for loop to calculate the average grade for a class of students.

```
// Example5_9
using System;

namespace csbook.ch5
{
    class GradeAverageCalculator
    {
        // calculate the average grade for the class.
        // pass in the number of students.
        public double CalculateAverage(int numberStudents){
            double avg = 0;

            // add up all the scores
            for (int i = 0; i < numberStudents; i++){
                Console.Write("Enter grade for student {0} ",
                                i);

                avg += double.Parse(Console.ReadLine());
            }

            // divide by the number of scores
            avg /= numberStudents;

            return avg;
        }
    }

    class Example5_9
    {
        static void Main(string[] args){
            try{
                // find out how many students in the class
                Console.Write("How many students? > ");
                int studentCount = int.Parse(Console.ReadLine());

                // calculate the class average
                GradeAverageCalculator calc =
                    new GradeAverageCalculator();

                double avg = calc.CalculateAverage(studentCount);

                // print the result
                Console.WriteLine("The class average is " + avg);
            }
            catch{
                Console.WriteLine("Bad input");
            }
        }
    }
}
```

Listing 5.9

Listing 5.9 shows an example using a for loop. The listing defines a class named GradeAverageCalculator that exposes a public method named CalculateAverage. The method takes a parameter that tells how many times the for loop should execute.

The method declares a double variable named *avg* and initializes it to 0. Then the for loop executes the specified number of times, prompting the user for a grade and accumulating the value into the total. After the loop exits, the total score is divided by the number of times the loop executed. Finally, the computed average is returned.

The second class in the listing is the driver of the program. Its name is Example5_9 and it contains the Main method. The first thing Main does is prompt the user to find out how many students are in the class. Then it creates an object of the GradeAverageCalculator class and calls its CalculateAverage method, passing the number read from the keyboard as the number of students to read grades for.

The value returned from the CalculateAverage method is stored in a variable and then printed out to the console. To guard against errors that may occur if the user types in a nonnumeric string for a grade, the entire Main method is enclosed in a try block.

Chapter 6 – Working With Classes

Classes are the blue prints that objects are constructed from. You have already written several classes in previous chapters. Classes contain properties and methods that are grouped together to represent an object or idea. You have hopefully noticed that even the minimal C# application requires at least one class definition that contains a Main method.

In this chapter, you will learn how to create and use classes. We will begin by defining a simple class and creating one of its objects. We will build on that class by providing different ways to initialize its members, defining methods and operators, properties, and indexers.

Creating Classes

You define a class by declaring the class with the *class* key word, specifying the name of the class, and providing a body. The body of the class contains all the data and methods of that class that you can use to work with the class and its objects.

Typically, a class represents something in the application that you are creating. In a payroll application, you might have an Employee class containing variables to store a name, social security number, and date of hire. In an online bookstore, you might have a Customer class, containing the email address, phone number, and billing address. The type of data you put in the class depends on what the class is to be used for. You can store any data in a class that you want to, even objects created from other classes.

Let's create a class that defines a Circle. The Circle class needs to store information that describes a circle, such as X and Y coordinates and a radius. The following class definition will get us started.

```
class Circle
{
    public int centerX;
    public int centerY;
    public int radius;

    public void PrintData()
    {
        Console.WriteLine("Center ({0},{1}) Radius {2}",
            centerX, centerY, radius);
    }
}
```

The Circle class is useful because it groups related data into an abstraction. Each object of Circle that is created will store its own centerX, centerY, and radius variables. During the lifetime of a Circle object, the values of those variables may change. At any given moment, those variables describe the Circle's current state. Member variables are often called *state variables* because the data they hold represents the state of the object. You will also see member variables called *Fields*.

The Circle class also contains a method named PrintData, which displays the current state information in the console window. All data and methods have been defined as public so that they are accessible from any code that can create a Circle object.

The listing for Example6_1.cs defines a Circle class.

```
// Example6_1.cs
using System;

namespace csbook.ch6{
    class Circle{
        public int centerX;
        public int centerY;
        public short radius;

        public void PrintData(){
            Console.WriteLine("Center ({0},{1}) Radius {2}",
                centerX, centerY, radius);
        }
    }

    class Example6_1{
        static void Main(string[] args){
            // create two circles
            Circle c1 = new Circle();
            c1.centerX = 10;
            c1.centerY = 20;
            c1.radius = 5;

            Circle c2 = new Circle();
            c2.centerX = 50;
            c2.centerY = 50;
            c2.radius = 20;

            // display their data
            c1.PrintData();
            c2.PrintData();
        }
    }
}
```

Listing 6.1

In the listing, the Main method creates two Circle objects and assigns values to their member variables. Then Main calls the PrintData method on each instance. The output is shown below.

```
Center (10,20) Radius 5
Center (50,50) Radius 20
```

Figure 6.1

Self Reference

The PrintData method was defined within the Circle class, giving it access to any other data or methods defined within the class. Another way to think of this is that each Circle object stores its own copy of that data. The copy of the member variables within the scope of the call to PrintData is the copy that belongs to the same object that the call was invoked through. In other words, calling *c1.PrintData* prints the data from c1 and calling *c2.PrintData* prints the data within c2.

A more explicit way to reference the member variable of the current object is by using the '*this*' keyword. The this keyword references the object that the current method call belongs to. The this keyword is implied and does not usually need to be used to reference a member variable. Consider the next example.

```
// Example6_2.cs
using System;

namespace csbook.ch6
{
    class ThisReferenceDemo
    {
        public int x;

        public void PrintX(int x)
        {
            Console.WriteLine(x);
            Console.WriteLine(this.x);
        }
    }
```

```
class Example6_2
{
    static void Main(string[] args)
    {

        ThisReferenceDemo demo = new ThisReferenceDemo();
        demo.x = 10;
        demo.PrintX(50);
    }
}
}
```
Listing 6.2

In Example6_2.cs the ThisReferenceDemo class contains a public integer named x. It also contains a method named PrintX that takes an integer argument named x. Within the scope of the PrintX call, the argument x overshadows the member variable x. The first WriteLine statement will demonstrate this by printing the value 50, the value passed as argument.

```
50
10
```

Figure 6.2

The second WriteLine statement uses the this keyword to explicitly state that the member variable x is the one desired.

Public and Private Access Modifiers

The Circle class from Example6_1.cs declared all its members to be public, giving all other classes direct access its implementation. In general, it is best not to give programs direct access to the implementation of the class. When client programs access the implementation directly, they become dependent on that implementation. Then if the implementation is changed those client programs may no longer work.

A better solution is to hide the data and methods that implement the class by declaring them with the private access modifier so that they can not be called directly from other classes. Then you can expose the data and functionality of your class through public properties and methods. The public properties and methods provide a way for client classes to interface with your class. This way you can change the implementation of a class (its private data and methods) without breaking the other programs. Properties are the topic of the next section.

Properties

Properties provide a public interface for the *state data* of your objects. However, they do more that just wrap the private variables. Properties contain blocks of code that get and set the data, giving you an opportunity to convert to other data types, screen for invalid data, or perform other operations.

To declare a property, you specify its data type and name. Then follow up with a block of code containing a *get* block and a *set* block. The next listing contains a new version of the Circle class that hides its implementation in private variables and uses properties to expose its state data.

```
class Circle
{
    private int x;
    private int y;
    private int radius;

    public int X // property definition
    {
        get { return x; }
        set { x = value; }
    }
```

```
public int Y // property definition
{
    get { return y; }
    set { y = value; }
}

public int Radius // property definition
{
    get { return radius; }
    set
    {
        if (value < 0)
        {
            throw
                new Exception("Radius must be positive");
        }

        radius = value;
    }
}
}
```

The Circle class has three properties named X, Y, and Radius. Each property contains a get block and set block. The get block simply returns the current value of the member variable. The set block takes a new value and assigns it to the member variable.

Each set block uses the *value* keyword to assign a new value to the member variable. The value keyword holds the value that is being assigned to the property. Its type must match the type in the property's declaration.

In the set block for the Circle's Radius property, we screen for invalid input. The if statement checks to see if the value is less than zero and if so, throws an exception.

We can now access the properties through the dot operator just as we would a member variable or method.

```
Circle c = new Circle();
c.X = 10;
c.Y = 25;
c.Radius = 5;
```

Object Initialization

When objects are created with the *new* operator, a special member method called a *constructor* is invoked to initialize the instance. Every class has at least one constructor. If you do not provide a constructor then the compiler will provide a default constructor for you, which takes no arguments and simply initializes member variables with their default values.

Providing your own constructor allows you to define your own way to initialize new objects of the class. For example, we may want our Circles to be initialized with values of 1 for the x, y, and radius instead of the default integer value of 0.

Defining a Constructor

Constructor methods always have the same name as the class itself and they have no return value. The following code defines a constructor for the Circle class.

```
public Circle()
{
        x = 1;
        y = 1;
        radius = 1;
}
```

The constructor has been declared as public so that it can be called from outside of the Circle class. In this example of the Circle's members is initialized with the value of one.

The next listing defines a new version of the Circle class that contains a constructor. The Main method creates an instance of Circle and

immediately prints out its state without changing anything to show
that the constructor initialization has taken place.

```
// Example6_3.cs
using System;

namespace csbook.ch6
{
    class Circle
    {
        private int x;
        private int y;
        private int radius;

        public Circle(){
            x = 100;
            y = 100;
            radius = 100;
        }

        public int X{
            get { return x; }
            set { x = value; }
        }

        public int Y{
            get { return y; }
            set { y = value; }
        }

        public int Radius{
            get { return radius; }
            set {
                if (value < 0)
                {
                    throw new Exception("Radius must be positive");
                }

                radius = value;
            }
        }

        public string GetXML(){
            string xml =
                "<Circle>\n"
                    + "\t<X>" + x + "</X>\n"
                    + "\t<Y>" + y + "</Y>\n"
                    + "\t<Radius>" + radius + "</Radius>\n"
                + "</Circle>";
            return xml;
        }
    }
```

```
class Example6_3
{
    static void Main(string[] args)
    {
        Circle c = new Circle();
        Console.WriteLine(c.GetXML());
    }
}
```

Listing 6.3

This version of the Circle has a convenience method named GetXML that generates an XML formatted string showing the values of all member variables. The Main method creates a Circle object and displays its XML string without setting any of the values. The output shows that the constructor has initialized all values to 100.

```
<Circle>
        <X>100</X>
        <Y>100</Y>
        <Radius>100</Radius>
</Circle>
```

Figure 6.3

Destructors

A destructor is a special method defined within a class to clean up any resources when the object is removed from memory. Technically a destructor is not necessary if your class is only using managed memory because the garbage collector will clean up those resources as well. Use of unmanaged code like COM components may require a destructor.

The destructor's method declaration looks a lot like a no-argument constructor accept that the destructor's name is preceded by the ~ character. Destructors take no arguments and cannot be overloaded. You can also not add any access modifiers to a destructor. The following method could be a destructor for the Circle class.

```
~Circle()
{
    Console.WriteLine("Circle destructor");
}
```

When a program is finished with an instance of Circle, it will either set its reference to null or just allow the variable to go out of scope. Either way the CLR will notice that there are no more references to the Circle object and it will mark the object for garbage collection. Eventually the .NET garbage collector will come along and release the object from memory. If there is a destructor implemented on an object, the garbage collector will call it at that time.

Destructors in C# use a *non-deterministic* model; you don't really know when the garbage collector is going to call them. The algorithm that the garbage collector uses is not something you have much control over. However, you can request a run from the garbage collector by calling the System.GC.Collect method. You might make such a request when you know that you have just finished using a large amount of memory or you know that your program is experiencing some down time. In general, you should not count on a destructor method for any critical processing since you do not know when that processing will be called. Adding unnecessary destructors can hurt the performance of your program by adding extra work to the garbage collector. So it is best not to use them if they are not necessary.

Static Data and Methods

A static variable is a class variable that is shared by all objects of the class. When one object changes the data, all the objects of that class will see those changes. Static variables do not store state data for an object since they do not belong to a specific object. You declare a static variable using the static keyword in the variable's declaration.

The following example uses a static variable to keep track of how many objects have been created.

```
// Example6_4.cs
using System;

namespace csbook.ch6
{
    class ReferenceCounter
    {
        public static long refCount = 0;

        public ReferenceCounter()
        {
            // each new one bumps up
            // the count
            refCount++;
        }
    }

    class Example6_4{
        static void Main(string[] args)
        {
            // create some ReferenceCounters
            new ReferenceCounter();
            new ReferenceCounter();
            new ReferenceCounter();

            // print the value of the static variable
            Console.WriteLine("Created {0} objects",
                    ReferenceCounter.refCount);
        }
    }
}
```

Listing 6.4

The example defines a ReferenceCounter class that contains a static variable named refCount. Each time a new ReferenceCounter object is created the constructor method increments refCount by 1. The refCount variable will keep track of how many objects have been created.

The Main method creates three ReferenceCounter objects and then writes out the value of refCount. Notice that the refCount variable is accessed through the class name instead of through a variable name. All static variables and methods are accessed through the class name.

The output of the program shows that three objects have been created.

```
Created 3 objects
```

Figure 6.4

Static Methods

Static methods belong to an entire class instead of any particular object of the class. Like static variables, you invoke them through the class name instead of an instance. In fact, they can be called without ever instantiating the class at all.

A good example of a static method is the Main method of any C# program. When the CLR executes a program, it loads the class into memory but it does not create an object of that class. It just calls the Main method through the class name. This is why Main must be declared as static. If it were not, the CLR would not be able to call it.

Because static methods do not belong to a particular instance, they do not have access to instance data or methods. Consider the following listing that attempts to call an instance method from Main.

```
// Example6_5.cs
using System;

namespace csbook.ch6
{
    class Example6_5
    {
        void PrintMessage(string msg)
        {
            Console.WriteLine(msg);
        }

        static void Main(string[] args)
        {
            // attempting to call a nonstatic method
            PrintMessage("Hello"); // fails to compile
        }
    }
}
```
Listing 6.5

The listing fails to compile because the Main method is static and does not have access to the nonstatic PrintMessage method. If we really want to call PrintMessage from Main then we have to either make PrintMessage a static method too or create an instance of the Example6_5 class and invoke the PrintMessage method through that instance.

```
static void Main(string[] args)
{
    Example6_5 example = new Example6_5();
    example.PrintMessage("Hello");
}
```

Static class members are useful for reference counting, constants, and methods that do not require access to fields. The need for static members depends on the requirements of your class. Keep in mind the following rules when using static members.

Rules For static methods
1. Static methods *can* access other static methods and data directly even if they are declared as private.
2. Static methods *cannot* access instance methods or data without creating or using an object.
3. Nonstatic methods *can* access static methods and data as well as other instance data and methods.

Value and Reference Parameters

Parameters that are passed to methods can either be passed by value or reference. By default, parameters are passed by value. When a parameter is passed by a value, a copy of it is passed to the method. Any modifications to the variable will change the copy, not the original variable. When a variable is passed by reference, it is the address of the original variable that is passed to the method and any changes to the parameter will affect the original variable passed.

Consider the following class definition. The SetValue class contains a single method named SetX, which assigns a value of 100 to the variable that was passed to it. However, the SetX method accepts the parameter by value, the default way. So it is the copy that we are really assigning 100 to, not the original variable that was passed to the method.

```
class SetValue
{
    public void SetX(int x)
    {
        x = 100;
    }
}
```

Below we see a code segment that calls the SetX method. It declares an int variable named myValue and initializes it to 0. Then myValue is passed to the SetX method, which attempts to modify it. Afterwards, we display the value with a WriteLine statement. The WriteLine statement will show that myValue will still be 0 after the call to SetX.

```
SetValue sv = new SetValue();

int myValue = 0;
sv.SetX(myValue);

Console.WriteLine("The value is " + myValue);
```

To pass a variable by reference you must use the *ref* keyword. The ref keyword must be used in two places. First it must be used when the method is declared, just before the variable declaration in the header of the method. It also must be used at the point where the method is being called. The next example is the same as the previous except that the integer is being passed by reference.

```
// Example6_6.cs
using System;

namespace csbook.ch6
{
    class SetValue{
        public void SetX(ref int x){
            x = 100;
        }
    }

    class Example6_6{
        static void Main(string[] args){
            SetValue sv = new SetValue();

            int myValue = 0;
            sv.SetX(ref myValue);

            Console.WriteLine("The value is " + myValue);
        }
    }
}
```

Listing 6.6

The Main method initializes myValue to zero. However, the output shows that after the call to SetX the value is 100.

```
The value is 100
```

Figure 6.5

Using out Parameters

In place of the ref keyword, you can also use the out keyword. Using out is a lot like using ref, but it has one big advantage. Generally C# requires you to initialize every variable before passing it off to a function but the out keyword informs the compiler that the method you are passing the variable to will initialize it for you.

The next example is the same as the previous except for using out in place of ref. Notice that this time we did not initialize myValue before passing it to the SetX method.

```
// Example6_7.cs
using System;

namespace csbook.ch6
{

    class SetValue{
        public void SetX(out int x)
        {
            x = 100;
        }
    }
```

```
class Example6_7{
    static void Main(string[] args)
    {
        SetValue sv = new SetValue();

        int myValue;
        sv.SetX(out myValue);

        Console.WriteLine("The value is " + myValue);
    }
}
```

Listing 6.7

The output shows that the value of the variable has been initialized to 100 by the SetX method.

```
The value is 100
```

Figure 6.6

Attributes

Attributes provide extra information to the compiler about methods, data, or other elements of your program. Most usages of attributes are for advanced programming practices so you may not need to work with them very much. One common use of an attribute is to access functions from an unmanaged DLL, such as the Windows API.

To apply an attribute you enclose it in square brackets just before the line of code that you want it applied to. Some attributes take arguments. The DllImport attribute takes the name of the DLL file containing the imported function as its argument.

```
[DllImport("User32.dll")]
public static extern Int32 SendMessage(IntPtr hwnd, Int32 wMsg,
                                        Int32 wParam, Int32 lParam);

[DllImport("User32.dll")]
public static extern Int32 FindWindow(string className,
                                        string windowName);
```

The SendMessage and FindWindow method declarations shown above have been declared as external methods that need to be loaded from a DLL. The DllImport attribute tells the compiler which DLL contains those functions.

Overloading Methods

You can define multiple methods with the same name within a class as long as they take different data types for their parameters. This is called *overloading* the method. Overloading is useful because often there are multiple ways to do the same thing and one of those ways may be better than others, depending on the circumstances.

In Listing 6.8, we overload the Add method of the AddNumbers class. The first version takes two double values and returns their sum. The second version takes three values.

```
// Example6_8.cs
using System;

namespace csbook.ch6
{
    class AddNumbers{
        public double Add(double x, double y)
        {
            return x + y;
        }

        // overload
        public double Add(double x, double y, double z)
        {
            return x + y + z;
        }
    }
```

```
class Example6_8{
    static void Main(string[] args)
    {
        AddNumbers add = new AddNumbers();
        double ans1 = add.Add(1, 2);
        double ans2 = add.Add(1, 2, 3); // call overload
        Console.WriteLine("ans1 is {0} and ans2 is {1}",
            ans1, ans2);
    }
}
```

Listing 6.8

The Main method creates an instance of the AddNumbers class. Then it creates two double values and initializes them with the return values of the Add methods. The first variable is initialized by the version of Add that takes two int parameters. The second variable is initialized by the version of Add that takes three integers. Finally, we display the results with a call to WriteLine. The output is shown below.

```
ans1 is 3 and ans2 is 6
```

Figure 6.7

Overloading Constructors

One of the most commonly overloaded methods is the constructor. This is because there are many ways in which you may want to initialize your objects. Each overload of the constructor provides a different way to initialize the object. The next example defines a class named StockPrice and overloads its constructor.

```
// example6_9.cs
using System;

namespace csbook.ch6{
    class StockPrice{
        // private data
        private double price;
        private string symbol;

        // public properties
        public double Price{
            get { return price; }
            set { price = value; }
        }

        public string Symbol{
            get { return symbol; }
            set { symbol = value; }
        }

        // constructor
        public StockPrice(){
            price = 0;
            symbol = "";
        }
        // overloaded constructor
        public StockPrice(string stockSymbol,
                          double stockPrice){
            symbol = stockSymbol;
            price = stockPrice;
        }
    }

    class Example6_9{
        static void Main(string[] args){
            // create with the no argument constructor
            StockPrice sp1 = new StockPrice();
            sp1.Symbol = "MSFT";
            sp1.Price = 50.00;

            // create with the overloaded constructor
            StockPrice sp2 = new StockPrice("MSFT", 50.00);
        }
    }
}
```

Listing 6.9

The StockPrice class of Listing 6.9 has two constructors. The first constructor takes no arguments and initializes the symbol and price members with an empty string and the value 0.00. The overloaded constructor takes a string and a double value as its arguments and uses them to initialize the values of its members. When you create an instance of StockPrice the compiler knows which version of the constructor to call by the types of the arguments that you provide, if you provide any at all.

The Exmaple6_9 class provides the Main method. Main creates two StockPrice objects. The first is created with the constructor that takes no arguments. The symbol and price members are then set using the Symbol and Price properties.

The second StockPrice object is created with the overloaded version of its constructor. The members are initialized from the constructor arguments. Not only does using the overloaded constructor require fewer lines of code, but it can also be more efficient. If you know what values you want to put in the properties at the time you create the object then you are better off initializing with those values instead of using default values only to change them later as we did with the first StockPrice object that we created.

The Default Constructor

All classes must have at least one constructor. If you do not provide any constructors then the compiler will provide one for you when it compiles your code. The default constructor that the compiler provides simply initializes members to their default values, which for reference types is null. If having null values in your object is a problem then you should provide a constructor of your own. In Listing 6.9 there is a default constructor that initialized the strings to empty strings instead of null references.

If you provide any constructors at all, the compiler will not provide a default constructor. This also must be considered when choosing which constructors to provide. If the StockPrice class from Listing 6.9 only had the constructor taking the string and double arguments then the compiler would not generate a no-argument constructor. The line

```
StockPrice sp1 = new StockPrice();
```

would generate a compiler error. Since the statement does not pass arguments to the constructor, the compiler assumes you are trying to call a no-argument constructor that does not exist.

When to Provide a Default Constructor
1. If the constructor is being overloaded and other parts of the program depend on a default constructor
2. If the class is going to be inherited by other classes
3. It is almost never wrong to provide a default constructor so why not just do it.

Calling an Overloaded Constructor

When you have overloaded constructors, you may find that you are duplicating some of the same logic in each constructor. It is possible to have one overloaded constructor to call another so that logic will only have to be written once. Consider this new version of the StockPrice class.

```
class StockPrice
{
    // private data
    private double price;
    private string symbol;

    // public properties
    public double Price
    {
        get { return price; }
        set { price = value; }
    }

    public string Symbol
    {
        get { return symbol; }
        set { symbol = value; }
    }

    // constructor
    public StockPrice()
        : this("", 0.00)
    {}

    // overload 1
    public StockPrice(string stockSymbol)
        : this(stockSymbol, 0.00)
    { }

    // overload 2
    public StockPrice(string stockSymbol, double stockPrice)
    {
        symbol = stockSymbol;
        price = stockPrice;
    }
}
```

This version provides three constructors. The first constructor is the no argument constructor. Its body is empty of any statements. None is needed because the constructor forwards the call to the overloaded constructor that takes a string and double as arguments. The syntax for a constructor to forward the call to an overloaded constructor is a colon after the argument list, followed by the *this* keyword. Used in this way, the *this* keyword tells the compiler to call a constructor for this class and provide the arguments in the parentheses.

The no-argument constructor in this example passes an empty string and the value 0.00 for the arguments to the overload. The second constructor takes a single string argument and forwards it to the overloaded constructor that accepts a string and double value. It passes the string that it receives to the overloaded constructor's string argument and passes 0.00 for the double value.

The third overloaded constructor is the one that the other two forward to. It is unchanged from the previous example. This constructor uses the string and double values that it receives to initialize its members. By overloading the constructors in this way you reduce the amount of code you write, isolating the initialization logic in one constructor and calling that one from the others.

Operator Overloading

When we add methods to a class that we created, we are really providing a means to perform operations on an object of that type. However, the C# language already has several operators built into the language. By overloading the existing operators, programming becomes more intuitive for users of your classes.

As an example, consider a class named Fraction. Each Fraction object contains a numerator and a denominator. There are several mathematical operations that one might need to perform on a Fraction object, such as addition, subtraction, multiplication, and division. One way to implement those operations is by providing a method such as

```
public Fraction Multiply(Fraction f)
{
    return new Fraction(numerator * f.numerator,
        denominator * f.denominator);
}
```

Then calling the operation would be like calling any other member function.

```
Fraction left = new Fraction(3, 4);
Fraction right = new Fraction(5, 8);
Fraction product = left.Multiply(right);
```

But it would be more intuitive to use the fraction with existing mathematical operators since the Fraction is a mathematical concept anyway. C# uses the * operator for multiplication. We would like to be able to write code like the following segment.

```
Fraction f1 = new Fraction(3, 4);
Fraction f2 = new Fraction(5, 8);
Fraction product = f1 * f2;
```

By default that code would not compile because there is no multiplication operator build into the language that knows how to handle objects of type Fraction, which is understandable since the class did not exist until I wrote it. Fortunately, C# provides the ability to overload operators using the operator keyword. In this way, I can extend the language to support my own classes with C#'s built-in operators.

The next listing implements a Fraction class that overloads the multiplication operator.

```
// Example6_10.cs
using System;

namespace csbook.ch6
{
    class Fraction
    {
        private int numerator;
        private int denominator;
```

```
// default to 0
public Fraction()
{
    numerator = 0;
    denominator = 1;
}


public Fraction(int n, int d)
{
    numerator = n;
    denominator = d;
}

public int Numerator
{
    get { return numerator; }
    set { numerator = value; }
}

public int Denominator
{
    get { return denominator; }
    set
    {
        if (value == 0)
        {
            throw new DivideByZeroException();
        }

        denominator = value;
    }
}

public static Fraction operator * (Fraction left,
                                   Fraction right)
{
    return new Fraction(
        left.numerator * right.numerator,
        left.denominator * right.denominator);
}

public Fraction Multiply(Fraction f)
{
    return new Fraction(numerator * f.numerator,
        denominator * f.denominator);
}
```

```
        public override string ToString()
        {
            return numerator.ToString()
                + "/"
                + denominator.ToString();
        }
    }

    class Example6_10
    {
        static void Main(string[] args)
        {
            // 3/4
            Fraction f1 = new Fraction(3, 4);

            // 5/8
            Fraction f2 = new Fraction(5, 8);

            // 15/32
            Fraction product = f1 * f2;

            Console.WriteLine(product.Numerator + "/"
                + product.Denominator);
        }
    }
}
```

Listing 6.10

The Fraction class first declares two private integers to store the numerator and denominator values. Next, the properties are defined to provide an interface for getting and setting those values. Notice that in the set block for the Denominator we check to see if the denominator is zero and throw a DivideByZeroException if that is the case.

The multiplication operator takes two arguments, both of them Fractions. The operator is defined as public and static and returns a new Fraction object. The operator keyword lets the compiler know we are defining an operator. We implement this operator by multiplying the numerators and denominators together and returning a new Fraction.

The listing also includes a Multiply method that does the same thing as the overloaded operator. It is always a good idea when you overload an operator to provide a public method that does the same thing because not all .NET languages support operator overloading and from those languages that do not, the operator would not be accessible.

The Main method creates two Fraction objects and multiplies them together using the overloaded multiplication operator. Then it prints the results out with a WriteLine statement. The output of the program is below.

```
15/32
```

Figure 6.8

Indexers

An indexer provides another way to access the data of an object. Indexers allow you to take one object and use it as a key to identify a member variable within the class. One use of indexers is to use strings as indexes for fields in the class. For example, a HealthDrinkMachine class might store an integer to hold the quantity of cartons of soymilk. To read or write that data you could use a property like the following statement.

```
healthDrinkMachine.SoyMilkQuantity = 10;
```

Or you could use an indexer to refer to the same field.

```
healthDrinkMachine["SoyMilk"] = 10;
int soyMilkQty = healthDrinkMachine ["SoyMilk"];
```

Here, instead of accessing the quantity of soymilk through a member variable or property we use the string "SoyMilk" as the key for an indexer.

The syntax for defining an indexer is similar to property syntax in that it has an access modifier, a return type, and has a block of code containing get and set blocks. What is different is the *this* keyword in the declaration of an indexer and the square brackets that contain the object to be used as the index.

```
public int this[string s]
{
    get
    {
        // get block
    }

    set
    {
        // set block
    }
}
```

The indexer is declared public and it returns an int. Within the square brackets, we must declare the type that will be used as an argument for the indexer. This example uses a string but any type can be used.

The get and set blocks within the indexer are used for getting and setting the data just like with properties. However, for the indexers to work properly you will need to test the object that was passed through the brackets and use it as a lookup key that maps to a field in the object.

Listing 6.11 provides a complete example that uses the HealthDrinkMachine class with an indexer. The HealthDrinkMachine class maintains an inventory of health drinks.

```
// Example6_11.cs
using System;

namespace csbook.ch6
{
    class HealthDrinkMachine
    {
        // member variables
        private int soyMilk;
        private int carrotJuice;

        // define some indexers
        public int this[string s]
        {
            get
            {
                if (s == "SoyMilk")
                    return soyMilk;
                else if (s == "CarrotJuice")
                    return carrotJuice;
                else return 0;
            }

            set
            {
                if (s == "SoyMilk")
                    soyMilk = value;
                else if (s == "CarrotJuice")
                    carrotJuice = value;
            }
        }
    }

    class Example6_11
    {
        static void Main(string[] args)
        {
            string drinkString = "";
            HealthDrinkMachine machine = new HealthDrinkMachine();

            machine["CarrotJuice"] = 5;
            machine["SoyMilk"] = 10;

            Console.WriteLine("We have CarrotJuice and SoyMilk.");
            Console.WriteLine("Which drink do you want?");
            drinkString = Console.ReadLine();
```

```
        // get the quantity
        int qty = machine[drinkString];
        if (qty == 0)
        {
            Console.WriteLine("Sorry, we are out of that.");
        }
        else
        {
            qty--;
            machine[drinkString] = qty;
            Console.WriteLine("We have {0} servings of {1} left.",
                qty, drinkString);
        }
    }
}
}
```

Listing 6.11

Within the Main method, the strings "CarrotJuice" and "SoyMilk" are used to set and then retrieve the values. We prompt the user to ask what they want to drink and whatever they type in is used as a key to the indexer. Then we read the quantity for that drink and subtract one from it. Finally, we update that quantity using the indexer. The output is shown below.

```
We have CarrotJuice and SoyMilk.
Which drink do you want?
SoyMilk
We have 9 servings of SoyMilk left.
```

Figure 6.9

Indexers are very useful for mapping data from one type to another. In Listing 6.11, we mapped a string to an integer that represents the quantity of a particular drink.

Multiple Files and References

So far all the programs we have written were contained within a single source file and compiled into a single executable file. To make our classes more accessible by other projects it is best to put classes into their own source files. Below we list two classes, each in their own source file. Then we compile both files into a single executable program.

First is the Greeting class. This class contains a single public method named SayHello with a one-line implementation that prints Hello to the screen. The class is defined within the greeting.cs file.

```
// greeting.cs
using System;

namespace csbook.ch6
{
    public class Greeting
    {
        public void SayHello()
        {
            Console.WriteLine("Hello");
        }
    }
}
```

Listing 6.12

The next listing is a client of the Greeting class. It is defined in the Example6_12.cs file.

```
// Example6_12.cs
using System;

namespace csbook.ch6
{
    class Example6_12
    {
        static void Main(string[] args)
        {
            Greeting g = new Greeting();
            g.SayHello();
        }
    }
}
```

Listing 6.13

Both of these files can be compiled into the same executable file with the following command line.

```
csc /out:Example6_12.exe Example6_12.cs Greeting.cs
```

Figure 6.11

The csc command is the command to execute the C# compiler. The first argument, */out:Example6_12.exe* says to name the output file Example6_12.exe. Then we list the C# source files that should be included in the compilation.

Partial Classes

With C# you can spread the implementations of your classes across multiple source files. This is especially convenient when your classes become large. The *partial* keyword in a class declaration informs the compiler that parts of the class' implementation exist in other source files. To compile a partial class you need to list all the files containing the partial implementations of the class at the command line.

The following example creates a new version of the Greeting class. This new version contains two methods, one to give a greeting in English and another in French. Each method is defined in a separate source file even though they are part of the same class. The English and French versions of SayHello are defined in separate source files.

The English version is defined in the greetingEnglish.cs file.

```
// greetingEnglish.cs
using System;

namespace csbook.ch6
{
    public partial class Greeting
    {
        public void SayHelloInEnglish()
        {
            Console.WriteLine("Hello");
        }
    }
}
```

Listing 6.14

The French version is defined in the greetingFrench.cs file.

```
// greetingFrench.cs
using System;

namespace csbook.ch6
{
    public partial class Greeting
    {
        public void SayHelloInFrench()
        {
            Console.WriteLine("Bon Jour");
        }
    }
}
```

Listing 6.15

Finally, we define the client of the Greeting class. The Example6_13.cs file contains the implementation of the Example6_13 class, which contains the Main method for the application.

```
// Example6_13.cs
using System;

namespace csbook.ch6
{
    class Example6_13
    {
        static void Main(string[] args)
        {
            Greeting g = new Greeting();
            g.SayHelloInEnglish();
            g.SayHelloInFrench();
        }
    }
}
```

Listing 6.16

To compile the application you must list all source files that contain partial class implementations for the Greeting class.

```
csc Example6_13.cs greetingEnglish.cs greetingFrench.cs
```

Figure 6.12

Partial classes are also used by the Visual Studio .NET Designer's code generator when you create Windows Applications later on. The designer uses partial classes to separate designer generated code from the code that you write.

Compiling and Using DLLs

Compiling all source code into a single executable file may make it easier to distribute your application because you only have to copy the one EXE file. However, if your classes are contained in separate DLL assemblies then those assemblies can be maintained separately and shared between applications.

To compile a class into a DLL you must change the target type for the csc command. By default the target type is EXE. To make a DLL you must change the target type to library. The following command compiles the greetingEnglish.cs and greetingFrench.cs files into a library named Greeting.dll.

```
csc /target:library /out:Greeting.dll greetingEnglish.cs
greetingFrench.cs
```

Figure 6.13

After running that command you should find the Greeting.dll file in your directory.

To use the Greeting class we must reference its DLL when compiling our executable file. You reference a DLL with the /reference parameter in the command line. The following command compiles the Example6_13.cs file, referencing Greeting.dll.

```
csc /out:Example6_13.exe Example6_13.cs
/reference:Greeting.dll
```

Figure 6.14

The command calls the C# compiler to produce an output file named Example6_13.exe and use Example6_13.cs as the input. It also tells the C# compiler to reference the Greeting.dll file. Without that reference Example6_13.cs would not compile because the compiler needs to know where the Greeting class is defined.

Chapter 7 – Object Oriented Programming

In the real world we tend to classify objects by the characteristics that they have in common. Dogs, cats, monkeys, and humans are all animals. Corvettes, Lamborghinis, and my old college roommate's orange Gremlin can all be classified as cars, although the Gremlin can also be classified as birth control. In other words they inherit some common attributes from a base class, such as animal or car. With object oriented programming, we can also pass common traits to classes through inheritance. In this chapter, we will dig deeper into object oriented programming using inheritance.

Inheritance

We use inheritance when we define a class that is derived from an existing class. The existing class is called the *base* class and the class that inherits it is called the *subclass.*

When you declare a class that inherits from another class you specify the base class after the class name in the declaration, separating the pair by a colon. The following segment shows the syntax for using inheritance.

```
class Fruit
{}

class Apple : Fruit
{}
```

We first defined a base class named Fruit. Next we define the Apple class, which inherits from Fruit. The declaration for the Apple class includes a colon after the class name followed by the name of the base class.

Think of a payroll system that involves different types of employees. We can define a parent class named Employee that provides common functionality and properties that all employees need. Then we can create different types of employees such as ManagerEmployee and HourlyEmployee that inherit the Employee base class.

```
class Employee{

    private string ssn;
    private string name;
    private DateTime hireDate;

    public string Ssn{
        get { return ssn; }
        set { ssn = value; }
    }

    public string Name{
        get { return name; }
        set { ssn = value; }
    }

    public DateTime HireDate{
        get { return hireDate; }
        set { hireDate = value; }
    }

    public Employee()
    {
        ssn = ""; name = ""; hireDate = new DateTime();
    }

    public void PrintEmployee() {
        string xml =
            "<Employee>\n"
                + "\t<SSN>" + ssn + "</SSN>\n"
                + "\t<Name>" + name + "</Name>\n"
                + "\t<HireDate>" + hireDate + "</HireDate>\n"
            + "</Employee>";

        Console.WriteLine(xml);
    }
}
```

Now that we have an Employee base class we can create different types of employees that inherit it. Below you can see that creating a new type of employee is a trivial amount of code.

```
class HourlyEmployee : Employee
{
    public HourlyEmployee(string nm, string s, DateTime hire)
    {
        HireDate = hire; Ssn = s; Name = nm;
    }
}
```

```
class ManagerEmployee : Employee
{
    public ManagerEmployee(string nm, string s, DateTime hire)
    {
        HireDate = hire; Ssn = s; Name = nm;
    }
}
```

The first subclass we defined is the HourlyEmployee class. Because HourlyEmployee inherits from Employee, it has the properties Ssn, Name, and HireDate. Even though they have not been explicitly declared within the HourlyEmployee class, they exist because they have been inherited. The HourlyEmployee class also inherited the PrintEmployee method.

You can see in the constructor that the public properties HireDate, Ssn, and Name are being initialized from the variables passed as arguments to the constructor. The ManagerEmployee constructor does exactly the same.

When you create an object of one of those subclasses you can access those inherited members just as you would if they were declared right in the class.

```
// create an manager
ManagerEmployee mgr =
    new ManagerEmployee("Anthony Francis",
                "345-67-8910",
                new DateTime(1990, 2, 18));

mgr.Name = "Tony Francis";

// print the data
mgr.PrintEmployee();
```

Inheritance and Type Casting

When a subclass inherits from a base class it gets more than just data and methods. A relationship is formed between the two classes such that the subclass is a specialized version of the base class. Because of this inherited relationship an instance of the derived class can be used whenever an instance of the base class is expected.

For example, we could declare an Employee reference and point it at a ManagerEmployee object. The compiler will allow this because a ManagerEmployee is derived from Employee. The next code segment declares an Employee base class reference but points it at an object of ManagerEmployee.

```
Employee emp = new ManagerEmployee("Jeff Suddeth",
              "123-45-1234", DateTime.Now);
```

The situation does not automatically work both ways. We know that every ManagerEmployee object is an Employee, but we do not know that every Employee object is a ManagerEmployee. The following assignment is not valid.

```
ManagerEmployee mgr = new Employee();  // not allowed
```

Nor can we pass a base class object where a subclass is expected, as the following code attempts to do.

```
void ShowManagerInfo(ManagerEmployee emp)
{
    emp.PrintEmployee();
}

Employee emp = new Employee();
ShowManagerInfo(emp); // not allowed. Must be ManagerEmployee!
```

The previous two cases were not valid because there will most likely be other classes that inherit from Employee, but not from

ManagerEmployee. There could be ContractEmployee, PartTimeEmployee, or TemporaryEmployee, all derived from Employee. If we write a method that assumes every employee object that it receives is a ManagerEmployee then not only would our method be useless for the other Employee types, but it would likely throw an exception if we call a method that ManagerEmployee implements but the others do not.

Still, there are valid cases when you need to cast from a base reference to a subclass reference. One case is when working with data collections such as the ArrayList, which you will read about in chapter 8. When you really need to cast a base reference to a subclass, you have two ways to explicitly perform the cast.

Explicit Casting

You can explicitly cast from a base class reference to a subclass using the type cast operation just as you would down cast from a long to an int. The following code attempts to retrieve a ManagerEmployee object from an ArrayList collection. The ArrayList returns the ManagerEmployee as the object type. So the code needs to cast the object reference to a ManagerEmployee reference before using it.

```
// create an array list to store managers
ArrayList managers = new ArrayList();

// create 3 managers and stick them in the ArrayList
managers.Add(new ManagerEmployee("Jeff",
                "555-12-3456", DateTime.Now));

managers.Add(new ManagerEmployee("Tony",
                "746-99-8765", DateTime.Now));

managers.Add(new ManagerEmployee("John",
                "345-87-9876", DateTime.Now));

// get the first manager from the list and display his info
ManagerEmployee me = (ManagerEmployee)managers[0];

me.PrintEmployee();
```

In the example we get the first ManagerEmployee in the list in the line

```
ManagerEmployee me = (ManagerEmployee)managers[0];
```

The explicit type cast is necessary since the call to managers[0] will return an object type, not the ManagerEmployee type. However, casting from an object type to a subclass is risky because if someone stuck an object in that list that is not a ManagerEmployee (or a class that inherits from it) then the cast operation will throw an InvalidCastException. So to do this method safely we should use a try catch block.

```
// get the first manager from the list and display his info
try
{
    ManagerEmployee me = (ManagerEmployee)managers[0];
    me.PrintEmployee();
}
catch (InvalidCastException ex)
{
    Console.WriteLine("Invalid Cast: " + ex.Message);

}
```

Casting With the 'as' Operator

If you do not want to worry about exceptions there is a second way to cast from a base type down to a subclass type. The *as* operator will check to see if the object inherits the type that you are trying to assign to before returning it. If the object does not inherit from that type, the operation will return a null reference. This means you must test the returned value for null before using the object.

```
// get the first manager from the list and display his info
ManagerEmployee me = managers[0] as ManagerEmployee;
if (me != null)
{
    me.PrintEmployee();
}
```

The two methods shown both provide safe mechanisms for casting from a base type to a subclass type. However, in general you should try to design your programs to minimize the necessity for explicit type casting. The extra work of type checking and casting can be quite a burden and affect the performance of time critical applications.

Testing the Runtime Type with the 'is' Operator

You can also check the runtime type of an object using the logical *is* operator. The *is* operator does not perform a cast, it just checks to see if the object's type matches the type you are testing for. The operation returns true if the object is or inherits from the type you are testing against. Otherwise it returns false.

```
void Test(object obj)
{
    if (obj is string)
    {
        Console.WriteLine("It is a string");
    }
}
```

Inheritance and Access Modifiers

In the Employee example shown earlier the subclasses initialized the base class data by calling on the public properties, not by assigning to the private data directly. This is because private data is not accessible from anywhere but within the class that contains it. Even subclasses cannot access private data.

If you want the subclasses to be able to access a piece of data then instead of declaring the data as private, use the *protected* modifier. The protected modifier prevents access to the variable or method; accept by the containing class or any subclasses.

The following example shows a Customer base class and an OnlineCustomer subclass that inherits Customer and adds an EmailAddress property. The name and accountNumber in the Customer class have been declared with the protected access modifier so that child classes can access them directly. However, they are still private to the rest of the world.

```
class Customer
{
    protected string name;
    protected string accountNumber;

    public Customer()
    {
        name = "";
        accountNumber = "";
    }

    public string Name
    {
        get { return name; }
        set { name = value; }
    }

    public string AccountNumber
    {
        get { return accountNumber; }
        set { accountNumber = value; }
    }
}

class OnlineCustomer : Customer
{
    protected string emailAddress;

    public OnlineCustomer(string custName,
                   string custAcct, string email)
    {
        emailAddress = email;
        name = custName;
        accountNumber = custAcct;
    }
```

```
public string Email
{
    get { return emailAddress; }
    set { emailAddress = value; }
}

}
```

In the constructor for OnlineCustomer we access the name and accountNumber fields directly instead of going through the public properties. The list of access modifiers is below.

Access Modifiers
1. public – Unrestricted access
2. protected – restricted to containing class and child classes
3. private – restricted to the containing class
4. internal – restricted to the same assembly (DLL or EXE containing the code)
5. protected internal – restricted to containing class and child classes in the same assembly

The ability to control which classes have access to data and methods is a powerful abstraction tool that you can use to minimize the dependencies between the classes in your applications. When used properly your programs will have fewer bugs and you will be able to change the implementation of classes without breaking other parts of your program.

Base Class Constructors

When a class is derived of a base class, it is important that the data declared within that base class be initialized properly. Since the constructor of the subclass may attempt to use base class data, it is important to initialize the data before the subclass constructor is even called. This is why whenever you construct an object, C# makes sure that the base class constructor is called first. Consider the next pair of classes.

```
class Shape
{
    public Shape()
    {
        Console.WriteLine("Shape constructor");
    }
}

class Triangle : Shape
{
    public Triangle()
    {
        Console.WriteLine("Triangle constructor");
    }
}
```

Shape is the base class. It provides no data or methods outside of the constructor, but it does contain a WriteLine statement to announce that its constructor is being called. The Triangle class is derived from Shape. It also provides no functionality other than a constructor method that contains a WriteLine statement. The next statement constructs a Triangle object.

```
Triangle t = new Triangle();
```

The Triangle constructor is called and you would intuitively expect to see its output. However, when the statement is executed you also see the output from the Shape constructor. Just as important is the order of the calls to the constructors. By the output you can see that the base class constructor is called first.

```
Shape constructor
Triangle constructor
```

Figure 7.1

If the Shape base class was derived of some other base class then we could consider that base to be the grandparent of Triangle. As you might guess, in that case the grandparent constructor would be called, then the Shape constructor, and finally the Triangle constructor.

In the preceding example there were actually three constructor calls made. The first was for the *object* class because all classes are derived from it. However, the object constructor did not write any output.

Overloaded Parent Constructors

As we just learned in the last chapter, we can overload constructor methods to provide different ways to initialize the objects. However, if there are overloaded constructors in the base class, then how does the compiler know which one to call when creating a child class object?

If we do not explicitly tell the compiler which base class constructor to call, it will assume that we want to call the no-argument constructor. That is fine, but there is a subtle point of interest here. You learned in the last chapter that if you provide a constructor that accepts arguments, then the compiler will not generate a default constructor for you. In that case, there would be no default constructor. Check out the next example.

```
class Fruit
{
    public Fruit(bool hasSeeds)
    { }
}

class Apple : Fruit
{
    public Apple()
    { }
}
```

The Fruit class has a constructor that takes a bool parameter. Therefore, the compiler will not generate a default constructor. However, we have added a subclass named Apple. The Apple constructor will attempt to call a default constructor for the Fruit class because we have not instructed it to do otherwise. Yet, no default constructor exists for the Fruit class. In this case the compiler forces a call to a no-argument constructor for the Fruit class even though no such constructor exists. Then the compiler issues an error about a nonexistent constructor call.

To fix the problem we need to tell the Apple constructor to call the Fruit constructor that takes a bool argument. We do that by using the colon operator again. The next segment is the correct way to specify which base class constructor we want to call.

```
class Fruit
{
    public Fruit(bool hasSeeds)
    { }
}

class Apple : Fruit
{
    public Apple() : base(true)
    { }
}
```

In the declaration for the Apple's constructor we follow it up with a colon and the *base* keyword. When the base keyword is used in the line of a constructor declaration it tells the compiler which base class constructor we want to call. We specify which base constructor to call by passing arguments in the parentheses. The compiler will know which base constructor to call by the types of those parameters. Since we pass a single bool value to the base call, the compiler will look for and find the Fruit constructor that takes a single bool.

If we want to call the base constructor that takes no arguments we could leave the arguments out of the base().

```
public Apple() : base()
{ }
```

But that would just be extra typing because the compiler calls that one
by default anyway.

Method Overriding

When a class inherits from a base class it gets all the public and
protected members of that base class, but that does not mean that we
have to leave them as they are. We have the ability to redefine those
members in anyway that fits our needs. Redefining an inherited
method is called *overriding*.

```
// Example7_4.cs
using System;

namespace csbook.ch7
{
    public class Vehicle
    {
        public void Drive()
        {
            Console.WriteLine("Driving the vehicle");
        }
    }

    public class Car : Vehicle
    {
        public new void Drive()
        {
            Console.WriteLine("Driving the Car");
        }
    }
}
```

```
class Example7_4
{
    static void Main(string[] args)
    {
        // create a Car
        Car c = new Car();
        c.Drive();
    }
}
```

Listing 7.4

Listing 7.4 contains three classes. The first class is the Vehicle class, which will be inherited. The Vehicle class defines a single public method named Drive that writes a line of text to the screen so that you know the Vehicle's version of the Drive method has been called.

The second class is the Car class, which inherits Vehicle. Since Car is a subclass of Vehicle, it inherits the Drive method. However, the Car class overrides the method. To override a method you include the *new* keyword in the method declaration. In the overridden version of Drive the statement printed to the screen makes it clear that the Drive method being called belongs to the Car class.

The final class defined in the listing is the Example7_4 class, which contains the Main method. It creates an instance of Car and calls its drive method. By the output you can tell that the version of the Drive method that was called really does belong to the Car.

```
Driving the Car
```

Figure 7.2

Calling the Base Class Version

It is often necessary for a child class to call the parent class' version of an overridden method. This is especially important when your program is inheriting classes from a library, such as the Windows Forms library where the base class' implementation of the method may have some important job to do. You can have an overridden subclass method call the base class' implementation using the *base* keyword.

```
public class Car : Vehicle
{
    public new void Drive()
    {
        Console.WriteLine("Driving the Car");

        // call parent class' implementation
        base.Drive();
    }

}
```

The Drive method of the Car class has been modified to call the Vehicle's version of the Drive class. In the listing you see that the Drive method still contains the new keyword indicating that this is an override of a subclass method. The second statement of Drive is a call to the base version. We use the *base* keyword followed by the dot operator and the method we want to call.

Now when the same Main method is executed, we see that both versions of the Drive method are called.

```
Driving the Car
Driving the vehicle
```

Figure 7.3

Overriding an inherited method is a useful way for a child class to customize a method for its own use. When an overridden method is called the compiler knows which version of the method to call by the type of the object invoked. If Drive is invoked on a Car reference then the Car version of Drive is called. If the object was a Vehicle reference then the Vehicle version of Drive is called. This is true even if you have a base class referring to a subclass.

```
Vehicle v = new Car();
v.Drive(); // calls vehicle version
```

In the statements above, the Vehicle reference is instantiated with a Car, a subclass of Vehicle. When the Drive method is called, it is the Vehicle version of that method that is invoked, because Vehicle is the data type for the variable referring to the object. However, you can also inform the compiler to invoke the version of Drive for the type of class instantiated, rather than the type that the reference was declared as. Doing so involves using *virtual methods*, which are bound at runtime instead of compile time.

Virtual Methods

A virtual method is not bound until runtime. This means that until the call is actually made at runtime we don't really know what type of object is implementing the method that we are calling. This is also called late binding.

Consider a method that takes a Vehicle object and calls its Drive method.

```
class Driver
{
    public void DriveTheVehicle(Vehicle v)
    {
        v.Drive();
    }
}
```

The DriveTheVehicle method takes a Vehicle object and calls its Drive method. Since Car inherits from Vehicle, we can also pass a Car object wherever a Vehicle object is expected.

```
Driver d = new Driver();
Car c = new Car();
d.DriveTheVehicle(c);
```

Reading the code, you would expect for the Car's Drive method to be called when DriveTheVehicle is invoked. However, that is not the case. The DriveTheVehicle method does not know anything about the Car. It only knows about the type in its declaration, the Vehicle. So that is the version of Drive that will be called.

We can tell the compiler not to bind the Drive call at compile time by declaring Drive as a *virtual method*. Virtual methods give us the ability to refer to an object by its base class but call the subclass implementation.

The following example defines Drive as a virtual method and overrides it in three different child classes.

```
// Example7_5.cs
using System;

namespace csbook.ch7
{
    public class Vehicle
    {
        public virtual void Drive()
        {
            Console.WriteLine("Driving the vehicle");
        }
    }
    public class Car : Vehicle
    {
        public override void Drive()
        {
            Console.WriteLine("Driving the Car");
        }
    }

    public class Boat : Vehicle
    {
        public override void Drive()
        {
            Console.WriteLine("Driving the Boat");
        }
    }

    public class SpaceShip : Vehicle
    {
        public override void Drive()
        {
            Console.WriteLine("Driving the SpaceShip");
        }
    }

    class Driver
    {
        public void DriveTheVehicle(Vehicle v)
        {
            v.Drive();
        }
    }
```

```
class Example7_5
{
    static void Main(string[] args)
    {
        // make a driver
        Driver d = new Driver();

        // make some vehicles
        Car c = new Car();
        Boat b = new Boat();
        SpaceShip s = new SpaceShip();

        // drive the vehicles
        d.DriveTheVehicle(c);
        d.DriveTheVehicle(b);
        d.DriveTheVehicle(s);
    }
}
```

Listing 7.5

In Listing 7.5, we define a Vehicle class that we use as the base class for three subclasses. The Vehicle class once again has a Drive method but this time we have made it virtual. The Car, Boat, and SpaceShip classes all inherit the Vehicle class and they all override the virtual method in their own way. When a method is virtual, we override it using the *override* keyword instead of *new* keyword that we used for the nonvirtual methods.

Next we declare a Driver class that contains a method named DriveTheVehicle. This method takes a reference to a Vehicle, the base class. Because the Car, Boat, and SpaceShip classes inherit Vehicle, objects of those classes can be passed to the DriveTheVehicle method.

The DriveTheVehicle method will behave differently depending on which type of object is passed to it. If we pass a Car object then Car's

Drive method will be called. If we pass a Boat object then the Boat's Drive method will be called. The Main method demonstrates this by creating one Car, one Boat, and one SpaceShip and passing each of them to the DriveTheVehicle method of the Driver object. The output is shown below.

```
Driving the Car
Driving the Boat
Driving the SpaceShip
```

Figure 7.4

The output is different depending on the type of object that is passed in at runtime. So the DriveTheVehicle method's behavior changes when we pass different types of Vehicles. We can change the behavior of DriveTheVehicle as many times as we want to without ever changing a line of its code. All we have to do is create a new class that inherits from Vehicle and override the virtual Drive method in a different way.

Try it! Create any class you want that inherits from Vehicle and overrides the virtual Drive method. Then create an object of that class and pass it to the DriveTheVehicle method.

Polymorphism

This technique of changing the behavior of code by passing in different subclass objects is called *polymorphism*. For a method to be polymorphic it must take a reference to a base class and call its virtual methods. In Example7_5.cs DriveTheVehicle was a polymorphic method.

Abstract Classes and Methods

When you think about it, what is a Vehicle, really? A Vehicle is not a concrete thing, but an idea. It is a generalization. It is an abstraction. The Car, Boat, SpaceShip objects are real. They are tangible. You can see yourself getting into a car and physically driving it, but you can't get into a Vehicle without knowing what kind of Vehicle it is. Is it a Car, a Boat, a SpaceShip, or something else?

Because a Vehicle is an abstraction, we may want to prevent other code from creating instances of Vehicles. The Vehicle class may exist as a parent class, but its only purpose is to provide an interface for common functionality that its subclasses will implement. We can declare references to Vehicles and point them at subclass objects, but we don't need to create Vehicles directly. We can enforce this usage of a class by defining the Vehicle class with the abstract keyword.

```
public abstract class Vehicle
{
    public virtual void Drive()
    {
        Console.WriteLine("Driving the vehicle");
    }
}
```

The abstract keyword tells the compiler that no one is allowed to create an instance of Vehicle. The Vehicle class will only be used as a base class to be inherited. If Vehicle is declared *abstract* then the next line of code will cause a compiler error.

```
// not allowed. Vehicle is abstract
Vehicle v = new Vehicle();
```

We can also define methods to be abstract. Think about it this way, how could we implement a method to Drive a Vehicle without knowing what type of Vehicle it is? We really need more information before we can attempt to drive it. Within the Vehicle class the Drive method provides an interface for common features that all Vehicle subclasses will support. Since all it does is provide the interface for the feature we don't have to provide an implementation for the Drive method within the Vehicle class. Instead we can define the method to be abstract.

An abstract method has no implementation. It must be implemented by a child class. If a child class does not provide an implementation for an abstract method then that child class must be defined as abstract as well, and therefore can also not be instantiated. We define a method to be abstract using the *abstract* keyword.

```
public abstract class Vehicle
{
    public abstract void Drive();
}
```

The Vehicle class is now a complete abstraction. It cannot be instantiated and its Drive method has no implementation. The Vehicle class serves only to provide a common interface for something that can be driven. That being the case, we can redefine Vehicle as an interface type. The next section talks about interfaces in C#.

Implementing Interfaces

The last section defined an abstract class named Vehicle that provided an interface for driving. C# supports the idea of an interface with special syntax that will help clean things up a bit. To define an interface you use the *interface* keyword followed by the name of the interface. Then you provide a block of code containing the declarations of the methods for the interface.

```
interface Vehicle
{
    void Drive();
}
```

The Vehicle interface contains a single method declaration, the Drive method. The Drive method is declared just as it was before, returning void and taking no arguments. The methods declared within an interface always have public access, but this is implied so you don't have to use the public access modifier. In fact, if you do the compiler considers that an error.

Implementing an interface is a lot like inheriting a class and overriding some of its methods. In fact the syntax for implementing an interface is the same as that for inheritance. You follow the class name with a colon and the name of the interface being implemented. The difference lies in the method implementation. When you implement an interface method you do not use the *new* or *override* keywords.

```
public class SpaceShip : Vehicle
{
    // implementing Vehicle's Drive method
    public void Drive()
    {
        Console.WriteLine("Driving the SpaceShip");
    }
}
```

Using an interface is simply a matter of declaring the interface reference and pointing it at an object that implements that interface. When you use a reference to an interface you can only call the methods defined within the interface. This seems like a restriction but it is actually a good one. If you were allowed to call methods defined in the implementation class then your code would depend on the implementation class. There could be many classes implementing the same interface and we would like to support them all. So if we restrict ourselves to only using methods declared in the interface then other programmers can create new implementation classes without breaking our code.

```
// Vehicle is an interface
// SpaceShip is the implementation class
Vehicle v = new SpaceShip();

// Calling an implementation method
v.Drive();
```

In the code segment we declare an interface reference for the Vehicle interface and point it at an implementation object of the SpaceShip class type. Because the variable we use when referring to the SpaceShip is of type Vehicle, we can only call methods declared in the Vehicle class. SpaceShip might have a method named JumpToLightSpeed, which is probably a cool method to call, but we can't call it through the Vehicle reference. We need to cast the object to the SpaceShip data type first.

```
SpaceShip s = (SpaceShip)v;
s.JumpToLightSpeed();
```

Sealed Classes and Methods

There may be times when you build a class in a library that you do not want other programmers to inherit. This gives you more control over how your classes are used by other programmers. If you do not want your class to be inherited by another class then you can use the *sealed* keyword in your class definition.

```
sealed class Apple
{
    // Apple implementation
    public void Test()
    {
        Console.WriteLine("Testing the apple");
    }
}
```

It is also possible to seal methods so they cannot be overridden by child classes. The following segment shows how this is done.

```
class Shape
{
    public sealed void Test()
    {
        Console.WriteLine("Testing the Shape");
    }
}

class Triangle : Shape
{
    public new void Test()
    {
        // can do this, Test has been sealed!
    }
}
```

In this segment the Test method is defined with the sealed keyword so it cannot be overridden in child classes. The Triangle class attempts to override it anyway and produces a compiler error.

The object Class and Its Methods

In C# all types inherit from the object class so it is beneficial to become acquainted with it. Since all types inherit from the object class, an object reference can refer to a variable of any type.

The following list shows some of the public methods defined within the object class. Since all types inherit from object, all types have these methods.

Public Methods of the object class
- Equals
- GetHashCode
- GetType
- ToString

Any of those methods can be overridden. The Equals method will take an object and compare it against itself. If you override the Equals method then you should also override the GetHashCode method or some of the classes in .NET's Collections namespace might not work correctly with your class.

The GetType method returns a Type object that contains information about the object's type at runtime. The Type class is used for reflection, a technique where an object examines information about itself.

By far the most commonly overridden method is the ToString method. The ToString method returns a string representation of an object. For numeric types like int and double, ToString will return the value of the variable as a string. This is why we can concatenate objects onto strings. The string's + operator can call the ToString method of an object and concatenate the returned string.

The object class also has a static method named ReferenceEquals. This method takes two object references as parameters and returns true if they are the same instance. Comparing references is not the same as comparing values. To compare the values you should use the Equals method.

Boxing and Unboxing

When we assign an object reference to a value type it is said that we are boxing the value type. A boxing example looks like this.

```
int x = 10;
object obj = (object)x;   // boxing
Console.WriteLine(obj);
```

In the code segment the x variable is boxed when it is cast as an object. Once it has been boxed we can use it like any other object. By placing it in the WriteLine statement the object's ToString method will be called to produce a readable string version of the boxed variable. The output of the WriteLine statement is

```
10
```

Figure 7.5

Boxing can be performed automatically. That is why we can use the x variable in the WriteLine statement without explicitly casting it to an object.

```
Console.WriteLine(x);
```

If we have an object reference that we know to be a boxed variable we can unbox the variable by casting the object back to its original type. Unboxing does not happen automatically. We must explicitly cast the object.

```
int y = (int)obj; // unboxing
Console.WriteLine(y);
```

Chapter 8 – Arrays and Collections

An array is a block of memory large enough to hold several variables of the same type. You reference the array in your program with a variable name. That name, along with an index to the element you want, gives you quick access to the individual elements it holds.

There are many applications for arrays. A customer has an array of orders. An order has an array of line items. The coffee bar has an array of menu items. A computer game has an array of sprites. The applications are endless. If you have a quantity of items that need to be stored in a structure that makes those items easily accessible then an array may be what you need. Once you create an array you can use it to sort, search, or modify your data.

There is an important consideration with an array. Since the array is a contiguous block of memory, you must specify how large that block of memory should be at the time you create the array. This means there is a finite number of items that the array will hold. This is a trade off for having fast access. If you need a data structure that will grow and shrink as you add and remove items then you should use one of the .NET collection classes instead.

The .NET Collection classes include the List, Stack, Queue, and Hashtable. Each is designed to structure data in a particular way to make it more efficient to access items in different situations. We will look at the collection classes later in the chapter.

Declaring and Using Arrays

Because arrays are objects and therefore reference types, creating an array is a two-step process. First you must declare the array and then you must create it with the *new* operator. To declare the array you must specify what type of data the array will hold and follow that type name with a pair of empty brackets. The brackets let the compiler know that you are declaring an array. Finally, you must give the array an identifier that you can use to reference it in code. The following line declares an array of integers.

```
int [] myArray;
```

But the array is not yet created, only declared. The value of *myArray* is null and trying to use it at this point would cause an exception to be thrown. The next line instantiates the array with the *new* operator.

```
myArray = new int[10];
```

You can also combine those two steps in a single line.

```
int [] myArray = new int[10];
```

Initializing the Array

When you create an array, its elements are initialized to the default value for the type in the array declaration. That would be 0, false, and null for numbers, bools, and references. After the array has been created, you can assign values to the elements with the index operator.

```
int [] myArray = new int[10];
myArray[0] = 100;
myArray[1] = 256;
myArray[2] = 15;
     ...
```

But if you know what the elements are going to be at the time you create the array, you can also provide an initialization list to initialize the values of the array when you create it.

```
double[] priceList = { 1.25, 1.55, 1.80 };
```

The initialization list is enclosed in the curly braces and contains a list of values of the appropriate type for the array. The elements in the list are separated by commas. The line of code above declares an array of double values and initializes it with a list of doubles.

Accessing Array Elements

To access an element of the array you use the name of the array followed by the pair of brackets containing the index of the element you want. Keep in mind that arrays are indexed starting from 0. For an array of 10 elements, the first element is at position 0 and the last element is at position 9.

The next example accesses the list of arguments typed at the command line of the program and prints them out.

```
// Example8_1.cs
using System;

namespace csbook.ch8
{
    class Example8_1
    {
        static void Main(string[] args)
        {
            for (int i = 0; i < args.Length; i++)
            {
                Console.WriteLine(args[i]);
            }
        }
    }
}
```

Listing 8.1

In Listing 8.1, the Main method accepts an array of strings that store the parameters that were typed at the command line when the user executed the program. The program loops through the elements of the array using a *for* loop. The array, itself being an object, contains a Length property telling how many elements it contains. We use that property in the logic of the *for* loop to figure out when the last element has been processed.

After compiling the program I ran it with the following command line, containing the names of some of my favorite coffees.

Example8_1 Sumatra Guatemala "Kenya AA"

The .NET CLR parses the command line on the spaces and stores the resulting strings in an array. Then the CLR passes the string array to the Main method as the *args* parameter. The quotation marks around the "Kenya AA" tell the CLR not to parse on the space so that "Kenya AA" is considered a single argument.

The output of the program is below.

```
Sumatra
Guatemala
Kenya AA
```

Figure 8.1

The foreach Loop

Looping through the elements of arrays and collections as in the previous example is so common that C# provides a special style of *for* loop just for that purpose. The *foreach* loop will iterate through an array or collection without using a counter variable. The *foreach* loop is designed to iterate through the elements of an array or collection but you cannot add or remove the elements from within the loop. The state of the array should remain unchanged while iterating over its elements.

The next code segment loops through the *coffees* array using a *foreach* instead of a counter variable.

```
string[] coffees = { "Kenya AA", "Guatamala", "Columbian" };

Console.WriteLine("Coffee List");
Console.WriteLine();
foreach (string s in coffees)
{
    Console.WriteLine(s);
}
```

The header of the loop declares a variable of the same type that is in the array. The example uses an array of strings, so the variable declared in the header must be of the string type as well. The body of the loop is executed for each item in the array. With each pass through the loop the *s* variable will reference the current string.

Array Methods

The Array class has a number of useful static and instance methods that you can use. These methods provide operations for searching, sorting, accessing elements, and efficient array copies.

Sorting and Searching

The next example demonstrates sorting and searching an array of strings.

```
// Example8_2.cs
using System;

namespace csbook.ch8
{
    class Example8_2
    {
        static void Main(string[] args)
        {
            string[] coffees =
                {
                    "Columbia",
                    "Kenya AA",
                    "Sumatra",
                    "Morning Blend",
                    "French Roast"
                };

            // sort them
            Array.Sort(coffees);

            // print them
            Console.WriteLine("Coffees sorted\n");
            for(int i=0; i<coffees.Length; i++)
                Console.WriteLine(i + ") " + coffees[i]);

            // search for one of my favorites
            int pos = Array.BinarySearch(coffees, "Kenya AA");
            Console.WriteLine("\n\nKenya AA is at position " + pos);
        }
    }
}
```

Listing 8.2

The Main method declares an array of strings to hold different types of coffee. The array is sorted with the static Sort method of the *Array* class. Then we print the elements of the array in their sorted order.

The static *BinarySearch* method takes a sorted array and an object, and then uses the binary search algorithm to find that item in the array. If the item is found then the position of that item in the sorted array will be returned. If the item is not found then the return value will be a negative number.

Copying Arrays

There may be times when you want to copy all the elements of one array into another. Since an array is a reference type, a simple assignment operation would not do the trick because that would only copy a reference to the array and not the array contents. One way to copy an array is to instantiate a new array and loop through all the elements, copying them into the new array one at a time.

```
string[] coffees2 = new string[coffees.Length];
for(int i=0; i<coffees.Length; i++)
{
    coffees2[i] = coffees[i];
}
```

However, this is not a very efficient way to copy an array. The quickest way to copy an array involves using pointers to memory, which we do not have in C#. Fortunately the Array class has a static method that handles Array copies efficiently for us. The static *Copy* method takes three parameters. The first is the source array for the copy operation. The second parameter is the destination. The final parameter is the number of items to be copied.

```
string[] coffees2 = new string[coffees.Length];

Array.Copy(coffees, coffees2, coffees.Length);

foreach (string s in coffees2)
    Console.WriteLine(s);
```

Table 8.1 – Array Methods

Method	Description	Example
Copy	Copies elements from one array to another	Array.Copy(src, dest, dest.Length);
BinarySearch	Searches for an element	pos = Array.BinarySearch(src, key);
Clear	Sets a range of elements to 0, false, or null	Array.Clear(src, 0, src.Length);
Length	Returns the number of elements in the array	arraySize = src.Length;

Example Using an Array of Data

A common use of an array is to store data records. These records may have been loaded from a database or the array could itself be used as the database, as in the next example. The example defines a *CoffeBar* class that uses an array of *Coffee* objects to store its product list. Each *Coffee* object is an entity that represents a type of coffee, storing the name of the coffee and the price.

The program lists its coffees to the console and asks the user if they want to order anything. The user can then type in the number for the type of coffee they want. The program continues to loop until the user wants to quit the program.

```
// Example8_3.cs
using System;

namespace csbook.ch8
{
    class Coffee
    {
        private string name;
        private double price;

        // constructors
        public Coffee() : this("", 0.0)
        {}

        public Coffee(string coffeeName, double coffeePrice)
        {
            name = coffeeName;
            price = coffeePrice;
        }

        public string Name
        {
            set { name = value; }
            get { return name; }
        }

        public double Price
        {
            set { price = value; }
            get { return price; }
        }
    }


    class CoffeeBar
    {

        private Coffee[] coffeeList =
                {
                    new Coffee("Kenya AA", 19.99),
                    new Coffee("Morning Blend", 16.97),
                    new Coffee("Decaff Hazelnut", 14.99),
                    new Coffee("French Vanilla", 12.99)
                };
```

```
public void Run() {
    while (OrderAgain())
    {
        Console.Write("\nEnter the number of the "
                        + "coffee you want>");
        try
        {
            int reply = int.Parse(Console.ReadLine());
            Console.WriteLine("\n{0,12} is {1:C2} "
                            + "per pound. Thank you.",
                        coffeeList[reply].Name,
                        coffeeList[reply].Price);
        }
        catch (FormatException)
        {
            Console.WriteLine("Bad format. Try again");
        }
        catch (IndexOutOfRangeException)
        {
            Console.WriteLine("Out of range. Try again");
        }
    }
}

private bool OrderAgain(){
    Console.WriteLine("\n\nHere are our coffees.");

    int id = 0;
    foreach (Coffee c in coffeeList)
    {
        Console.WriteLine("{0}) {1} - {2:C2} per pound",
            id++, c.Name, c.Price);
    }

    Console.Write("\nWould you like to order? (Y or N)>");
    string reply = Console.ReadLine();
    if (reply.ToUpper()[0] == 'Y')
    {
        return true;
    }

    return false;
}
```

```
class Example8_3  {
    static void Main(string[] args)
    {
        CoffeeBar cb = new CoffeeBar();
        cb.Run();

    }
  }
}
```

Listing 8.3

The *Coffee* class is defined to have the Name and Price properties. It has no methods defined other than the constructors. The no-argument constructor simply forwards the call to the overloaded constructor, passing some default arguments.

The *CoffeeBar* class declares an array of Coffee objects and uses it as a data source. The array is initialized with an initializer list at the time it is declared. Because the array contains reference types, each element is initialized with the new operator.

The CoffeeBar has one public method named Run. The Run method contains the main loop of the program. It calls the OrderAgain method to prompt a customer for an order and continues to loop until OrderAgain returns false, which happens when the user chooses not to order.

The *Example8_4* class is the driver of the application. It contains the Main method, which gets things rolling for us. Main creates an instance of the CoffeeBar and calls its Run method. The output below shows a sample run of the application.

```
Here are our coffees.
0) Kenya AA - $19.99 per pound
1) Morning Blend - $16.97 per pound
2) Decaff Hazelnut - $14.99 per pound
3) French Vanilla - $12.99 per pound

Would you like to order? (Y or N)>y
Enter the number of the coffee you want>1
Morning Blend is $16.97 per pound. Thank you.

Here are our coffees.
0) Kenya AA - $19.99 per pound
1) Morning Blend - $16.97 per pound
2) Decaff Hazelnut - $14.99 per pound
3) French Vanilla - $12.99 per pound

Would you like to order? (Y or N)>n
```

Figure 8.2

Sorting Arrays of Objects

Earlier we sorted an array of strings that contained the names of different coffees. In the last section our example used an array of Coffee objects. What if we want to sort that array too?

Before we can sort an array of Coffee objects we have to know how to compare Coffee instances. We need to know what makes one Coffee object have a higher value than another Coffee object - and that depends on what question we are asking when we request the sorting operation. Coffee objects have more than one field and we can define sorts on any of them. For starters, let's come up with a way to sort Coffee objects alphabetically by the name of the coffee. Then we will sort them again by price.

The IComparable Interface

One way to sort the array of objects is to have the Coffee class implement the *IComparable* interface, which is used by the *Array.Sort* method. The *IComparable* interface has one method named CompareTo that accepts an object reference. The method should be defined to cast the object parameter to its own type and then compare the object against itself. Listing 8.4 defines a Coffee class that implements IComparable.

```
// Example8_4.cs
using System;

namespace csbook.ch8
{
    class Coffee : IComparable
    {
        private string name;
        private double price;

        // constructors
        public Coffee()
            : this("", 0.0)
        { }

        public Coffee(string coffeeName, double coffeePrice)
        {
            name = coffeeName;
            price = coffeePrice;
        }

        public string Name
        {
            set { name = value; }
            get { return name; }
        }

        public double Price
        {
            set { price = value; }
            get { return price; }
        }
```

```
        public int CompareTo(object obj)
        {
            Coffee c = obj as Coffee;
            if (c == null)
            {
                throw
                    new ArgumentException("object is not a Coffee");
            }

            return name.CompareTo(c.name);
        }
    }


class Example8_4
{
    static void Main(string[] args)
    {
        Coffee[] coffeeList =
            {
                new Coffee("Kenya AA", 19.99),
                new Coffee("Morning Blend", 16.97),
                new Coffee("Decaff Hazelnut", 14.99),
                new Coffee("French Vanilla", 12.99)
            };

        Array.Sort(coffeeList);

        foreach (Coffee c in coffeeList)
        {
            Console.WriteLine("{0}\t\t{1}",
                c.Name, c.Price);
        }
    }
}
```

Listing 8.4

In our implementation of the *CompareTo* method we cast the object to a Coffee instance using the 'as' operator. If the object passed at runtime is not a subclass of Coffee then 'as' will return null. In that case we throw an exception. If the object is derived from Coffee then we compare it to the current object by calling the *CompareTo* method on the name property. The *Array.Sort* method can then treat our Coffee object as an IComparable and sort an array of Coffees.

There are two problems with this method of sorting. First, it requires us to change our Coffee class by implementing an interface. Not only might we not want to change the class, we may not even have access to the source code to change it. The other problem is that there is only one *CompareTo* method in the *IComparable* interface, so we can only define one way to sort the objects through this method. What we really need is to define a separate class that knows how to sort Coffee objects. For this purpose, .NET provides the *IComparer* interface.

The IComparer Interface

The *IComparer* interface contains a single method named Compare that takes two objects as parameters. If we create a class that implements this interface, we can define the Compare method to treat the objects as Coffee instances and compare them in any way we want. We can even create multiple classes that implement *IComparer* so that we can compare Coffee objects in different ways, allowing us to define multiple sorts.

An overloaded version of the *Array.Sort* method accepts an *IComparer* reference as a second parameter and uses it to compare the objects in the array as it sorts them. The next example defines two classes that implement *IComparer*. The first implements the Compare method to compare Coffee objects by their name. The second compares Coffee objects by price.

```
// Example8_5.cs
using System;
using System.Collections;

namespace csbook.ch8
{
    class Coffee
    {
        private string name;
        private double price;
```

```
        // constructors
        public Coffee()
            : this("", 0.0)
        { }

        public Coffee(string coffeeName, double coffeePrice){
            name = coffeeName;
            price = coffeePrice;
        }

        public string Name{
            set { name = value; }
            get { return name; }
        }
        public double Price{
            set { price = value; }
            get { return price; }
        }
    }
class CoffeeSortByName : IComparer
{
    public int Compare(object x, object y)
    {
        Coffee left = x as Coffee;
        Coffee right = y as Coffee;

        if (left == null || right == null)
        {
            throw new ArgumentException("object is not a Coffee");
        }

        if (left.Name.CompareTo(right.Name) < 0)
            return -1;
        else if (left.Name.CompareTo(right.Name) == 0)
            return 0;

        return 1;
    }
}

class CoffeeSortByPrice : IComparer
{
    public int Compare(object x, object y)
    {
        Coffee left = x as Coffee;
        Coffee right = y as Coffee;

        if (left == null || right == null)
        {
            throw new ArgumentException("object is "
                        + " not a Coffee");
        }
```

```
                if (left.Price < right.Price)
                    return -1;
                else if (left.Price == right.Price)
                    return 0;

                return 1;
            }
    }

    class Example8_5
    {
        static void Main(string[] args)
        {
            Coffee[] coffeeList =
                {
                    new Coffee("Kenya AA", 19.99),
                    new Coffee("Morning Blend", 16.97),
                    new Coffee("Decaff Hazelnut", 14.99),
                    new Coffee("French Vanilla", 12.99)
                };

            // sort by name first
            Console.WriteLine("Sorted by Name\n");
            Array.Sort(coffeeList, new CoffeeSortByName());
            foreach (Coffee c in coffeeList)
            {
                Console.WriteLine("{0}\t\t{1}",
                    c.Name, c.Price);
            }

            // now sort by price
            Console.WriteLine("\n\nSorted by Price\n");
            Array.Sort(coffeeList, new CoffeeSortByPrice());
            foreach (Coffee c in coffeeList)
            {
                Console.WriteLine("{0}\t\t{1}",
                    c.Name, c.Price);
            }
        }
    }
}
```

Listing 8.5

The Main method defines an array of Coffee objects and then sorts it in two different ways. First it creates a *CoffeeSortByName* object and passes it to the *Array.Sort* method. A foreach loop then prints out the properties of each element in the array so that you can see they are in fact sorted by name.

Next the Main method sorts the array, this time using a *CoffeeSortByPrice* object. Once again it prints the Coffees to the console showing that they are sorted by price.

```
Sorted by Name

Decaff Hazelnut            14.99
French Vanilla            12.99
Kenya AA                  19.99
Morning Blend             16.97


Sorted by Price

French Vanilla            12.99
Decaff Hazelnut           14.99
Morning Blend             16.97
Kenya AA                  19.99
```

Figure 8.4

Multidimensional Arrays

Arrays can also be expanded in multiple dimensions. You can define an array of two or three dimensions, or more if you can wrap your brain around it. Multidimensional arrays can be defined in two ways. The first type is used when all lengths of a dimension are the same, such as a rectangular shaped two-dimensional array. The two-dimensional array is declared using a comma in the array brackets to separate the dimensions. The lengths of those dimensions are not specified until the array is created with the *new* keyword.

```
int[,] timesTable = new int[13, 13];
```

The *timesTable* array is a two-dimensional array with 13 rows and 13 columns of integers. We can access an element of the array by specifying the index of both dimensions.

```
timesTable[4, 3] = 12;
```

The next example generates a multiplication table in a two dimentional array and prints it to the console.

```
// Example8_6.cs
using System;

namespace csbook.ch8
{
    class Example8_6
    {
        static void Main(string[] args)
        {
            int[,] timesTable = new int[13, 13];

            for (int i = 0; i < 13; i++)
                for (int j = 0; j < 13; j++)
                    timesTable[i, j] = i * j;


            for (int i = 1; i < 13; i++)
            {
                for (int j = 1; j < 13; j++)
                {
                    Console.Write("{0,4}", timesTable[i, j]);
                }
                Console.WriteLine();
            }

        }
    }
}
```

Listing 8.6

The listing first creates the timesTable array as a two-dimensional array of integers with 13 rows and 13 columns. Then it loops through the rows and columns with the i and j counter variables, setting the current value to the product of i and j.

The second set of nested for loops loops through the rows and columns again, this time printing them out. The result is a multiplication table.

```
1    2    3    4    5    6    7    8    9   10   11   12
2    4    6    8   10   12   14   16   18   20   22   24
3    6    9   12   15   18   21   24   27   30   33   36
4    8   12   16   20   24   28   32   36   40   44   48
5   10   15   20   25   30   35   40   45   50   55   60
6   12   18   24   30   36   42   48   54   60   66   72
7   14   21   28   35   42   49   56   63   70   77   84
8   16   24   32   40   48   56   64   72   80   88   96
9   18   27   36   45   54   63   72   81   90   99  108
10   20   30   40   50   60   70   80   90  100  110  120
11   22   33   44   55   66   77   88   99  110  121  132
12   24   36   48   60   72   84   96  108  120  132  144
```

Figure 8.5

Jagged Arrays

The second type of multidimensional array is the Jagged Array. A jagged array is an array where the lengths of the dimensions can be different. A jagged array is really an array of arrays. The extra dimensions must be created separately.

```
// jagged array
string[][] jag = new string[3][];

// create the second dimension
jag[0] = new string[2];
jag[1] = new string[4];
```

```
jag[2] = new string[3];
```

In the segment above the jag array has been declared as *an array of string arrays.* When we create the array with the new operator we only create the first dimension. For the other dimension we must create each separately since they will have different lengths. The result is an array shaped like the following image.

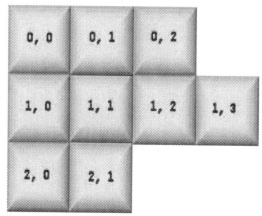

Figure 8.6

Accessing the elements of a jagged two-dimensional array can be trickier than rectangular shaped two-dimensional arrays because each row has a different number of columns (or each column has a different number of rows, depending on how you look at it).

The next example uses a jagged array of strings. It loops through the rows and columns twice, once to initialize the values and once to print them out.

```
// Example8_7.cs
using System;

namespace csbook.ch8
{
    class Example8_7 {
        static void Main(string[] args) {
            // jagged array
            string[][] jag = new string[3][];

            // create the second dimension
            jag[0] = new string[2];
            jag[1] = new string[4];
            jag[2] = new string[3];

            // initialize the elements
            for (int i = 0; i < jag.GetLength(0); i++){
                for (int j = 0; j < jag[i].GetLength(0); j++){
                    jag[i][j] = string.Format("({0,2}, {1,2})", i, j);
                }
            }

            // print the elements
            foreach (string[] strArray in jag) {
                foreach (string s in strArray)
                {
                    Console.WriteLine(s);
                }
            }
        }
    }
}
```

Listing 8.7

The first set of nested *for* loops initializes each element in the array
with a string containing its row and column number. Notice that the
condition statement in the *for* loop checks the *GetLength* method of
the array to figure out how many elements to loop over. The second
set of nested loops uses nested foreach loops to print the elements out.

```
( 0,  0)
( 0,  1)
( 1,  0)
( 1,  1)
( 1,  2)
( 1,  3)
( 2,  0)
( 2,  1)
( 2,  2)
```

Figure 8.7

Using .NET Collections

Arrays provide very fast access to data. The only trade off is that their size is fixed at the time you create them. You can only add as many elements to the array as it was created to store. .NET provides several collection classes that can store as many elements as needed. They are all stored in the System.Collections namespace. Each collection type stores and retrieves data in its own way, making your data storage more efficient in different circumstances. Internally, the elements of a collection are stored as object references. Since all types are derived from object, any data type can be stored in any collection class. This section looks at several of the collections provided by .NET.

The ArrayList

The ArrayList is like an array that has no bounds. It has methods for adding, removing, and retrieving elements. You can use the Count property to find out how many elements are in the ArrayList at a given time. You use the index operator to access an element at a given index, just like an array. Because you can remove elements from an ArrayList, the index of each element can change as the items are shifted around.

When you create an ArrayList, it initially creates a number of placeholders for data and adds more when necessary. If you want to know how many spaces are in an ArrayList, as opposed to the number of elements currently stored, you can use the ArrayList's Capacity property. Table 6.2 shows some of the useful properties and methods of the ArrayList.

Table 8.2 – ArrayList Methods

Method	Description	Example
Add	Add an object to the list	list.Add(customer);
Remove	Remove an object	list.Remove(customer);
RemoveAt	Remove by index	list.RemoveAt(5);
Count	The number of objects in the list	int num = list.Count;
[ ] operator	Gets or sets object at the index	list[2] = new Customer();
ToArray	Returns elements in an array	int [] intArray = list.ToArray(typeof(int));
Clear	Removes all elements	list.Clear();
Sort	Sorts elements. There are Overloads of this method.	list.Sort(new CoffeeSorter());
BinarySearch	Searches with binary search algorithm	int pos = ArrayList.BinarySearch("Sumatra");

The following example uses an ArrayList to store some string objects.

```
// Example8_8.cs
using System;
using System.Collections;

namespace csbook.ch8
{
    class Example8_8
    {
        static void Main(string[] args)
        {
            ArrayList list = new ArrayList();
            list.Add("alpha");
            list.Add("beta");
            list.Add("gamma");
            list.Add("delta");

            // print the first element
            string first = (string)list[0];
            Console.WriteLine("First Element: {0}", first);

            // print the last element
            string last = (string)list[list.Count - 1];
            Console.WriteLine("Last Element: {0}", last);

            // remove 'beta'
            list.RemoveAt(1);

            // print all elements
            foreach (string s in list)
            {
                Console.WriteLine(s);
            }
        }
    }
}
```

Listing 8.8

The Main method of Example8_6 creates an ArrayList and uses its Add method to add some strings. It then uses the index operator to retrieve the reference to the first element in the collection and store it in a variable named *first*. The element is returned as an object type and must be cast to string for the assignment statement to be valid. Then the listing uses the Console.WriteLine method to display the string.

Next the Main method gets the last element in the ArrayList using the index operator. The Count property returns the number of items in the ArrayList but we subtract one because the ArrayList is indexed from zero. We cast the object to a string type and store its reference in the *last* variable. Then we print it.

Next we use the ArrayList's RemoveAt method to remove an item from the collection. The RemoveAt method removes an item at a specified index. Finally, we print out the remaining items in the ArrayList with a foreach loop. Be careful not to remove items from a Collection while a foreach loop is iterating through the items, or the iterator used by foreach will become invalid, giving you unexpected results. Also, notice that the program uses the System.Collections namespace, where ArrayList is defined.

```
First Element: alpha
Last Element: delta
alpha
gamma
delta
```

Figure 8.8

ArrayLists are very useful data structures but there are times when other data structures may be better suited, such as the Stack or Queue data structures. The next section talks about the Stack data structure.

The Stack

The Stack data structure brings to mind a stack of plates at the line for the buffet. When clean plates are added to the stack, they are always added to the top. When you take a plate you must take the one on top, the last one added. This algorithm for storing and retrieving data (or plates for the buffet) is called Last In, First Out or *LIFO*.

You push items onto the Stack with its Push method. To retrieve the last item from the Stack you use the Pop method. The Pop method removes the item from the Stack and returns its reference. You can get the last item added without removing it from the Stack by calling the Peek method. Table 8.3 shows some Stack properties and methods.

Table 8.3 – Stack Methods

Method	Description	Example
Count	Number of objects on the stack	int x = s.Count;
Clear	Empties the stack	s.Clear();
Contains	Returns true if an object is in the stack	bool hasJeff = s.Conains("Jeff");
Peek	Gets the object on top of the stack without removing it.	nextCust = (Customer)s.Peek();
Push	Pushes an object on the head of the stack	s.Push(new Customer());
Pop	Pops from head of the stack	next = (Customer)s.Pop();

Stacks are useful data structures for storing things that need to be reversed, or undone. They are also used in algorithms for solving mazes or evaluating mathematical expressions. The next example pushes some strings onto a Stack and then Pops them off, printing them in reverse order.

```
// Example8_9.cs
using System;
using System.Collections;

namespace csbook.ch8
{
    class Example8_9
    {
        static void Main(string[] args)
        {
            Stack s = new Stack();
            s.Push("one");
            s.Push("two");
            s.Push("three");
```

```
            // print the last one
            string myString = (string)s.Pop();
            Console.WriteLine(myString);

            // pop off the rest and print them too.
            while (s.Count > 0)
            {
                myString = (string)s.Pop();
                Console.WriteLine(myString);
            }
        }
    }
}
```

Listing 8.9

The output of the program shows the strings printed in the reverse order.

```
three
two
one
```

Figure 8.9

The Queue

The Queue uses a First In, First Out (FIFO) algorithm for storing and retrieving objects. A queue is like the line of customers waiting at the buffet. The customer who has been waiting the longest gets to go next.

The next example shows the use of a Queue. The example places some strings onto the queue. Then it prints the strings as it removes them from the queue. In the output you can see that the strings were printed in the same order they were added – FIFO.

```csharp
// Example8_10.cs
using System;
using System.Collections;

namespace csbook.ch8
{
    class Example8_10
    {
        static void Main(string[] args)
        {
            Queue q = new Queue();
            q.Enqueue("one");
            q.Enqueue("two");
            q.Enqueue("three");

            //print them out in the order
            // they come off
            string s;
            while (q.Count > 0)
            {
                s = (string)q.Dequeue();
                Console.WriteLine(s);
            }
        }
    }
}
```

Listing 8.10

You place objects onto the Queue by calling its Enqueue method. You remove items from the Queue with the Dequeue method. You can also get the object at the head of the Queue without removing it with the Peek method. Some useful Queue methods are outlined below in table 8.4.

Table 8.4 – Queue Methods

Method	Description	Example
Count	The number of objects in the queue	int x = q.Count;
Enqueue	Add object to queue	q.Enqueue("Jeff");
Dequeue	Remove object from queue	string next = (string)q.Dequeue();
Peek	Gets object at head of queue without removing it	string head = (string) q.Peek();
Clear	Removes all objects from the queue	q.Clear();

The Hashtable

You have seen how an array or ArrayList can be used to retrieve objects using their position in the list as the key to that object. The only problem is the position of an object in an ArrayList may change as objects are added to and deleted from the list.

A Hashtable is a data structure that uses an object as a unique key to identify a stored value. For instance, a string that holds a Customer object's account number could be used as the key to identify that Customer. Unlike the Customer's position within an ArrayList, the account number will not change when items are added to or deleted from a HashTable.

The Hashtable key can be of any type, as can the value. You can use the index operator to get or set an object in the Hashtable for a given key. The following example uses a Hashtable to store some monthly bills.

```
// Example8_11.cs
using System;
using System.Collections;

namespace csbook.ch8
{
    class Example8_11
    {
        static void Main(string[] args)
        {
            Hashtable myBills = new Hashtable();
            myBills["GAS"] = 125.00;
            myBills["WATER"] = 40.00;
            myBills["PHONE"] = 62.00;
            myBills["CABLE"] = 32.00;

            Console.Write("Which Bill would you like to see?");
            string bill = Console.ReadLine().ToUpper();

            if (myBills.ContainsKey(bill))
            {
                double amount = (double)myBills[bill];

                Console.WriteLine("{0}: {1,7:C2}",
                    bill, amount);
            }
            else
            {
                Console.WriteLine("That is not a real bill");
            }

        }
    }
}
```

Listing 8.11

The program uses string objects as the keys and double values for the values in the Hashtable. We create a Hashtable named *myBills*. The double values added represent the amount of a bill and a string is used as the key to identify that amount. The program prompts the user to enter a string for the bill that they would like to see and uses that string to lookup the amount in the Hashtable.

```
double amount = (double)myBills[bill];
```

Because the items are stored in the Hashtable as objects, they must be cast back to the proper type when we retreive them.

```
Which Bill would you like to see?phone
PHONE:   $62.00
```

Figure 8.10

Table 8.5 – Hashtable Properties and Methods

Method	Description	Example
[] operator	Gets or sets an object in the Hashtable	cust = (Customer) hash[101];
Count	Returns the number of objects in the Hashtable	int x = hash.Count;
Add	Adds a key and value	hash.Add(101, new Customer());
Clear	Clears the hashtable	hash.Clear();
ContainsKey	Returns true if the key is in the Hashtable	bool hasJeff = hash.ContainsKey("Jeff");
ContainsValue	Returns true if the value is in the Hashtable	bool hasCustomer = hash.ContainsValue(cust);
Remove	Removes an object from the Hashtable by its key	hash.Remove(key);

The *ContainsKey* and *ContainsValue* methods use the Equals method of the key and value objects to determine equality. Therefore, if you are designing a class that will be used in a *Hashtable* you may want to override the Equals and *GetHashCode* methods of that class. Otherwise the version of those methods inherited from object will be called.

Generics

The collections shown so far were already available in the .NET 1.1 framework. They are very good at keeping your data organized for you, but with that utility comes a price. The collection classes store references as references to the *object* base type. That is how they can store any data type. It also creates two issues to think about. First, there is a performance hit because every time you retrieve an item it must be cast to the appropriate type. The other risk is that you are sacrificing type safety when using collections in this way, because anything can be added to these collections. In general, casting from a base class to a subclass is risky and should be avoided.

.NET 2.0 addresses these issues with generics, a set of strongly typed collections. When you instantiate a generic collection you provide the *class name* of the data type that the collection will hold. Only objects of that type can be added to the collection, enforcing type safety. Also, because the collection knows what data type it is holding, it knows what type to return, so casting is not necessary, giving generic collections better performance than their predecessors.

All generics are declared in the *System.Collections.Generic* namespace. Table 8.6 outlines some of the available classes.

Table 8.6 – Generic Collection Classes

Collection Class	Description
List	Use this where you would have used an ArrayList.
SortedList	A List that stays in sorted order
Queue	Adds and removes items with a FIFO algorithm
Stack	Adds and removes items with a LIFO algorithm
Dictionary	Uses Key-value pairs. Use this instead of a Hashtable

Creating an instance of a generic class is not much different from instantiating any other class. The only difference is that the data type includes information about the type (or types) of objects being stored. This type information is enclosed within < > symbols.

The next lines of code show how to instantiate some of the generic collection classes.

```
// create a list of integers
List<int> myInts = new List<int>();

// create a queue of strings
Queue<string> stringQueue = new Queue<string>();

// create a stack of Cards
Stack<Card> pokerDeck = new Stack<Card>();

// create a Dictionary customers
Dictionary<int, Customer> custerTable =
                       new Dictionary<int, Customer>();
```

Notice that the type information is passed as arguments when the instance is declared and also to the constructor. The type information is necessary in both places because it is essentially part of the class name. Queue, Queue<int>, and Queue<string> are all names of different classes. Once the generic collection is created, you access its methods and properties as you would with the other collections.

Using a Generic Class

The next example demonstrates the generic collections List<T> and Dictionary<T> to store the names of employees.

```
// Example8_12.cs
//
using System;
using System.Collections.Generic;

namespace csbook.ch8
{
    class Example8_12
    {
        static void Main(string[] args)
        {
            // store names in list
            List<string> names = new List<string>();
            names.Add("Jeff");
            names.Add("Becky");
            names.Add("Mike");

            foreach (string nm in names)
            {
                Console.WriteLine(nm);
            }

            // store names with job title as key
            Dictionary<string, string> employees
                = new Dictionary<string, string>();
            employees["Manager"] = "Becky";
            employees["Cashier"] = "Mike";
            employees["Barista"] = "Jeff";

            foreach (string key in employees.Keys)
            {
                Console.WriteLine("{0}\t: {1}", key,
                    employees[key]);
            }

        }
    }
}
```

Listing 8.12

Listing 8.12 uses two generic collections. The first is a List<T>, which stores a list of whatever type you specify when you declare your reference. In the example we declare a list of strings, declared as List<string>.

You add objects to the List<T> like you would with the ArrayList, but when using the List<T> the type of the objects you add must be the same that was specified as the T when you declared your List<T>. The main advantages of using the List<T> instead of the ArrayList are type safety and performance.

After adding some names to the list, we print them out using a simple foreach loop. The names will be printed out in the order that they were added. By default, the List<T> does not store its items in sorted order, but you can sort them by calling the Sort method on the List<T>.

Next the example demonstrates the generic *Dictionary<Key, Value>* class. The Dictionary is like the Hashtable. It maps keys to values. The types of the objects that can be used as keys and values must be the same types specified when the Dictionary is declared.

The example creates a Dictionary object that uses strings for its keys and its values. Then we add some employee names to the Dictionary using their job title as the key. Finally, we print out the names of all employees with their title using the foreach loop. The loop iterates through the keys of the Dictionary and uses each key to look up its associated value. Figure 8.11 Shows the program's output.

```
Jeff
Becky
Mike
Manager : Becky
Cashier : Mike
Barista : Jeff
```

Figure 8.11

Defining a Generic Set Class

You can also define your own generic classes. To define a generic class you take a type parameter list enclosed in the < > operators immediately following the class name in the declaration. A generic Set class could be declared as

```
class Set<T> { /* implementation */ }
```

Within the implementation of the class you can declare and use variables of type T, the type parameter passed in at compile time. The next example defines a generic Set class. A Set is defined as a data structure that stores items in sorted order, disallowing duplicates.

```
// Example8_13.cs
//
using System;
using System.Collections.Generic;

namespace csbook.ch8
{
    class Set<T>
    {
        private List<T> list = new List<T>();

        public void Add(T t)
        {
            if (!list.Contains(t))
            {
                list.Add(t);
                list.Sort();
            }
        }

        public void Remove(T t)
        {
            if (list.Contains(t))
            {
                list.Remove(t);
            }
        }
```

```
public T GetAt(int idx)
{
    if (idx < 0 || idx >= list.Count)
    {
        throw new ArgumentOutOfRangeException();
    }
    return list[idx];
}

public int IndexOf(T t)
{
    int idx = -1;
    for (int i = 0; idx < list.Count; idx++)
    {
        if (list[i].Equals(t))
        {
            idx = i;
            break;
        }
    }
    return idx;
}

// create a readonly indexer
public T this[int idx]
{
    get
    {
        return list[idx];
    }
}

public int Count
{
    get { return list.Count; }
}
}

class Example8_13
{
    static void Main(string[] args)
    {
        Random r = new Random();

        // create a set of integers
        Set<int> mySet = new Set<int>();

        for (int i = 0; i < 20; i++)
        {
            mySet.Add(r.Next(100));
        }
```

```
        for (int i = 0; i < mySet.Count; i++)
        {
            Console.Write("{0} ", mySet[i]);
        }
    }
  }
}
```

Listing 8.13

The example defines a generic Set class accepting the type T as a type parameter. This type is used to create a generic List that we will use to store our items. The first two methods will Add and Remove items from the list. The Add method makes sure that the item is not already in the list before adding it. After an item is added the list is resorted.

The GetAt method accepts an integer and uses it as an index into the list to return an item. If the specified index is invalid then we throw an ArgumentOutOfRangeException. The last method is the IndexOf method. IndexOf takes a T and tries to find that item in the list. If the item is found then the index of that item is returned.

There is also a readonly indexer defined that takes an integer and uses it to retrieve an item from an index in the list. Finally, the Set<T> class implements a Count property. The Count property is a read-only property that returns the number of elements currently in stored in the Set.

The Main method of the program creates a Set of integers and adds some random numbers to it. Then it prints the list out. The numbers are printed in order since that is how they are stored in the list. As we loop through the items in the Set to print them we use the indexer to access the element being printed.

```
1 12 22 28 29 31 39 45 46 50 54 56 71 79 81 92 96
```

Figure 8.12

Chapter 9 – Delegates and Events

Method calls must often be bound at runtime instead of compile time so that methods called by your application can support different implementations. One way to do this is by defining an interface for classes to implement, as we have already seen in chapter 5. Implementing interfaces works well in many cases but there are times when other solutions work better. These other solutions include the use of delegates and events.

In this chapter we look at an example that makes dynamic method calls to objects watching for price changes for a security in the stock market. First we will implement the example using an interface. Then we will use delegates and events to implement the same application.

Dynamic Method Calls

Under the hood and beneath the layers of .NET, a C# Method is really just an address of memory. At the object code level, when we call a method we push a return address onto the stack along with whatever arguments are being supplied to that method call. The structure holding the return address and method arguments is called the *Stack Frame*. The Stack grows and grows as methods call other methods, pushing more data onto the stack. As methods complete their execution and return, the stack frame for that method is popped from the stack and the stack shrinks.

Since a method is just an address of memory it makes sense that we should be able to declare a method and point it to the address of different implementations. This way, at runtime our program can have different behavior depending on which implementation our declared method is actually pointing to.

In the C language, we give these assignable methods the name *function pointers*. In object oriented languages we use virtual methods to accomplish the same thing. That *virtual* keyword is actually telling the compiler to store this method's address in a table so that it can be reassigned at runtime. As chapter 5 showed, C# supports the notion of dynamically binding methods via virtual methods and interfaces. C# also supports the dynamically binding of methods through use of a delegate, which is basically a class that encapsulates a function pointer.

Dynamically bound methods are ideal for asynchronous programming, such as event handling.

The Stock Market Example

Consider a class that tracks the price of a security in the stock market. We can call this class the *Market* class. When the price is updated the object should send notification of the change to one or more client objects that are registered for such notifications. We need a way for objects to *register* themselves with a Market object, without having the Market class depend on the type of object listening for these price changes.

Each client object would do something different with the price notification that it receives. One client might print it to the console or update a chart. Another might send the new price to a relational database. In other words, the method called by the Market object to send a price change notification could have many implementations. It needs to be bound at runtime.

We know of a few ways to dynamically bind a method call in C#. We can use virtual methods, delegates, or events. In the next section we review the object oriented approach of using virtual interface methods. After that we implement the same example using delegates and then events.

The Object Oriented Approach

One way to call a method whose implementation is not known until runtime is to define the method virtual, or better yet, define a C# *interface* and an implementation class. Then client classes can communicate with the implementation class through the interface.

In this section, we create a Market class that encapsulates a price. Whenever a client of that object changes the price, all the other clients need to be notified of that change.

A Market Observer Example

The interface we will define will be named IMarketObserver. It will only contain a single method, OnPrice. The Market class will call that method to notify an observer of the price change, passing the old price and the new price. In the image below, the Market class uses a reference to an IStockObserver to call its OnPrice method. However, IStockObserver is implemented by a different class, perhaps unknown to the Market that provides the implementation of OnPrice.

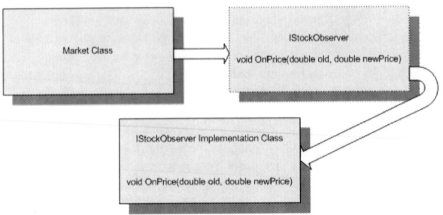

Figure 9.1

The Market class must contain a price and some list of IStockObserver objects. There should also be a method that allows an object that implements IStockObserver to register itself with the market.

In this example we will have three different implementations of the IStockObserver interface. Objects of each will be created and registered with the Market. When the price changes, all three objects will be notified and each will have its own way of handling the price change.

```
// Example9_1.cs
using System;
using System.Collections;

namespace csbook.ch9
{
    interface IStockObserver
    {
        void OnPrice(double oldPrice, double newPrice);
    }

    class Market
    {
        private double currentPrice;
        private double oldPrice;
        private ArrayList observers;

        public Market()
        {
            currentPrice = 0;
            observers = new ArrayList();
        }

        public double Price
        {
            get { return currentPrice; }

            set
            {
                oldPrice = currentPrice;
                currentPrice = value;
                NotifyAll();
            }
        }

        public void Register(IStockObserver obs)
        {
            if (observers.Contains(obs) == false)
                observers.Add(obs);
        }

        protected void NotifyAll()
        {
            foreach (IStockObserver obs in observers)
            {
                obs.OnPrice(oldPrice, currentPrice);
            }
        }
    }
```

```
class Observer1 : IStockObserver{
    public void OnPrice(double oldPrice, double newPrice){
        Console.WriteLine(
            "Observer1: old {0,7:C2} new {1,7:C2}",
            oldPrice, newPrice);
    }
}

class Observer2 : IStockObserver{
    public void OnPrice(double oldPrice, double newPrice){
        Console.WriteLine(
            "Observer2: old {0,7:C2} new {1,7:C2}",
            oldPrice, newPrice);
    }
}

class Observer3 : IStockObserver{
    public void OnPrice(double oldPrice, double newPrice){
        Console.WriteLine(
            "Observer3: old {0,7:C2} new {1,7:C2}",
            oldPrice, newPrice);
    }
}

class Example9_1{
    static void Main(string[] args){
        // create the market
        Market m = new Market();

        // create some observers
        Observer1 ob1 = new Observer1();
        Observer2 ob2 = new Observer2();
        Observer3 ob3 = new Observer3();

        // register them with the market
        m.Register(ob1);
        m.Register(ob2);
        m.Register(ob3);

        // watch the price change
        m.Price = 100.00;
        m.Price = 101.00;
        m.Price = 102.25;
        m.Price = 101.99;

        Console.WriteLine("Market Closed!");
    }
}
```

Listing 9.1

Listing 9.1 declares the IStockObserver interface. As we defined earlier, the IStockObserver interface has only a single method.

Next the listing declares the Market class, which must store an ArrayList of IStockObserver objects. The Market also declares two private double values. The first stores the current price. The second stores the previous price.

The Market has a public property named *Price*. You will notice that the set block of the property does more than just set the new price. It first stores the current price as the old price, then sets the new price. Then it calls the *NotifyAll* method, which uses a foreach loop to send out notifications of the price change.

The Main method of the program creates a Market object and then creates objects of three different classes that implement IMarketObserver. All three objects are registered with the Market and then we start changing the price. You will notice in the output that our price changes trigger calls to the OnPrice method of each of the objects that have been registered.

```
Observer1: old $100.00 new    $0.00
Observer2: old $100.00 new    $0.00
Observer3: old $100.00 new    $0.00
Observer1: old $101.00 new $100.00
Observer2: old $101.00 new $100.00
Observer3: old $101.00 new $100.00
Observer1: old $102.25 new $101.00
Observer2: old $102.25 new $101.00
Observer3: old $102.25 new $101.00
Observer1: old $101.99 new $102.25
Observer2: old $101.99 new $102.25
Observer3: old $101.99 new $102.25
Market Closed!
```

Figure 9.2

There are two things interesting about this program. First, there is a separation of interface from implementation, allowing the Market object to call each market observer through the defined interface method without having knowledge of the type of class implementing the object being invoked. It is also interesting to see that these *OnPrice* methods were executed, not because the Main method called them, but in response to the Main method changing the price.

Dynamic Calls Using Delegates

A delegate is a class that encapsulates the address in memory of a method. We can use a delegate to invoke a method, just as we can call the method directly. The advantage of using the delegate is that we can point the delegate at different methods when the program runs, giving us another way to bind method calls at runtime.

While you could accomplish the same dynamic binding through an interface, there are advantages to using delegates. If a method is going to be called through an interface then the object containing that method must have implemented that interface. However, there are times when we are given classes to work with but cannot change them to implement new interfaces. The nice thing about delegates is that they can be bound to any method with the correct signature, regardless of the type of class that contains it.

Declaring delegates

The C# compiler has special support for delegate classes making it easy to define them in a single line of code. A delegate is bound to a method of a specific signature. The *signature* of a method is a term used to describe a method by the types of arguments it accepts and the return type. So if we create a delegate that is designed to call a method that takes one string for an argument and returns void, then we can only call methods with that signature through that delegate.

As an example, consider the following method.

```
class Greeting
{
    public static void SendGreeting(string s)
    {
        Console.WriteLine("<Greeting>{0}</Greeting>", s);
    }
}
```

Suppose we want to call that method through a delegate. First we must define a delegate to work with methods of that signature. You declare a delegate with the delegate keyword, followed by what looks like a method declaration but is actually defining the signature of the method that the delegate will call.

```
delegate void Caller(string s);
```

We have just defined a delegate named Caller. This delegate can only be bound to methods that take one string as argument and return void.

Using a delegate

To instantiate the delegate we use the new operator. The delegate's constructor takes as its argument a method that has the correct signature. Once we have the definition of a delegate we can bind it to a method by instantiating it. Then we can call the method through the delegate.

```
Caller caller = new Caller(Greeting.SendGreeting);
caller("Bon jour.");
```

Above, the *Caller* delegate is instantiated. The instance is given the name caller. The argument being passed to the delegate's constructor is the static method named SendGreeting from the Greeting class.

Once we have created the delegate object we can invoke the method through it. To pull this example together for you, see the complete listing below.

```
// Example9_2.cs
using System;

namespace csbook.ch9
{
    delegate void Caller(string s);

    class Greeting{
        public static void SendGreeting(string s){
            Console.WriteLine("<Greeting>{0}</Greeting>", s);
        }
    }

    class Example9_2{
        static void Main(string[] args){
            Caller caller = new Caller(Greeting.SendGreeting);
            caller("Bon jour.");
        }
    }
}
```

Listing 9.2

But C# delegates are not just dressed up function pointers. A delegate can encapsulate more than one method address, giving you the ability to call several methods with a single method call. Here is how it works.

There is an overloaded += operator for the delegate that allows you to append a method to the list of methods that a delegate will call. Listing 9.3 demonstrates this.

```
// Example9_3.cs
using System;

namespace csbook.ch9{

    delegate void GreetingDelegate();

    class Greeting{
        public static void SendFrenchGreeting(){
            Console.WriteLine("Bon Jour!");
        }

        public static void SendEnglishGreeting(){
            Console.WriteLine("Hello!");
        }

        public static void SendSpanishGreeting(){
            Console.WriteLine("Hola!");
        }
    }

    class Example9_3
    {
        static void Main(string[] args)
        {

            // create a delegate
            GreetingDelegate caller =
                new
            GreetingDelegate(Greeting.SendEnglishGreeting);

            // add some more delegates
            caller +=
            new GreetingDelegate(Greeting.SendFrenchGreeting);

            caller +=
            new GreetingDelegate(Greeting.SendSpanishGreeting);

            // call them all!
            caller();
        }
    }
}
```

Listing 9.3

The Main method in Listing 9.3 instantiates the *GreetingDelegate* with the static method *Greeting.SendEnglishGreeting* and names the instance *caller*. Then two other delegates are instantiated and added into the first delegate using the += operator. The result is that when we invoke the caller delegate all the delegates it contains will be invoked as well. The output is shown below.

```
Hello!
Bon Jour!
Hola!
```

Figure 9.4

The StockMarket with delegates

The next example implements the stock market application again, this time with delegates. There is no interface defined. There is no need for one because the delegates are bound to method signatures, not types.

```
// Example9_4.cs
using System;

namespace csbook.ch9
{
    delegate void OnPrice(double oldPrice, double newPrice);

    class Market
    {
        private double currentPrice;
        private double oldPrice;
        private OnPrice delegates;

        public void Register(OnPrice newDelegate)
        {
            if (delegates == null)
                delegates = newDelegate;
            else
                delegates += newDelegate;
        }
```

```
        protected void NotifyAll()
        {
            if (delegates != null)
                delegates(oldPrice, currentPrice);
        }

        public double Price
        {
            get { return currentPrice; }
            set
            {
                oldPrice = currentPrice;
                currentPrice = value;
                NotifyAll();
            }
        }
    }

class MarketObserver
{
    // the method that implements the delegate
    public void OnPriceImp1(double oldPrice,
                                    double newPrice)
    {
        Console.WriteLine(
                "Impl1 old {0,7:C2} new {1,7:C2}",
                oldPrice, newPrice);
    }


    public void OnPriceImp2(double oldPrice, double newPrice)
    {
        Console.WriteLine("Impl2 old {0,7:C2} new {1,7:C2}",
            oldPrice, newPrice);
    }

    public void OnPriceImp3(double oldPrice, double newPrice)
    {
        Console.WriteLine("Impl3 old {0,7:C2} new {1,7:C2}",
            oldPrice, newPrice);
    }
}

class Example9_4
{
    static void Main(string[] args)
    {
        Market m = new Market();

        // make the observer
        MarketObserver ob = new MarketObserver();
```

```
// register the delegates
m.Register(new OnPrice(ob.OnPriceImp1));
m.Register(new OnPrice(ob.OnPriceImp2));
m.Register(new OnPrice(ob.OnPriceImp3));

// make some price changes
m.Price = 100.00;
m.Price = 101.25;
m.Price = 102.50;
m.Price = 101.99;

Console.WriteLine("The market is closed!");
     }
   }
}
```

Listing 9.4

Listing 9.4 does not define several MarketObserver classes, only one. However, we could have defined more because a method signature does not include the class name.

In the listing we created a class called MarketObserver that contains three methods with the same signature as the OnPrice delegate, declared at the top of the namespace. Each of those methods is a candidate to be called through an instance of the OnPrice delegate.

The Market class still contains an old and new price. However, this time instead of an ArrayList of market observers, the class contains a single delegate. The Register method accepts an OnPrice delegate instead of an interface. If our own delegate is null then we store this delegate as our own. If we already have a delegate then we just append the new delegate to our existing one with the += operator.

The NotifyAll method invokes the contained delegate, which in turn will invoke each of the delegates that it contains. The result is that each of the OnPriceImp method handlers whose delegates have been registered will be called.

The Main method creates one Market object and one MarketObserver object. Then it creates three delegates, binding each to a method of the MarketObserver object. Each delegate is passed to the Market's Register method. Although the methods that the delegate is bound to are instance methods, that is not a requirement. We could also have bound the OnPrice delegate to a static method as long as it had the correct signature. Finally, the Main method changes the price a few times to trigger some calls to our delegates.

```
Impl1 old    $0.00 new $100.00
Impl2 old    $0.00 new $100.00
Impl3 old    $0.00 new $100.00
Impl1 old $100.00 new $101.25
Impl2 old $100.00 new $101.25
Impl3 old $100.00 new $101.25
Impl1 old $101.25 new $102.50
Impl2 old $101.25 new $102.50
Impl3 old $101.25 new $102.50
Impl1 old $102.50 new $101.99
Impl2 old $102.50 new $101.99
Impl3 old $102.50 new $101.99
The market is closed!
```

Figure 9.4

Anonymous Method Calls

If you are defining a method whose only purpose is to be called through a delegate then you can simplify your program by using an anonymous method instead. An anonymous method is a method with no name. It is defined inline when a delegate is instantiated and can only be invoked through the delegate it was created for.

Consider a delegate declared with the following signature.

```
public delegate void PrintString(string s);
```

The PrintString delegate has a signature of returning a void and accepting a string parameter. We can instantiate this delegate using an anonymous method with the following syntax.

```
PrintString ps = delegate(string s)
{
    Console.WriteLine(s);
};
```

In the code segment above we declare a PrintString delegate named ps and point it at a delegate that wraps an anonymous method. The anonymous method accepts a string parameter named s. The block of code containing the WriteLine statement is the body of the anonymous method. To call the method we invoke the *ps* delegate as follows.

```
ps("Foo");
```

Listing 9.5 shows a complete example using the PrintString delegate.

```
// Example9_5.cs
using System;

namespace csbook.ch9
{
    class Example9_5
    {
        public delegate void PrintString(string s);

        public static void Main(string[] args)
        {
            PrintString ps = delegate(string s)
            {
                Console.WriteLine(s);
            };

            ps("Foo");
        }
    }
}
```

Listing 9.5

Using Anonymous Methods for Threads

Anonymous delegates are especially useful when creating new Threads, the topic of Chapter 17. In short, your program can execute multiple tasks concurrently by launching each task in its own thread of execution. The Thread class uses a delegate named *ThreadStart* to invoke a method in its own thread. The signature of the ThreadStart delegate returns void and accepts no arguments. Prior to the introduction of Anonymous methods in .NET 2.0 the code to create a new thread looked like the following segment.

```
ThreadStart threadDelegate = new ThreadStart(myThreadMethod);
Thread thread = new Thread(threadDelegate);
thread.Start();
```

The code instantiates the ThreadStart delegate and passes it to the constructor for the Thread class. Then it calls the thread object's Start method to begin execution. The myThreadMethod would be declared elsewhere in the same class.

```
// elsewhere in the class
private void myThreadMethod()
{
    // do some work ...
}
```

Since the myThreadMethod is only used as the starting point of a thread it seems overkill to have it hanging around. A better solution is to define it as an anonymous method. The following example launches a new Thread using an anonymous delegate.

```
// Example9_6.cs
using System;
using System.Threading;

namespace csbook.ch9
{
    class Example9_6
    {
```

```
public static void Main(string[] args)
{
    // name the main thread
    Thread.CurrentThread.Name = "Main Thread";

    Thread thread = new Thread(delegate()
    {
        for (int i = 0; i < 5; i++)
        {
            Console.WriteLine("My name is " +
                Thread.CurrentThread.Name);

            Thread.Sleep(0);
        }
    });

    // name the new Thread and start it up
    thread.Name = "Thread1";
    thread.Start();

    // do some processing of my own
    for (int i = 0; i < 5; i++)
    {
        Console.WriteLine("My name is " +
            Thread.CurrentThread.Name);
        Thread.Sleep(0);
    }
}
```

Listing 9.6

The Main method in Listing 9.6 runs two threads concurrently. Each thread is given a name so that when output occurs you can tell which thread produced it. The Main method begins by naming the current thread "Main Thread". Then it creates a new thread using an anonymous method. The body of the thread's method simply loops ten times, printing its name to the screen. With each pass through the loop it calls the Sleep method to give up its CPU time and let another thread take over.

When the thread's Start method is called the thread will begin executing. Meanwhile the main thread will continue executing the Main method. Like the other thread, the main thread loops ten times, printing its name to the screen. After each pass through the loop it calls the Sleep method to give some other thread a chance to run.

The output of the program shows that both threads are running at the same time.

```
My name is Thread1
My name is Main Thread
My name is Thread1
My name is Main Thread
My name is Thread1
My name is Main Thread
My name is Thread1
My name is Main Thread
My name is Thread1
My name is Main Thread
```

Figure 9.5

Using Events

The Market example that we have so far implemented twice, is an example of event-based programming. In both cases we have seen, the Main method did not call the methods that produced the output, but instead changed a state variable, the price. It was that event, the changing of the price that resulted in calls we implemented to handle such an event.

Event-based programming is useful for many types of applications. In fact, user interfaces are almost always event based. Rather than polling all input devices to see if a user moved the mouse or pressed a key, the operating system will generate an event. If you have delegate registered for that event then the *event handler*, the method that the delegate is bound to, will be invoked through the delegate by the CLR.

Handling Events

To handle an event you first must create a method of the correct signature for the delegate that the event uses. For example, the Timer class uses a delegate named *ElapsedEventHandler* to handle its Elapsed event. The correct signature for the ElapsedEventHandler delegate is to return void and take two arguments, an *object* type that will refer to the object signaling the event and an *ElapsedEventArgs* type, which contains information about the event. The following method could be used as the event handler for the Timer's *Elapsed* event.

```
static void Timer_Elapsed(object sender, ElapsedEventArgs e)
{
    Console.WriteLine(DateTime.Now.Second);
}
```

By convention the delegates for handling .NET events use a signature that returns void and accepts two arguments as shown. The first argument is always of *object* type and will always be a reference to the object that signaled the event. The second argument will either be an *EventArgs* instance or some class that inherits from EventArgs. The ElapsedEventArgs class that is used in the Timer_Elapsed method above is derived from EventArgs and it contains information about the timer that has triggered the event.

The following example uses a Timer event to print a line to the console every second. After 5 seconds the program terminates.

```
// Example9_7.cs
using System;
using System.Timers;

namespace csbook.ch9
{
    class Example9_7
    {
        public static void Main(string[] args)
        {
            Timer t = new Timer(1000);
            t.Elapsed += new ElapsedEventHandler(Timer_Elapsed);
            t.Start();

            // go to sleep for 5 seconds and then exit
            System.Threading.Thread.Sleep(5000);
        }

        static void Timer_Elapsed(object sender, ElapsedEventArgs e)
        {
            Console.WriteLine(DateTime.Now.Second);
        }
    }
}
```

Listing 9.7

Listing 9.7 uses the System.Timers namespace to create a Timer object. The Main method creates the Timer, giving it a time of 1 second. Then we create an ElapsedEventHandler delegate instance and bind it to our Timer_Elapsed method. In the same line of code we add that delegate to the Elapsed event using its overloaded += operator. After we call the Timer's Start method the event will fire once each second, calling our Timer_Elapsed event handler. Meanwhile, the Main method goes to sleep for 5 seconds. After those 5 seconds are up, the entire application exits.

Defining Custom Events

Because events use delegates, to define an event you must first define the delegate that it will use to call any event handler registered with it. If you are following the conventions then you might also want to define class that inherits from EventArgs to store any extra parameters about your event. Once you have the delegate and event argument class defined you can create the event in a single line of code.

```
public event MessageHandler MessageEvent;
```

The *MessageEvent* event has been declared as a public member. It uses a delegate named *MessageHandler* to call any event handling methods that are registered with it.

The following example fires a custom event whenever the TriggerEvent method is called.

```
// Example9_8.cs
using System;

namespace csbook.ch9
{
    delegate void MessageHandler(object sender, EventArgs e);

    class EventSender
    {
        public event MessageHandler MessageEvent;

        protected void OnMessageEvent()
        {
            if (MessageEvent != null)
            {
                MessageEvent(this, new EventArgs());
            }
        }

        public void TriggerEvent()
        {
            OnMessageEvent();
        }
    }

    class Example9_8
    {
        public static void Main(string[] args)
        {
            // create the object that has an event
            EventSender sender = new EventSender();
```

```
            // register an event handler
            sender.MessageEvent += new MessageHandler(
                    Example9_8.EventSender_MessageHandler);

            // now make a call that triggers the event
            sender.TriggerEvent();
        }

        static void EventSender_MessageHandler(object sender,
                                                EventArgs e)
        {
            Console.WriteLine("The event has been handled!");
        }
    }
}
```

Listing 9.8

Listing 9.8 declares a delegate named MessageHandler that follows the convention of taking an object and an EventArgs parameter and returning void. The EventSender class declares an event named MessageEvent. There is a protected method named OnMessageEvent, which signals the event if it is not null. The event is signaled using the event's name followed by a pair of parentheses that contains the parameters to be passed to any event handler methods that are registered.

The Main method does three things. First it creates an instance of the EventSender class. Then it hooks its *EventSender_MessageHandler* method to the *MessageEvent* event. Finally, it calls the *TriggerEvent* method, which results in the triggering of the event. The output is shown in Figure 9.6.

```
The event has been handled!
```

Figure 9.6

The Event Based Market Observer

Now that we have handled events and created our own custom events we can create a new version of our stock market application that uses events to notify observers of a change in price.

Listing 9.9 implements an event based market. First it defines the PriceChangeArgs class, which contains the parameters for the price change event. The class derives from the EventArgs class and stores two double values for the old and new price. Next the listing defines a delegate that takes an object as its first parameter and a PriceChangeArgs instance as its second.

The Market class declares an event named PriceChangeEvent, which is based on the PriceChange delegate. The protected OnPriceChange method signals the event whenever it is called, which happens to be whenever the Price property is changed.

Next we create a MarketObserver class that contains three methods of the correct signature to be bound to the PriceChange delegate. Each one simply displays the parameters it receives in the PriceChagneArgs object to the console.

The Main method first creates a Market object. Then it creates a MarketObserver object and registers its methods as event handlers for the Market's PriceChangeEvent event. Finally, Main makes things interesting by changing some prices to trigger calls to our event handlers.

```
// Example9_9.cs
using System;

namespace csbook.ch9
{
    class PriceChangeArgs : EventArgs
    {
        public double oldPrice;
        public double newPrice;

        public PriceChangeArgs(double d1, double d2)
        {
            oldPrice = d1;
            newPrice = d2;
        }
    }

    delegate void PriceChange(object sender, PriceChangeArgs e);

    class Market
    {
        private double currentPrice;
        private double oldPrice;

        public event PriceChange PriceChangeEvent;

        public Market(){         }

        protected void OnPriceChangeEvent()
        {
            if (PriceChangeEvent != null)
                PriceChangeEvent(this,
                    new PriceChangeArgs(oldPrice, currentPrice));
        }

        public double Price
        {
            get { return currentPrice; }
            set
            {
                oldPrice = currentPrice;
                currentPrice = value;
                OnPriceChangeEvent();
            }
        }
    }
}
```

```
class MarketObserver
{
    // the method that implements the delegate
    public void OnPriceImpl(object sender, PriceChangeArgs e)
    {
        Console.WriteLine("Impl1 old {0,7:C2} new {1,7:C2}",
            e.oldPrice, e.newPrice);
    }

    public void OnPriceImp2(object sender, PriceChangeArgs e)
    {
        Console.WriteLine("Impl2 old {0,7:C2} new {1,7:C2}",
            e.oldPrice, e.newPrice);
    }

    public void OnPriceImp3(object sender, PriceChangeArgs e)
    {
        Console.WriteLine("Impl3 old {0,7:C2} new {1,7:C2}",
            e.oldPrice, e.newPrice);
    }
}

class Example9_9
{
    static void Main(string[] args)
    {
        Market m = new Market();

        // make the observer
        MarketObserver ob = new MarketObserver();

        // hook up the event handlers
        m.PriceChangeEvent += new PriceChange(ob.OnPriceImpl);
        m.PriceChangeEvent += new PriceChange(ob.OnPriceImp2);
        m.PriceChangeEvent += new PriceChange(ob.OnPriceImp3);

        // make some price changes
        m.Price = 100.00;
        m.Price = 101.25;
        m.Price = 102.50;
        m.Price = 101.99;

        Console.WriteLine("The market is closed!");
    }
}
```

Listing 9.9

The output of the program shows that our event handlers were called by the CLR with each change of the Market's *Price* property.

```
Impl1 old    $0.00 new $100.00
Impl2 old    $0.00 new $100.00
Impl3 old    $0.00 new $100.00
Impl1 old $100.00 new $101.25
Impl2 old $100.00 new $101.25
Impl3 old $100.00 new $101.25
Impl1 old $101.25 new $102.50
Impl2 old $101.25 new $102.50
Impl3 old $101.25 new $102.50
Impl1 old $102.50 new $101.99
Impl2 old $102.50 new $101.99
Impl3 old $102.50 new $101.99
The market is closed!
```

Figure 9.7

Chapter 10 – Exception Handling

Being able to detect and handle erroneous conditions is very important. Defensive programming is all about being able to detect and handle error conditions gracefully so that your program does not crash; or worse, continue executing under erroneous conditions producing invalid results. A crash is actually preferable to incorrect output because at least with a crash the user will know that there is a problem! However, we would prefer to avoid a crash too.

There are a number of defensive programming strategies but one technique, the use of *Exceptions*, is built into the C# language. You will no doubt encounter exceptions early on in your learning so it is best to get them out in the open now.

Listing 10.1 shows a perfectly legitimate C# program that reads a string from the keyboard, converts it to an integer, and prints a message saying if the value is even or odd.

```
// Example10_1.cs
using System;

namespace csbook.ch10
{
        public class Example10_1
        {
                public static void Main(String [] args)
                {
                        Console.Write("Enter an Integer: ");
                        string input = Console.ReadLine();

                        int x = int.Parse(input);
                        if (x % 2 == 0)
                                Console.WriteLine(
                                        "The value is even");
                        else
                                Console.WriteLine("The value is odd");
                }
        }
}
```

Listing 10.1

The first statement in Main prompts the user to enter an integer. Then the ReadLine method reads a line of text from the keyboard and returns it as a string. Before we can use a math operator on the value, we must first parse it into an int type. The int.Parse method takes a string such as "5" and returns the integer value. We then store that value in the *x* variable.

Next we use the modulus operator to see if the number is a multiple of 2. The modulus operator returns the remainder after integer division. If the remainder is 0 then we know that the number is a multiple of 2, and therefore even.

If the value is even then the program prints a message to the screen saying so. Otherwise it prints a message saying that the value is odd. The modulus operator is covered in chapter 3. *If* statements are covered in chapter 5.

If you run that program and type *5* at the prompt the program will work as expected. However, defensive programming means that you must be prepared for the unexpected. Run it again and type *5.0*. You will probably see an error screen like the following.

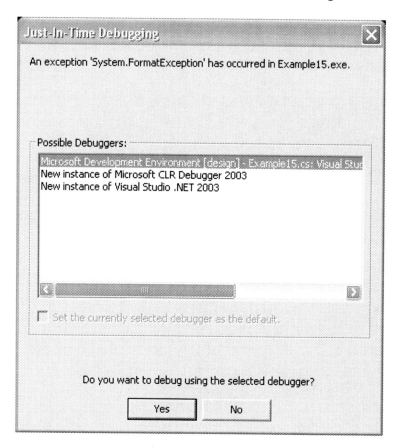

Figure 10.1

The problem here is that the int.Parse method was expecting a string in the format of an integer, but we gave it a string that had a decimal point, the format of a floating point number. Not knowing what else to do, the int.Parse method threw a FormatException, an error object that lets us know that our input string was formatted incorrectly.

Since we have no control over what the user types when prompted by the program the best we can do is catch any exception thrown by the int.Parse method and handle the error as gracefully as possible.

To catch an exception you enclose the code that may throw the exception in a *try* block. Then define a *catch* block that catches an exception of the type we want to handle.

```
// Example10_2.cs
using System;

namespace csbook.chapter1
{
  public class Example10_2
  {
        public static void Main(String[] args)
        {
                Console.Write("Enter an Integer: ");
                string input = Console.ReadLine();

                try
                {
                        int x = int.Parse(input);

                        if (x % 2 == 0)
                          Console.WriteLine("The value is even");
                        else
                          Console.WriteLine("The value is odd");

                }
                catch (FormatException ex)
                {
                        Console.WriteLine("Not an Integer! {0}",
                                        ex.Message);
                }
        }
  }
}
```

Listing 10.2

```
Enter an Integer: 5.0
Not an Integer! Input string was not in a correct
format.
```

Figure 10.2

Listing 10.2 is the same as the previous listing with the addition of the try block around the code that may throw the exception. If an exception is thrown then the .NET runtime will jump to a catch block that catches the appropriate exception type. The listing will catch exceptions of type FormatException.

As you can see in Figure 10.2 the exception thrown by the int.Parse method was handled in the catch block by printing a helpful error message. With its exception handling code, Listing 10.2 is much safer than Listing 10.1, as long as the only exception thrown is a FormatException. To make the code even better guarded against exceptions we can define additional catch blocks to handle other types of exceptions as well.

Catching Multiple Exception Types

Sometimes you will write a block of code that needs to be able to handle different types of exceptions. To handle multiple types of exceptions you can create a separate catch block for each exception you want to handle.

```
try
{
    // guarded code
}
catch (FormatException ex)
{
    Console.WriteLine(ex.Message);
}
catch (OutOfMemoryException ex)
{
    Console.WriteLine(ex.Message);
}
catch (OverflowException ex)
{
    Console.WriteLine(ex.Message);
}
catch (Exception ex)
{
    Console.WriteLine(ex.Message);
}
```

The code segment above has separate catch blocks to handle exceptions of type FormatException, OutOfMemoryException, and OverflowException, but there are many other exception types defined in .NET that the CLR can throw. Fortunately, all the exceptions inherit from the Exception base class. The last catch block in the code segment is a catchall. It is declared to handle objects of the Exception class but thanks to inheritance, it will handle any object that inherits from Exception too. Any thrown exception that is not handled by the previous catch blocks will fall throw to this one.

The Finally Block

When an exception is thrown from a try block the point of execution will jump to the first exception handler found that can handle that type of exception. None of the code in the try block after the point where the exception was thrown will be executed. This could be a problem if there was very important code in that block, such as code that closes a file or releases a lock on a synchronization object. If you have code that absolutely must be executed then the finally block is the place to put it.

The finally block will be executed every time the try block exits, whether an exception occurred or not. The following code segment uses the finally block to guarantee that a very important message is written to the screen.

```
try
{
    // code that may throw
}
catch (Exception ex)
{
    Console.WriteLine(ex.Message);
}
finally
{
    Console.WriteLine("Important Message");
}
```

Throwing an Exception

To throw an exception you simply create an instance of an exception class and throw it.

```
throw new IndexOutOfRangeException();
```

A typical scenario for throwing an exception is when a user of your class is asking for data with an invalid parameter. The following segment is a method that can be called to look up a string using an index. If the caller passes an invalid index then the method throws an IndexOutOfRangeException.

```
public string GetString(int x)
{
    if (x < 0 || x >= data.Length)
    {
        throw new IndexOutOfRangeException();
    }

    return data[x];
}
```

The method uses an if statement to test if the value of x is less than 0 or greater than or equal to the length of the data array. If x is outside that range then the block following the if statement will execute, throwing the exception.

Defining Your Own Exceptions

There may be times when you want to provide more specific error information than these built-in exceptions provide. You could always use the overloaded constructor of the Exception class that accepts a string parameter. The string you pass would be returned from Exception object's Message property. While this is useful for displaying error details to a user, you might find it even more useful to create your own class that inherits from Exception.

```
class MyException : Exception
{
    public MyException() : base("Warning: There was an error")
    {}
}
```

The constructor for the MyException class calls the Exception class' overloaded constructor that accepts a string argument. The string passed in will be returned when an exception handler catches a MyException object and accesses the Message property.

The following listing is a complete example that demonstrates the use of exceptions.

```
// Exmaple10_3.cs
using System;

namespace csbook.ch6
{
    class MyException : Exception
    {
        public MyException() : base("Warning: There was an error")
        {}
    }

    class Example10_3
    {
        static void Main(string[] args)
        {
            try
            {
                if (args.Length > 0)
                {
                    switch(int.Parse(args[0]))
                    {
                        case 1:
                            throw new IndexOutOfRangeException();

                        case 2:
                            throw new MyException();

                        case 3:
                            throw new IndexOutOfRangeException();
                    }
                }
            }
            catch (IndexOutOfRangeException ex)
            {
                Console.WriteLine(ex.Message);
            }
            catch (MyException ex)
            {
                Console.WriteLine(ex.Message);
            }
            catch (Exception ex)
            {
                Console.WriteLine("Exception: "
                    + ex.GetType().ToString());
            }
```

```
            finally
            {
                Console.WriteLine("Finally block");
            }
        }
    }
}
```

Listing 10.3

The listing first defines the MyException custom exception type. The Main method tests to see if there is a command line argument and if so, converts it to an integer. It will throw a different type of exception, depending on the resulting value of the integer. If the value of the argument is not the format of an integer then the int.Parse method will throw a FormatException. Since we do not explicitly handle a FormatException it will be handled by last catch block, which handles the Exception objects. The finally block will be executed every time.

The output in Figure 10.3 shows multiple runs of the program.

```
C:\>Example10_3 1
Index was outside the bounds of the array.
Finally block

C:\>Example10_3 2
Warning: There was an error
Finally block

C:\>Example10_3 3
Index was outside the bounds of the array.
Finally block

C:\>Example10_3 hello
Exception: System.FormatException
Finally block
```

Figure 10.3

When the value 2 is passed as the command line argument our custom exception will be thrown. The output in Figure 10.3 shows that the value of the Message property is the string that the MyException constructor passes to the Exception's overloaded string constructor.

Chapter 11 – The Visual Studio Environment

You can certainly write C# programs without a pricey development environment, but the features that Visual Studio .NET provides will help you design, write, test, and debug your code much more quickly so you can spend more time developing features for your product and less time troubleshooting bugs.

In this chapter we will develop a library to manage an accounts receivable database. We will also create two client applications and along the way explore some of the features of Visual Studio .NET.

Creating Solutions and Projects

Solutions and projects are Visual Studio's way of organizing the source code for the applications and libraries that you create. A solution contains one or more projects that are typically related to each other. Each project is a DLL or executable file that makes up a part of your application. Whenever you create a project, Visual Studio

.NET will also create a solution to contain that project. You can also add a new project to an existing solution.

There are different types of projects that you can create and each has its own requirements. So far in this book most of our projects have been Console Applications. We also created some Class Libraries at the end of Chapter 6. Choosing a project type will generate a starter application for you and it will also set up the compiler command with the correct settings so that you can build the program from the menu. Table 11.1 lists some different types of projects.

Table 11.1 – Visual Studio .NET Project Types

Project Type	Description
Windows Application	An executable with a Windows user interface. Compiled to an EXE file.
Class Library	A library that is loaded at runtime containing classes that your program can use. Compiled to a DLL file.
Windows Control Library	A library that contains graphical controls that can be used by windows applications
Web Control Library	A library of graphical controls for ASP.NET applications
Console Application	A Dos console program compiled as an EXE file
Windows Service	An EXE program that can be installed as a Windows Service. A Windows Service can be started and stopped by the Service Control Applet.
Empty Project	A project that has no files

The first project we will create will be a class library. Begin by clicking on the File menu and choosing New and Project. You should see the New Project dialog box where you can enter information about the type of project you want to create.

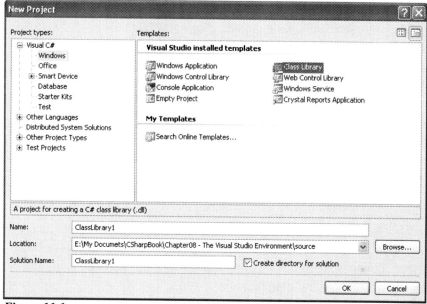

Figure 11.1

Choosing the Project Type and Setting Its Properties

The tree to the left side of the dialog groups the different types of projects. Make sure that the Windows group is selected and on the right side click on the Class Library project. Then look towards the bottom of the dialog.

Near the bottom of the dialog you see the Name property for the project. The Name that you specify in the text area will be the name of the binary file created by your project. It will also be the default namespace used when adding new classes to your project. Leaving the default value of ClassLibrary1 will result in a file named ClassLibrary1.dll - not very descriptive. We are creating an accounts receivable system so go ahead and change the name of the project to *AccountsReceivable*.

The *Location* is the directory where your solution will be created. You can set that directory to be any that you like. Click the Browse button if you want to navigate to a different directory or you can just type it in.

The Solution Name is the name of your solution file. It will also appear at the root of the Solution Explorer window when loaded into Visual Studio. If you check the box that says Create directory for solution then your solution will be in its own directory, which is a little easier to work with since you know that everything in that directory is part of your solution. Set the solution name to *AccountsReceivableSystem*. Make sure that the checkbox is checked to create a directory for the solution and click OK to create your project. You should get a window similar to the following one with your open solution and project.

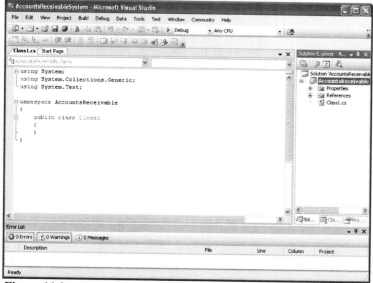

Figure 11.2

The Solution Explorer

You have just created a solution named AccountsReceivableSystem
that contains one class library project. Your window may look
different because Visual Studio .NET is highly configurable and the
windows within it can be moved around, but hopefully one of the
windows you see is the *Solution Explorer* window, shown on the right
side of Visual Studio in Figure 11.2. If you do not see the Solution
Explorer on your window then click on the *View* menu and choose
Solution Explorer.

The Solution Explorer is a tree view of your solution. At the root of
the tree you see your solution. When the root node is expanded you
can see all the projects contained within the solution. We only have
one so far. Expanding the project node reveals nodes belonging to the
project.

The Properties node contains a file named AssemblyInfo.cs. This file contains attributes that provide information about your project such as version information. This file has been generated for you and it is not necessary to modify it.

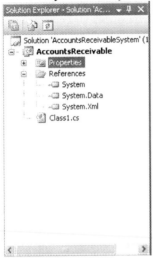

Figure 11.3

If you expand the references node, you can see all the other assemblies that your project contains references to. By default the environment generated a project that has references to the System, System.Data, and System.Xml assemblies. Those assemblies implement the primitive types and classes contained in the System namespace.

The final node in the tree is a source code file that Visual Studio generated to get us on our way programming. By default the file is named Class1.cs. In a moment we will change that file name to something more meaningful.

The Code Window

The largest part of the window is the code editor window. This window can contain one or more tabs, each with an editor window to write your source code. By clicking on the tabs you can quickly navigate between the open files.

Figure 11.4

You can also see two combo boxes at the top of the tab. These combos provide another way to navigate through your application. The combo on the left contains the names of the classes for your project. Currently there is only one class named Class1. The combo to the right will list any methods that belong to whatever class currently selected. Because we have not started writing any code yet there are no methods to list. So let's take care of that right now.

Implementing Account.cs

First let's rename our Class1.cs file to something that makes sense. This is an Accounts Receivable application. So the first thing we will do is define an Account class. In the Solution Explorer, right click the

Class1.cs file and choose *Rename*. Then type Account.cs for the new file name. If Visual Studio .NET asks you if you want to change the name of the Class1 class to Account, go ahead and say yes. Or you can change the class name by just typing it in. While we're at it, change the namespace to *csbook.ch11* to be consistent with the example.

We will define an Account class to have four properties defined as follows.

- long RecordNumber – A unique identifier for the Account
- string Name – A name on the account
- double Balance – The balance on the account
- DateTime DueDate – The date when the balance must be paid.

To start off, add private variables to store these values and then add public properties to expose them. The following listing shows the Account.cs file.

```
// Account.cs
using System;
using System.Collections.Generic;
using System.Text;

namespace csbook.ch11
{
    public class Account
    {
        private long recno;
        private string name;
        private double balance;
        private DateTime dueDate;

        public long RecordNumber
        {
            get { return recno; }
            set { recno = value; }
        }
    }
}
```

```
        public string Name
        {
            get { return name; }
            set { name = value; }
        }

        public double Balance
        {
            get { return balance; }
            set { balance = value; }
        }

        public DateTime DueDate
        {
            get { return dueDate; }
            set { dueDate = value; }
        }
    }
}
```

Listing 11.1

We are going to want to store our Account objects in a list, sorted by RecordNumber. So we will need to define a way to compare different instances of Account. We will need the Account class to implement the IComparable interface.

Change the declaration of the Account class so that it implements IComparable.

```
public class Account : IComparable
```

Next implement the CompareTo method in the Account class as shown.

```
public int CompareTo(object obj)
{
    if (obj is Account)
    {
        Account acc = obj as Account;
        if (recno == acc.recno)
        {
            return 0;
        }
        else if (recno > acc.recno)
        {
            return 1;
        }
        else
        {
            return -1;
        }
    }
    throw new ArgumentException();
}
```

The CompareTo method first makes sure that the object passed is in fact, an instance of Account. If it is not then an ArgumentException is thrown. Otherwise it compares the record number of the object against the current one. If the record numbers match then the objects are considered equal, in which case we return 0. If the object received has a smaller record number then the current one is considered greater and we return 1. Otherwise the current object is smaller and we return -1. The list containing all the Account objects will call this method for comparing Accounts during searching and sorting operations.

Next we will implement the constructors. Because the account data will be loaded from a tab delimited text file we will create a constructor that accepts a tab delimited string and uses it to initialize its members. We will also create a no-argument constructor that invokes the overloaded one with a string of default values. The format of the string will be RecordNumber, Name, Balance, DueDate, each separated by tab characters.

The next code segment contains the constructors as you should implement them.

```csharp
public Account()
    : this("-1\t\t0.0\t1/1/2006")
{
}

public Account(string text)
{
    try
    {
        // spit on the tab characters
        string[] data = text.Split('\t');
        recno = int.Parse(data[0]);
        name = data[1];
        balance = double.Parse(data[2]);
        dueDate = DateTime.Parse(data[3]);
    }
    catch (Exception)
    {
        // if any exceptions, just default
        recno = -1;
        name = "";
        balance = 0;
        dueDate = DateTime.Today;
    }
}
```

The no-argument constructor passes a literal string to the overloaded version with some default values. The default values are -1 for the record number, "" for the name, 0.0 for the balance, and 1/1/2006 for the due date.

In the overloaded constructor we first split the string into an array of strings by parsing on the tab character. The Split method of the string object handles the parsing for us. We only need to tell it which character to parse on. The fields will be separated into an array of strings named *data*. Then we can use those strings to initialize our fields using int.Parse, double.Parse, and DateTime.Parse.

Finally, we need a way to generate a tab delimited string containing the fields so that the Account data can be written back into the file. We would also like to display an Account to the console in XML format. The following two methods will produce string representations of the Account object. First implement the GetPersistentString method to generate the tab delimited string for database persistence. Then override the ToString method to generate XML for pretty printing. The final version of your Account.cs file is shown below.

```
// Account.cs
using System;
using System.Collections.Generic;
using System.Text;

namespace csbook.ch11
{
    public class Account : IComparable
    {
        private long recno;
        private string name;
        private double balance;
        private DateTime dueDate;

        public Account()
            : this("-1\t\t0.0\t1/1/2006")
        {
        }

        public Account(string text)
        {
            try
            {
                // spit on the tab characters
                string[] data = text.Split('\t');
                recno = int.Parse(data[0]);
                name = data[1];
                balance = double.Parse(data[2]);
                dueDate = DateTime.Parse(data[3]);
            }
            catch (Exception)
            {
                // if any exceptions, just default
                recno = -1;
                name = "";
                balance = 0;
                dueDate = DateTime.Today;
            }
        }
```

```
public long RecordNumber
{
    get { return recno; }
    set { recno = value; }
}

public string Name
{
    get { return name; }
    set { name = value; }
}

public double Balance
{
    get { return balance; }
    set { balance = value; }
}

public DateTime DueDate
{
    get { return dueDate; }
    set { dueDate = value; }
}

public int CompareTo(object obj)
{
    if (obj is Account)
    {
        Account acc = obj as Account;
        if (recno == acc.recno)
        {
            return 0;
        }
        else if (recno > acc.recno)
        {
            return 1;
        }
        else
        {
            return -1;
        }
    }
    throw new ArgumentException();
}

public string GetPersistentString()
{
    StringBuilder sb = new StringBuilder();
    sb.AppendFormat("{0}\t{1}\t{2}\t{3}",
        recno, name, balance,
        dueDate.ToShortDateString());

    return sb.ToString();
}
```

```
    public override string ToString()
    {
        StringBuilder sb = new StringBuilder();
        sb.Append("<Account>\r\n");
        sb.AppendFormat("\t<RecordNumber>{0}</RecordNumber>\r\n",
                                    recno);

        sb.AppendFormat("\t<Name>{0}</Name>\r\n", name);
        sb.AppendFormat("\t<Balance>{0}</Balance>\r\n", balance);
        sb.AppendFormat("\t<DueDate>{0}</DueDate>\r\n",
                    dueDate.ToShortDateString());
        sb.Append("<Account>\r\n");

        return sb.ToString();
    }
    }
}
```

Listing 11.2

Compiling the Program

Next save your file and compile it to make sure there are no mistakes.
To compile the code, click on the Build menu and choose *Build
AccountsReceivable*. If there were any errors they will be listed in the
Errors List at the bottom of the window. You can double click an
error in that list and the editor will bring you to the very line where
the error occurred.

Adding a New File to the Solution

So far we have a class that represents a single Account. Now we will
create a class that encapsulates a list of accounts. This class will be
called AccountsReceivable. It will provide methods to load accounts
from a file and persist them back to the file. It will also provide
methods to Add, Delete, Get, and Update Accounts. It will also
provide methods to get the first, last, next, and previous accounts for
basic navigation.

Add a new source file by right clicking on the AccountsReceivable project node in the Solution Explorer and choosing *Add* and *New Item*. The Add New Item dialog box will appear showing all the things you can add to your project.

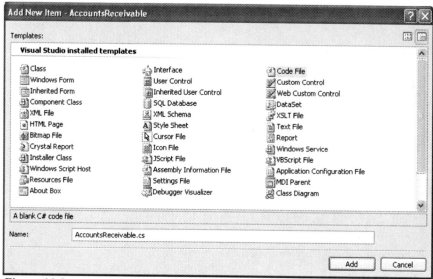

Figure 11.5

Select the Code File in the list of items and enter the name AccountsReceivable.cs. There will be a new node added to the tree in your Solution Explorer and the AccountsReceivable.cs file will be open in an editor window.

Create the AccountsReceivable class by entering the code from the following listing.

```
using System;
using System.Collections.Generic;
using System.Text;
using System.IO;

namespace csbook.ch11
{
    public class AccountsReceivable
    {
        private List<Account> accounts;

        public AccountsReceivable()
        {
            accounts = new List<Account>();
        }

        public void LoadAccounts(string filename)
        {
            accounts.Clear();

            if (File.Exists(filename))
            {
                StreamReader reader = new StreamReader(filename);

                string input = reader.ReadLine();
                while (input != null && input.Length > 0)
                {
                    Account a = new Account(input);
                    accounts.Add(a);

                    input = reader.ReadLine();
                }

                accounts.Sort();
            }
        }

        public void SaveAccounts(string filename)
        {
            StreamWriter writer = new StreamWriter(filename);

            foreach (Account a in accounts)
            {
                writer.WriteLine(a.GetPersistentString());
            }
            writer.Close();
        }
```

```
public Account GetAccount(long recno)
{
    Account key = new Account();
    key.RecordNumber = recno;
    int position = accounts.BinarySearch(key);

    Account returnValue = accounts[position];

    return returnValue;
}

public Account GetFirst()
{
    return accounts[0];
}

public Account GetLast()
{
    return accounts[accounts.Count - 1];
}

public Account GetNext(long currRecnum)
{
    Account a = new Account();
    a.RecordNumber = currRecnum;
    int position = accounts.BinarySearch(a);

    if (position != accounts.Count - 1)
    {
        return accounts[position + 1];
    }
    return null;
}

public Account GetPrevious(long currRecnum)
{
    Account a = new Account();
    a.RecordNumber = currRecnum;
    int position = accounts.BinarySearch(a);

    if (position != 0)
    {
        return accounts[position - 1];
    }
    return null;
}

public void AddAccount(Account a)
{
    accounts.Add(a);
    accounts.Sort();
}
```

```
public void DeleteAccount(long recno)
{
    Account key = new Account();
    key.RecordNumber = recno;
    int position = accounts.BinarySearch(key);
    accounts.RemoveAt(position);
}

public void UpdateAccount(Account a)
{
    Account key = new Account();
    key.RecordNumber = a.RecordNumber;
    int position = accounts.BinarySearch(key);
    accounts[position] = a;
}

public long GetNextAccountNumber()
{
    long last = accounts[accounts.Count - 1].RecordNumber;
    return last + 1;
}
}
}
```

Listing 11.3

Build your project again to make sure there are no mistakes. We now
have a library for managing Accounts. If you look in your project's
directory you will see bin directory that contains another directory
named Debug. The Debug directory is the output directory for your
compiled files. You will find a file there named
AccountsReceivable.dll.

Now you are ready to add a Console Project to the solution to test
your library.

Adding a New Project to the Solution

Right click on the root node in the Solution Explorer and choose *Add*
and *New Project*. You are going to add a Console Application to the
solution to test the class library you just created. Choose Console

Application from the list of available project types and enter
AccountsReceivableTest for the project's name. Then click OK to
generate the project.

Rename the Program.cs file to something applicable like
TestClient.cs. Then type the following code into TestClient.cs.

```
// TestClient.cs
using System;
using System.IO;

namespace csbook.ch11
{
    class AccountLoader
    {
        static void Main(string[] args)
        {
            AccountsReceivable ar = new AccountsReceivable();
            ar.LoadAccounts(@"c:\receivable.txt");

            Account acc = ar.GetAccount(101);

            Console.WriteLine(acc);

            Account acc2 = new Account();
            acc2.RecordNumber = ar.GetNextAccountNumber();
            acc2.Name = "Larry";
            acc2.Balance = 5.5;
            acc2.DueDate = DateTime.Today;

            ar.AddAccount(acc2);

            // walk the list forward
            Account ac3 = ar.GetFirst();
            while (ac3 != null)
            {
                Console.WriteLine(ac3);
                ac3 = ar.GetNext(ac3.RecordNumber);
            }

            ar.SaveAccounts(@"c:\saved.txt");
        }
    }
}
```

Listing 11.4

The program creates an instance of AccountsReceivable and tests some of its methods. First it loads the accounts from a file named c:\receivable.txt, which is a tab delimited text file containing sample data that you will create. To create the sample data you can open any text editor and type the data for each record on its own line. Each field should be separated by a tab.

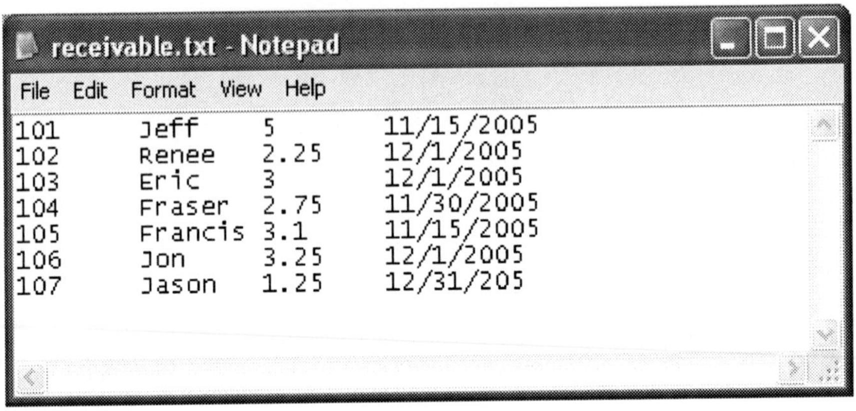

```
receivable.txt - Notepad
File  Edit  Format  View  Help
101      Jeff      5        11/15/2005
102      Renee     2.25     12/1/2005
103      Eric      3        12/1/2005
104      Fraser    2.75     11/30/2005
105      Francis   3.1      11/15/2005
106      Jon       3.25     12/1/2005
107      Jason     1.25     12/31/205
```

Figure 11.6

You can also create a spread sheet with a program like Microsoft Excel. Consider each row in the spreadsheet a separate record and type each field into a separate column. If you use Excel then be sure to save the file tab delimited text. Also be sure to pay attention to the path where the file is saved. The test program is expecting the file to be located at c:\receivable.txt. Make sure you close Excel after saving the file. Otherwise Excel will lock the file and your test program will not be able to open it.

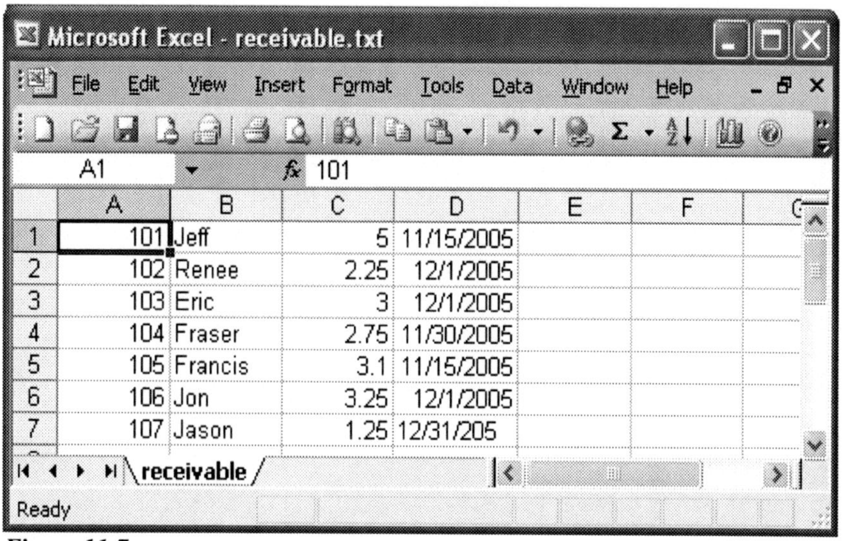

Figure 11.7

After loading the file the program retrieves account number 101 by its account number and prints that account to the screen. Then the program creates a new account, sets its properties and adds it to the AccountsReceivable object. Next the program tests the functionality of iterating over the accounts using the GetFirst and GetNext methods. Finally, the AccountsReceivable is written to a file named saved.txt. When the program is finished you can open that file in a text editor or Microsoft Excel to see that the new account was added correctly.

Adding References

Once you have your test program and your test data, there is one thing left to do before you can run the program. The test program uses objects from the AccountsReceivable.dll so you must set a reference to that DLL from the AccountsReceivableTester project.

To add the reference right click on the References node of the AccountsReceivableTester project in the Solution Explorer. Then choose Add Reference. The Add Reference Dialog box will appear with several tabs. Each tab gives you a different way to add a reference.

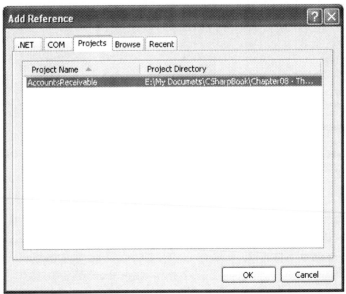

Figure 11.8

The .NET tab allows you to set a reference to a .NET assembly. The COM tab allows you to set a reference to a COM object. The Browse tab can be used to browse the file system for an assembly, such as a third party library you might have purchased.

Because the file we want to reference is from a project loaded in the same solution the easiest way to add a reference is to choose the Projects tab and select the AccountsReceivable project. Then click OK.

After clicking OK the References node in the Solution Explorer tree under the AccountsReceivableTester project will contain a node for AccountsReceivable.

Figure 11.9

Compiling and Running the Test Program

You can now build and run the test program. With the TestClient.cs file active in the editor window choose the Build menu and select *Build AccountsReceivableTester*. You can also right click in the Solution Explorer on the AccountsReceivableTester project node and select *Build*. Because the AccountsReceivable project is referenced from AccountsReceivableTester, if there were any changes to AccountsReceivable since the last time it was compiled then it will be recompiled before building the tester program.

After you successfully build your test program, you are ready to run it. When you have multiple projects in the solution, you have to tell Visual Studio .NET which project is the startup project. To set your test program as the startup program, right click on the

AccountsReceivableTester project node in the Solution Explorer and choose *Set as startup project*.

Now run the program by selecting *Start Without Debugging* from the Debug menu or just press CTRL+F5.

Below is part of the output from the test program. You should also notice that a new file has been created that stores the accounts after they have been resaved in tab delimited format.

```
<Account>
     <RecordNumber>106</RecordNumber>
     <Name>Jon</Name>
     <Balance>3.25</Balance>
     <DueDate>12/1/2005</DueDate>
<Account>

<Account>
     <RecordNumber>107</RecordNumber>
     <Name>Jason</Name>
     <Balance>1.25</Balance>
     <DueDate>12/31/0205</DueDate>
<Account>

<Account>
     <RecordNumber>108</RecordNumber>
     <Name>Larry</Name>
     <Balance>5.5</Balance>
     <DueDate>11/11/2005</DueDate>
<Account>
```

Figure 11.10

Debugging

One of the most powerful features of Visual Studio .NET is the debugger. Without a real debugger troubleshooting programs can be a grueling process of putting WriteLine statements all over your program to print out variables until you find the problem. On top of that you have to go back and remove all those statements before you release your program or your user will see your debug messages. With the debugger you can step through your code line by line, checking the values of each variable as you go. In this section we will use some of the debugging features to fix a buggy program.

Let's start by creating a Console Application in Visual Studio .NET. Name the project Example11_3. After the project has been generated rename Program.cs to Example11_3.cs and type in the code from the following listing. The listing contains a logical error. If you detect it as you are typing then you are doing great! But to experience the debugging tools we need a bug to fix, so type the code as-is and leave the bug in there.

```
// Example11_3.cs
using System;
using System.Collections.Generic;
using System.Text;
using System.IO;

namespace csbook.ch8
{
    class ProductList
    {
        private struct Product
        {
            public long prodID;
            public string name;
            public double price;
        }

        private Product[] products;
```

```
public void LoadProducts()
{
    // creat an array of products
    products = new Product[5];

    // load the array from the file
    int currentRecord = 0;

    StreamReader infile =
            new StreamReader(@"c:\products.txt");

    string input = infile.ReadLine();

    while (input != null && input.Length > 0)
    {
        string[] data = input.Split('\t');

        products[currentRecord].prodID =
            long.Parse(data[0]);

        products[currentRecord].name = data[1];

        products[currentRecord].price =
            double.Parse(data[2]);


    }
}

public void PrintProducts()
{
    for (int i = 0; i < products.Length; i++)
    {
        if (products[i].prodID > 0)
        {
            Console.WriteLine("{0}\t{1,20}{2,20}",
                    products[i].prodID,
                    products[i].name,
                    products[i].price);
        }
    }
}
```

```
        public void Run()
        {
            Console.WriteLine("Ben's Toy Shop");
            LoadProducts();
            PrintProducts();
        }

    }

    class Example11_3
    {
        static void Main(string[] args)
        {
            ProductList prodList = new ProductList();
            prodList.Run();
        }
    }
}
```

Listing 11.5

The listing loads an array of products from a tab delimited text file named c:\products.txt. You will need to create that file too. Using a text editor or spreadsheet, create the file with the following test data.

```
101    Action Figure      6.99
102    Building Blocks     9.99
103    Toy tools     12.99
104    Work Bench    19.99
```

Figure 11.11

Remember to use tabs between the fields, not spaces.
After loading the file the program prints the list of products to the screen. Now let's run the program. From the Debug menu click on "Start Debugging" or just press F5. If the Debugger toolbar is visible you can also click the green triangle. You will notice a serious problem. The only output you will see will be "Ben's Toy Shop". The program will appear to 'hang' at that point. You can kill the program by selecting its console window and pressing CTRL+C. You can also

stop the program through the debugger by clicking on "Stop Debugging" from the Debug menu or hold Shift and press F5. Now let's find the problem and fix it.

Using Break Points

A Break Point is a way to interrupt your program and let the debugger take control of its execution, giving you the opportunity to step through the code and find a problem. To set a Break Point you can set your cursor to the line you want to break on and press F9. You can also click your mouse in the grey margin to the left of your editor window. When the Break Point is set you will see a red dot in that grey area.

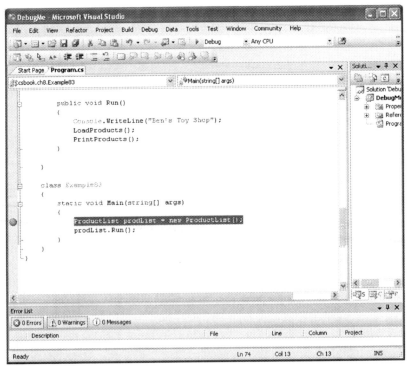

Figure 11.12

Now when you run the program with debugging the program will stop at that Break Point and turn over control to the debugger. Run the program by pressing F5 or by using the Debug menu.

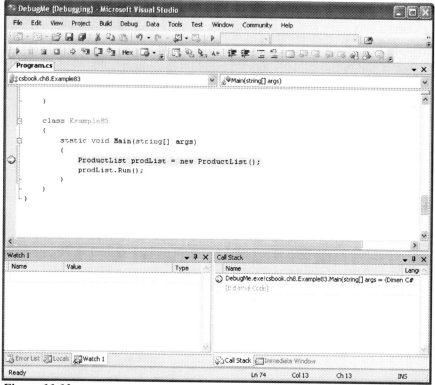

Figure 11.13

The program now waits at a Break Point, giving you time to examine the state of the program and its variables. While we are at a Break Point the bottom part of the window has changed. There are some debugging windows now visible.

To the left you have three tabs; the Error List tab contains any error information. The Locals tab will show the values of any local variables in the current method. The Watch tab allows you to set watches for any variable so that you will see its value when it comes into focus.

To the right you have the Call Stack, a very useful window that shows you the chain of methods that have been called up to the point where the current line of execution is. Since we are just inside the Main method our Call Stack has Main at the top of its stack.
The other tab is the immediate Window. The Immediate Window allows you to execute statements. For instance, you can display variables or change values while you are at a Break Point.

Stepping Through the Code

Now that the program is at a Break Point we want to step through it so we can find the error. There are two ways to step through the code. You can either step over the current line as it is executed or you can step into the current line. There three ways to step over the current line.

1. Pressing F10
2. Clicking "Step Over" from the debug menu
3. Clicking on the Step Over button on the debug toolbar

The ProductList class uses the default constructor generated by the compiler, so there is nothing to step into. Press F10 to step over the constructor call.

Now the yellow bar that shows the current line should be on top of the call to the Run method. We want to step into that method because that is where the logic takes place. There are three ways you can step into a method.

1. Press F11
2. Select "Step Into" from the Debug menu
3. Clicking the "Step Into" button on the Debug toolbar

Press F11 now to step into the run method. You will notice two things. First, you will notice that the point of execution jumped to a line just inside the Run method. You will also notice that the Call Stack window changed. Now Run is at the top of the stack.

Go to LoadProducts method and set a Break Point on the line that calls the Split method. This will allow us to see what the input string looks like with teach pass through the loop. Press F5 to continue running the program to that Break Point. When you hit the break, click on the Locals tab at the bottom of the window.

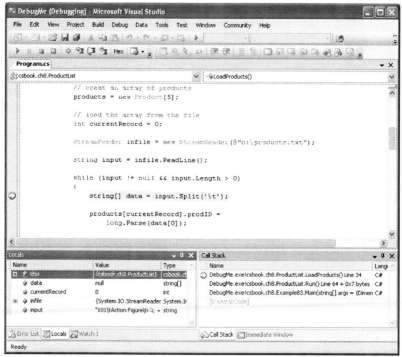

Figure 11.14

The Locals window automatically lists all variables within the scope of the current method. You can see that the value of the input string is a tab delimited string that begins with record number 101. You can also check the value of the string by hovering the mouse over the variable because Visual Studio will then display something like a tooltip that shows you the current value of the variable.

For a better look at the value of the variable you can display the quick watch window. To display the Quick Watch Window you can right click the variable and choose Quick Watch from the popup menu.

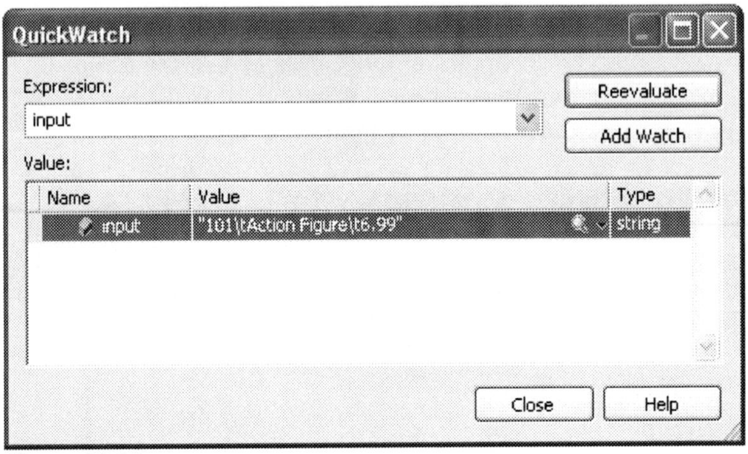

Figure 11.15

The Quick Watch Window will even allow you to change the value of a variable while in display. Select the value and change it to whatever you want. In this case the value is as it should be so you shouldn't change anything. Click Close to dismiss the QuickWatch dialog.

Press F10 to step over the Split method. The *data* variable is an array of strings containing the data for the product record. If you right click on data and choose "Add Watch," the array will be added to the Watch Window at the bottom of the Window. Because the variable is an array you need to expand the tree to view the items in the array.

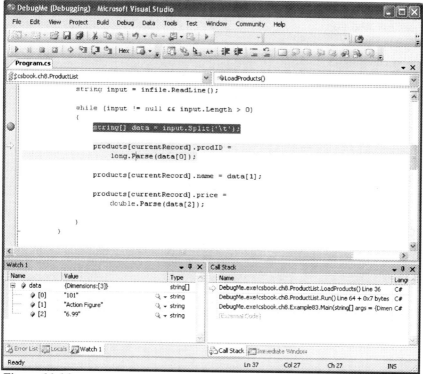

Figure 11.16

In the lower left window of Figure 11.16 you can see the watch on the data array. The array has been expanded so each string value is displayed. The string in the first position shows that the record number is 101. The name of the product is "Action Figure". The price of the product is 6.99.

Press F10 a couple of times to complete the first iteration of the loop. When you loop around and the yellow bar is back on the call to the Split method again, stop and look in the Watch Window again.

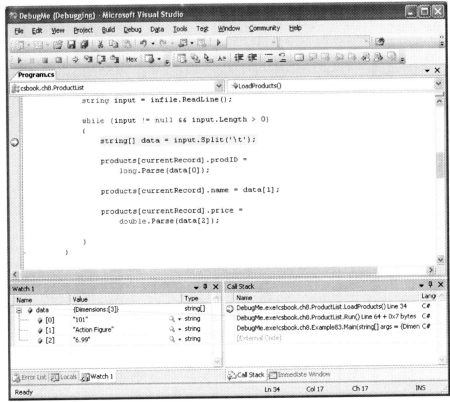

Figure 11.17

Do you see the problem? We are about to parse the string into the next record but look at the values in the Watch Window. They are the same. They will always be the same because we forgot to read the next line from the file. Since the input string is always the same it will never be null and its length will always be greater than 0. So we are stuck in an infinite loop.

How can we fix this? The last thing that should be done in the block of the while loop should be to read the next line of the file. Then when we hit the end of the file, ReadLine will return null and our while loop can exit. We also need to increment the currentRecord variable or we will always over write the first record in the array. Stop the program by choosing *Stop Debugging* from the Debug menu and change the while loop to look like the following code segment.

```
while (input != null && input.Length > 0)
{
    string[] data = input.Split('\t');

    products[currentRecord].prodID = long.Parse(data[0]);
    products[currentRecord].name  = data[1];
    products[currentRecord].price = double.Parse(data[2]);

    input = infile.ReadLine();// read next line
    currentRecord++; // move to next position
}
```

Recompile the program and run it again without the debugger using CTRL+F5 or by choosing *Start Without Debugging* from the Debug menu. If you did everything correctly you should see output similar to this,

Ben's Toy Shop		
101	Action Figure	6.99
102	Building Blocks	9.99
103	Toy tools	12.99
104	Work Bench	19.99

Figure 11.18

That is the basic process of debugging an application. To summarize, debug your applications using the following steps.

1. Set a Break Point in your application
2. Run with the debugger (F5)
3. Step through the code, stepping over or into method calls as necessary (F10 or F11)
4. Examine variables using the following debug windows
   a. The Call Stack
   b. The Locals Window
   c. The Quick Watch Window
   d. The Watch Window
5. Find and correct the problem
6. Run with the debugger again to verify that your fix worked

Using Regions to Hide Code

One of the difficulties of programming is reading through lots of code, trying to find the parts that are pertinent to your current problem. Visual Studio .NET makes it easier by providing many ways to search and browse through your code with the Solution Explorer and the Class Explorer. It also supports collapsible regions of code so you can unclutter the editor window by hiding code that you don't need to see, such as designer generated code or code that you already know works.

You define collapsible regions in your code using the #region compiler directive. The #region directive does not affect your program but the Visual Studio editor recognizes it and creates a tree structure around a region of code so you can collapse it.

```
namespace region
{
    class Program
    {
        static void Main(string[] args)
        {
            #region Hide This Code!

            Console.WriteLine();

            #endregion
        }
    }
}
```

Figure 11.19

In Figure 11.19, a region has been defined with the label "Hide This Code!" To the left of the editor screen, you see the small node box with the dash in it. If we click that box the region will be collapsed.

```
using System.Text;

namespace region
{
    class Program
    {
        static void Main(string[] args)
        {
            Hide This Code!
        }
    }
}
```

Figure 11.20

Figure 11.20 shows the same source code with the region collapsed. One thing you should know about collapsing a region is that when you search your code using Quick Find from the Edit menu or by pressing Control+F you want to make sure that the "Search Hidden Text" option is selected or the collapsed text will not be searched.

Creating a Windows Project

For the final section of this chapter we will create a Windows application that browses through the accounts receivable file that we created earlier. In the beginning of this chapter we created a solution named AccountsReceivableSystem containing two projects. There was an AccountsReceivable project that defined the Account class and the AccountsReceivable class in a DLL. There was also a Console Application that used the AccountsReceivable class to display the accounts to the console. Now we will create a Windows application in the same solution to display the account information.

Creating the Project

Let's now run Visual Studio .NET and open the AccountsReceivableSystem solution that we created in the beginning of this chapter. Right click on the solution node in the Solution Explorer and choose *Add*. From the cascading menu that appears, choose *New Project*.

From the New Project Dialog choose *Windows Application* as the project type. Then type in *AccountsReceivableBrowser* as the name of the project.

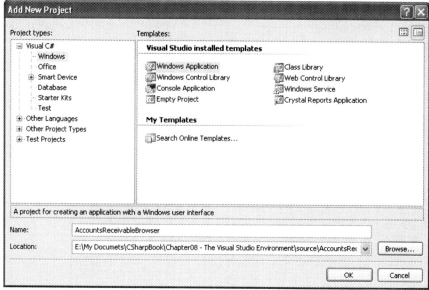

Figure 11.21

After clicking the OK button the environment will generate your project and open the main Form for your application in design mode. The default name of your application's first Form is Form1.

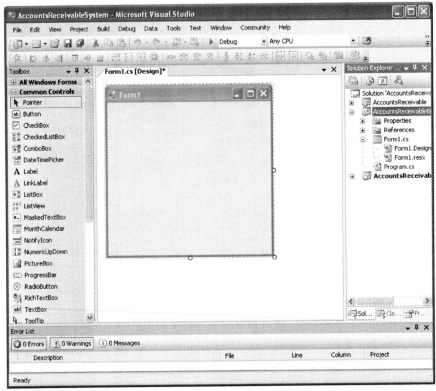

Figure 11.22

Viewing your form in design mode makes it easy to develop the user interface of your application. You can drag and drop graphical controls from the Toolbox to your form and position them exactly how you want them. If you want to view the source code behind your form then you can do that too by right clicking anywhere on the form and selecting "View Code" from the context menu that appears.

Look at the Solution Explorer window. The tree under the AccountsReceivableBrowser project has a node named Form1.cs, which is the source code file containing the implementation of Form1. The Form1.cs node has two child nodes named Form1.Designer.cs and Form1.resx. All three of those files work together to implement your form. The Visual Studio .NET environment uses each of these files to store different kinds of information about your form. Form1.cs contains logic and event handlers. Form1.Designer.cs contains code generated by the designer. Form1.resx contains resource information about your form. Mostly you will either work with the designer or the Form1.cs file.

The Toolbox

Figure 11.22 shows the Windows Form Designer. In the center is the designer editor for the main form of our application. There is also a Toolbox window on the left side of the Window. If your Toolbox is not showing you can display it from the View menu or by holding down the control key and pressing 'W' then 'X'. If you find the Toolbox too invasive in your space then you can also make it slide out of the way by toggling the Pushpin icon at its top.

The Toolbox contains a set of components that you can drag and drop on your form. When you drop a component on your form the designer will create a member variable in your Form's class and initialize the instance of that component in a method named InitalizeComponent in the Form1.Designer.cs file. The InitializeComponent method is called from your form's constructor. It is a method that was generated by the designer so you should not edit it yourself. To change the way the form or a component is initialized you can change its properties using the Property Window, covered in the next section.

The Property Window

The Property Window is where you can modify the design time properties of the forms and components of your application. Normally the Property Window is displayed in the lower right corner but since the environment is very configurable, it is possible that yours has been moved. If the Properties Window is not visible in your environment then you can display it from the View menu or hold down Control and press 'W' then 'P'.

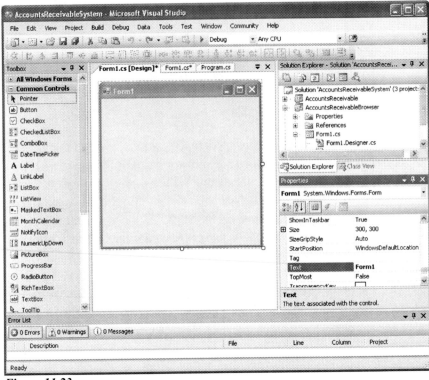

Figure 11.23

The Property Window displays the properties for which ever object is currently selected in the designer. In Figure 11.23 the selected object is Form1. The Property Window shows Form1 as the selected object in a combo box at the top. The combo box also shows the data type of the selected object, which for Form1 is System.Windows.Forms.Form.

The icons near the top of the Property Window let you sort the properties alphabetically or grouped. If you click the lightening bolt icon the Property Window will show all the events supported by the selected object. From that view you can create an event handler by double clicking on the event that you want to handle.

The User Interface

Now that you know about the Toolbox and Property Windows let's use them to implement a user interface for browsing our accounts receivable file. We won't add or edit accounts at this time because that would involve some techniques outside the scope of this chapter.

Look on the Toolbox for the Label control. Place a Label on the form either by double clicking the Label on the Toolbox or by dragging it from the Toolbox on to the Form. Select the Label you just placed on the form and look in the Property Window for the Text property. Set the Text to *Account Number*. You will notice that the text changed on the Label in the designer.

Add three more Labels and set their text properties to *Name, Balance,* and *Due Date*. Align the Labels across the form near the top. Next add four more Labels, placing one beneath each of the previous Labels you added so that the top Label will be column heading for the bottom Label. See Figure 11.21 for the finished screen. The four new Labels should have their Name property set to lblAccountNumber, lblName, lblBalance, and lblDueDate respectively.

Go back to the Toolbox and find the Button control. Add three Buttons to the form. The buttons should be named previousButton, nextButton, and closeButton. Change the text properties of those buttons accordingly.

Finally, click some place on Form1 so that its properties are displayed in the Property Window. Change the form's name property to frmBrowser. Then change the Text property to "Accounts Receivable Browser". The Text property of a Form sets the text displayed in the

Form's title bar. The user interface should look similar to Figure 11.24.

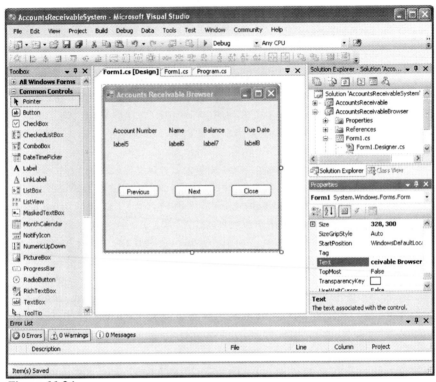

Figure 11.24

The Code Behind the User Interface

This application will create an AccountsReceivable object and do two things with it. The Next button will move to the next account and display its values in the Labels. The Previous button will move to the previous record and display its values. That's it. Using our AccountsReceivable library we wrote earlier we can accomplish this in just a few lines of code. The Close button will close the application.

Because its implementation is the most trivial, let's implement the event handler for the closeButton click event first. To handle the event, select the Close button so that its properties are displayed in the Properties Window. Then click the lightening bolt to display the events. Then double click the Click event. Visual Studio .NET will create an event handler method named closeButton_Click and open the Form1.cs file, placing the cursor inside the closeButton_Click method so you can write the code to handle this event. In this case it is a one-liner. Simply call the Close method, a method that your frmBrowser class has inherited from the Form class. This method will close the window, making the program shutdown.

```
private void closeButton_Click(object sender, EventArgs e)
{
    Close();
}
```

In case you are wondering how this event handler is triggered, you may want to re-read chapter 9 on delegates and events. It is exactly the same. If you need convincing you should look in the InitializeComponent method in Form1.Designer.cs for the following line:

```
this.closeButton.Click += new
System.EventHandler(this.closeButton_Click);
```

You probably need to expand the region labeled as "Windows Form Designer Generated Code" to see it. That line is designer generated code that instantiates the EventHandler delegate and appends it to the Click event of the closeButton object. The EventHandler delegate comes predefined in Framework Class Library.

Next we need to add the browsing functionality. First, add a project reference for AccountsReceivable by right clicking on the references node for your project in the Solution Explorer. Click on Add Reference and then select the Projects tab. Choose AccountsReceivable and click OK.

Open Form1.cs in an editor window and prepare to write some code. The project will be completed in 6 steps.

1) Unless you change the namespace of your application to the same that we used for the AccountsReceivable project you will need to announce that you are using that namespace. Add the following using statement near the top of Form1.cs.

```
using csbook.ch11;
```

2) Declare an AccountsReceivable instance and an Account instance inside your frmBrowser class.

```
private AccountsReceivable ar;
private Account currentAccount;
```

3) In the constructor add the following lines of code after the call to InitializeComponent.

```
// intialize the objects
ar = new AccountsReceivable();
ar.LoadAccounts(@"c:\receivable.txt");
currentAccount = ar.GetFirst();

DisplayCurrentRecord();
```

4) Implement the DisplayCurrentRecord method as a member of the frmBrowser class.

```
private void DisplayCurrentRecord()
{
    if (currentAccount != null)
    {
        // set the user interface properties
        lblAccountNumber.Text =
                currentAccount.RecordNumber.ToString();

        lblName.Text = currentAccount.Name;

        lblBalance.Text
            = string.Format("{0,7:C2}", currentAccount.Balance);

        lblDueDate.Text
            = currentAccount.DueDate.ToShortDateString();
    }
    else
    {
        lblAccountNumber.Text = "";
        lblName.Text = "";
        lblBalance.Text = "";
        lblDueDate.Text = "";
    }
}
```

5) Add the event handler for clicking on the Next button. You can add the event handler as you did for the Close button or you can double click the Next button. Double clicking the control in the designer adds an event handler for the default event of the control. For Buttons, the default event is Click, which is what we want in this case. Implement the event handler as follows.

```
private void nextButton_Click(object sender, EventArgs e)
{
    if (currentAccount == null)
    {
        currentAccount = ar.GetFirst();
    }
    else
    {
        currentAccount = ar.GetNext(currentAccount.RecordNumber);
    }
    DisplayCurrentRecord();
}
```

6) Add the event handler for the previousButton click event. Implement the event like the following code segment.

```
private void previousButton_Click(object sender, EventArgs e)
{
    if (currentAccount == null)
    {
        currentAccount = ar.GetLast();
    }
    else
    {
        currentAccount = ar.GetPrevious(currentAccount.RecordNumber);
    }
    DisplayCurrentRecord();
}
```

Guess what. You're done.

Running the Application

Make sure that your AccountsReceivableBrowser application is selected as the startup project in the Solution Explorer by right clicking its project node and selecting *Set As Startup Project*. Also make sure that you did not move or delete the c:\receivable.txt file since that is the file used to load the accounts from.

Now press F5 to run the application.

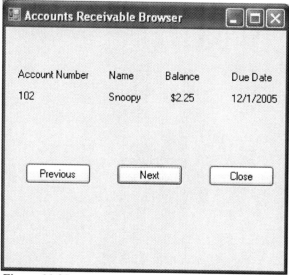

Figure 11.25

You can click on the Next and Previous buttons to browse through the accounts. When you are finished, click the Close button to exit the application.

Chapter 12 – Windows Forms Programming

The user interface of your application is possibly the most important part because it controls the way the user interacts with your business logic. The user interface also happens to be the only part of the application that your user actually sees. You could have a most elegant set of classes on the backend but it won't make a bit of difference if the front end of your application gives your users a miserable experience.

Most of the programs we have written up to this point have been console applications that use character input and output for the user interface. A user interface that is uses character input and output is called *CHUI*. With Windows applications we create a user interface using graphics that provide a way to gather input from the user, accept commands from the user, and present the results of an operation. Programs that use a graphical user interface are called *GUI* applications.

This chapter lays the ground work for Windows programming with C#. In this chapter we will look at the Form class, drawing in a window, and child controls. We start out with a program that was written without the Visual Studio .NET designer so that we can dissect it and understand the basic structure of Windows applications in C#. Then we go back into the Visual Studio .NET environment so that we can work with the tools that it provides.

The Simplest Windows Program

Perhaps the simplest Windows program we can come up with would be to display an empty Form. While the program itself might not be very interesting, its source code will at least reveal the minimal work required to create a Windows application.

```
// Example12_1.cs
//
using System;
using System.Windows.Forms;

namespace csbook.ch12
{
        class Example12_1
        {
                public static void Main(string [] args)
                {
                        Application.Run(new Form());
                }
        }
}
```

Listing 12.1

When you compile and run this application you will see a blank window like the one shown in Figure 12.1.

Figure 12.1

Even though this window provides no useful functionality it actually does quite a lot. You can click in the title bar of the window and drag the window around your desktop. There are three control boxes in the upper right corner that allow you to minimize, maximize, normalize, and close the window. You can also double click the title bar to toggle between maximum and normal state. In the upper left corner there is an icon that when clicked, will display a system menu. You can also click on the border of the window and drag it to resize the form. All this functionality is pre-built into the form so you get it for free.

The basic Window consists of a title bar, a border, and the client area. The client area is the part of the window your application will use the most for drawing and displaying its user interface.

Now let's look at the source code. To create a window we must work with the Form class or a class that inherits Form. The Form class is defined in the *System.Windows.Forms* namespace so we include that namespace at the top of the program.

The Main method only requires a single line of code.

```
Application.Run(new Form());
```

This one line does it all. It creates a new Form object and passes that object to the Application.Run method. That is where the magic happens.

Window Messages

Windows applications respond to events generated by user input, such as the keyboard and mouse. Every key press, mouse movement, or click will generate one or more *event messages* that are delivered to the message queue for the application that owns Window that was active at the time the event occurred. The Application.Run method contains a loop that dequeues the messages and processes them. If the message is about an event that the application has registered a delegate for, that delegate will be called.

Inheriting the Form Class

Normally to create a Windows program you would not instantiate the Form class directly since it does not provide any functionality specific to your application. A more typical solution is to create a new class that inherits Form and provides all the methods and user interface elements that your program needs, as the next example demonstrates.

```
// Example12_2.cs
//
using System;
using System.Windows.Forms;

namespace csbook.ch12
{
    class frmExample12_2 : Form
    {
        public frmExample12_2()
        {
            Text = "Here is my Form!";
        }

        public static void Main(string [] args)
        {
            Application.Run(new frmExample12_2());
        }
    }
}
```

Listing 12.2

This listing for Example12_2.cs creates a class named frmExample12_2 that inherits Form. Because frmExample12_2 is a specialized version of Form, it inherits all the public and protected data, properties, methods, and events of a Form. In the constructor the example sets the Text property so that when the window is displayed you will see the window text in the title bar.

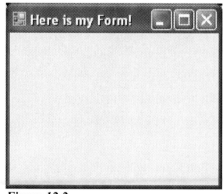

Figure 12.2

Window Controls by Hand

The last example we will look at before moving back into the Visual Studio environment is a window that contains a control. A *control* is a type of window that provides a way for the user to interact with your program. Buttons and Textboxes controls. To use a control in your application you need to instantiate the type of control you want, set is properties so that it has the size and location that you want, and add the control to the window that will contain it. You add a control to a window by adding it to the window's *Controls* collection.

Each control has its own properties, methods, and events that it supports. For instance, the Button class has a Click event. To handle the Click event for a button you must register a delegate with that Button object.

The next listing creates a window that that contains a single button and handles its Click event by displaying a message box.

```
// Example12_3.cs
//
using System;
using System.Windows.Forms;

namespace csbook.ch12
{
    class frmExample12_3 : Form
    {
        private Button myButton;

        public frmExample12_3()
        {
            this.Text = "Form with a Button";

            myButton = new Button();
            myButton.Location = new System.Drawing.Point(102, 87);
            myButton.Text = "Hello";
            myButton.Click += new EventHandler(myButton_Click);

            Controls.Add(myButton);
        }
```

```
        private void myButton_Click(object sender, EventArgs e)
        {
            MessageBox.Show(this, "Hello", "Click Event",
              MessageBoxButtons.OK, MessageBoxIcon.Information);
        }

        public static void Main(string [] args)
        {
            Application.Run(new frmExample12_3());
        }
    }
}
```

Listing 12.3

The class implementing the main form is named frmExample12_3. It declares a private Button instance named myButton. The constructor for frmExample12_3 instantiates the button and set the Button's Location and Text properties. Then it registers a delegate, binding it to the myButton_Click method. Finally, the constructor adds myButton to the Controls collection inherited from the Form class.

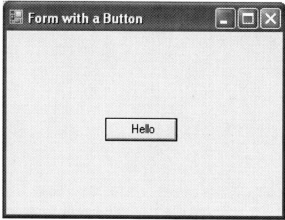

Figure 12.3

When the user clicks on the Hello button the Button's Click event will invoke its delegate, resulting in a call to the myButton_Click method. The myButton_Click method displays a message box announcing the click event.

299

```
private void myButton_Click(object sender, EventArgs e)
{
    MessageBox.Show(this, "Hello", "Click Event",
        MessageBoxButtons.OK, MessageBoxIcon.Information);
}
```

The MessageBox class has several overloaded versions of the static Show method. The version called in this listing takes five parameters. The first is a reference to a parent window. Next is the string that will appear in the center of the message box. The third argument is the text that will appear in the title bar of the message box. The last two arguments are enumerations that affect the appearance of the message box. The MessageBoxButtons.OK value tells the MessageBox to display only an OK button. The MessageBoxIcon.Information value tells it to display an icon showing that this is useful information. The message box created with these parameters is shown in Figure 12.4.

Figure 12.4

The remainder of the examples in this chapter will use the Visual Studio .NET development environment. Much of the code you have written so far will actually be generated by the designer and may look a little different. However, if you read the designer-generated code carefully you will see that it is doing exactly the same things that we have been doing already.

The Form Class

The Form class is used to create your program's main window. You pass an instance of Form to the Application.Run method to begin the message processing loop and you close the Form to end the message processing loop. There are certain key events during the lifetime of the Form that you may want your application to respond to. For instance, the Load and FormClose events may be used to initialize and clean up data or resources that your program uses.

To handle a Form event you need to register a delegate. To register a delegate in design mode you click on the Form so that its properties appear in the Properties Window. Then Click the lightening bolt at the top of the Properties Window to list the events for the Form. Double click the event you want to handle and the designer will do the rest. The designer will generate an event handler method with the correct signature for that event and then register a delegate to call that method. Then the designer will open the source code in an editor window with the cursor located inside the event method so that you can immediately write the code to handle the event.

The following code shows a typical event method that handles the FormClosing event. By convention all event handler delegates return void and accept two arguments. The first is always a reference to the object that fired the event and is always named *sender*. The second parameter will either be an EventArgs reference or a class derived from EventArgs. It is also by convention that event methods are named with the object they are registered with, followed by an underscore and the name of the event.

```
private void Form1_FormClosing(object sender, FormClosingEventArgs e)
{
    // ask if they really want to close
    if (MessageBox.Show(this, "Do you really want to exit?",
            "Closing",
            MessageBoxButtons.YesNo,
            MessageBoxIcon.Question) == DialogResult.No)
    {
        e.Cancel = true;
    }
}
```

The FormClosing event is triggered by the Form when it is about to close, giving the user the opportunity to make sure that closing is what she really intends. The second argument of this method is a FormClosingEventArgs instance, which inherits from EventArgs. The FormClosingEventArgs object contains a Cancel property that we can set to true if we want to cancel the closing event.

The MessageBox.Show method returns a value from the DialogResult enumeration. DialogResult contains many values that can be returned by dialog boxes. In our case the message box will contain a Yes button and a No button. If the user clicks No then MessageBox.Show will return DialogResult.No. The example above tests for that case and cancels the closing event if the user clicked No. Table 12.1 lists some of the events that you can handle from forms.

Table 12.1 – Form Events

Event	Description
Load	The form has loaded from memory. It has created its child controls so it is safe to initialize their properties.
Activated	The form has just received focus
Paint	The form needs to repaint itself
Shown	The form has just shown itself for the first time since being loaded
FormClosing	The form is going to close but this gives the opportunity to cancel the closing
FormClosed	The form has closed

Drawing in Forms

Years ago when programmers needed to draw computer graphics they had to use a different programming library for each video card. This made things difficult for application programmers because they had to ship drivers for every video card and printer they wanted to support. Microsoft addressed the issue by providing a layer of abstraction between the video hardware and the programs that used it. This layer of abstraction was a portion of the Windows API called the GDI or *Graphics Device Interface*.

With the GDI, the program would draw its graphics to something called a Device Context instead of writing directly to the video card. Then the operating system would take the drawing from the Device Context and transfer it to the video card or printer, allowing application programmers to focus on their own business logic and not on proprietary hardware drivers.

Using the GDI involved creating certain operating system resources, such as Pens and Brushes, and then using them to draw shapes and text. The operating system maintained handles to those resources and unfortunately, it only had a limited number of handles. So when you were finished using these resources you needed to remember to release them or the operating system would run out of handles.

Working with the GDI was not difficult but the extra layer of abstraction did slow things down a bit, which is why Microsoft eventually created DirectX for game developers. DirectX is a set of interfaces that provide speedy access to hardware, as well as support for all the 3D rendering that today's games offer. For most other Windows Applications, GDI worked just fine.

.NET includes a managed version of GDI called GDI+. With GDI+ you do your drawing with an object of the Graphics class. A Graphics object represents a drawing surface, such as a form or printer document. It contains many methods for drawing shapes, lines, text, and displaying images.

Normally you put your drawing code inside the Paint event for a form. The Paint event receives an argument of type PaintEventArgs, which contains a Graphics object for the Form that triggered the event. Using that Graphics object you can then perform any drawing necessary for your application.

Drawing Text

The Graphics object has the DrawString method for drawing text. There are several overloads for this method but generally you use it by giving it a string to display along with a font, brush, and the location where you want the string displayed.

As an example, create a Windows application and add an event handler for the Paint event of your main form. Then implement the Paint event as follows.

```
private void Form1_Paint(object sender, PaintEventArgs e)
{
    Graphics g = e.Graphics;

    // create the font and choose my brush
    string text = "Hello, GDI+";
    Font font = new Font("Arial", 16);
    Brush brush = Brushes.Blue;
    Point point = new Point(50, 100);

    // draw the text
    g.DrawString(text, font, brush, point);

}
```

Listing 12.4

The method uses three classes from the System.Drawing namespace. The Font class stores information about the font used to display the string. The Font has a family name and size. You can also specify if you want the font to be underscored, bold, italic, or crossed out. The brush contains a color or pattern used to perform the drawing. The point class represents a location on the client area of the window where the drawing will occur. The top left corner of the Form's client region contains the point 0, 0. The X and Y coordinate values increase as you move right and down respectively. Figure 12.5 shows what the Form will look like with the Paint event from above.

Figure 12.5

Drawing Lines

You can draw lines using the Graphics object's DrawLine method. The DrawLine method takes a Pen object and two points that it uses as the starting and stopping points for the line. The next listing shows a Paint event handler that will draw 10 crimson lines in increasing length.

```
private void Form1_Paint(object sender, PaintEventArgs e)
{
    // get the graphics
    Graphics g = e.Graphics;

    // get a pen
    Pen pen = Pens.Crimson;
    Point start = new Point(20, 250);
    Point stop = new Point(20, 200);

    // draw 10 lines
    for (int i = 0; i < 10; i++)
    {
        start.X = start.X + 20;
        stop.X = stop.X + 20;
        stop.Y = stop.Y - 20;
        g.DrawLine(pen, start, stop);
    }
}
```

Listing 12.5

The window drawn with the paint event handler from listing 12.5 is shown in Figure 12.6.

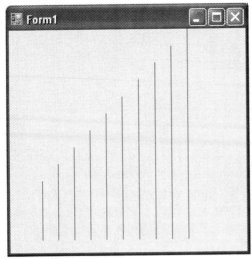

Figure 12.6

Drawing Shapes

The next example shows a Paint event handler that draws two solid shapes in a Form. The example first draws a circle with a brush using the color BurlyWood. Then it draws a rectangle with the color CadetBlue.

The Graphics class provides the FillOval method for drawing solid ovals. To use FillOval you supply a rectangle for the bounding region of the oval and the Graphics object handles the actual drawing. If the bounding rectangle you supply happens to be a perfect square then your oval will be a circle.

The FillRectangle method fills a rectangular region contained by the bounding rectangle supplied as the second argument.

```
private void Form1_Paint(object sender, PaintEventArgs e)
{
    Graphics g = e.Graphics;

    // draw an BurlyWood colored circle
    SolidBrush azureBrush = new SolidBrush(Color.BurlyWood);
    Rectangle circleBounds = new Rectangle(10, 10, 50, 50);
    g.FillEllipse(azureBrush, circleBounds);

    // draw a CadetBlue rectangle
    SolidBrush beigeBrush = new SolidBrush(Color.CadetBlue);
    Rectangle rectBounds = new Rectangle(10, 90, 50, 100);
    g.FillRectangle(beigeBrush, rectBounds);

    // dispose of the brushes
    azureBrush.Dispose();
    beigeBrush.Dispose();
}
```

Listing 12.6

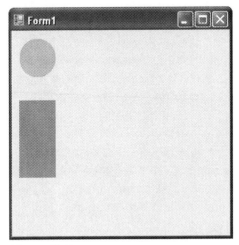

Figure 12.7

The Graphics class has many methods for drawing lines or shapes.
You can also set clipping regions and create graphics paths and
regions to define your own shapes. The Graphics class is a very
powerful class for working with computer graphics and we can hardly
scratch the surface of it in this one chapter.

Cleaning Up Resources

Graphics objects, such as Brushes and Pens contain unmanaged
operating system resources that the .NET garbage collector will not
know to release. Classes that contain unmanaged resources that need
to be explicitly released normally implement the IDispose interface.
IDispose declares the Dispose method that classes implement to
release unmanaged resources, such has Pen and Brush handles. The
last two lines of the Paint event handler clean up resources by calling
the Dispose method on the two brushes.

```
// dispose of the brushes
azureBrush.Dispose();
beigeBrush.Dispose();
```

While the Paint event handler above appears to do the responsible thing by calling Dispose, there is a possibility that an exception can be thrown, causing the Form1_Paint method to exit unexpectedly before calling Dispose. If the method exits before calling Dispose then the program will leak resources. To guard against resource leaks, C# provides a way to define a block of code that guarantees the Dispose methods will be called.

The *using* block creates a protected section of code where the resources are allocated. When the block exits the Dispose methods will be called automatically on the objects created in the header of the code block. The Paint event from Listing 12.6 could be rewritten to make it safer as in Listing 12.7.

```
private void Form1_Paint(object sender, PaintEventArgs e)
{
    Graphics g = e.Graphics;

    // draw an BurlyWood colored circle
    using (SolidBrush azureBrush = new SolidBrush(Color.BurlyWood),
                beigeBrush = new SolidBrush(Color.CadetBlue))
    {
        Rectangle circleBounds = new Rectangle(10, 10, 50, 50);
        g.FillEllipse(azureBrush, circleBounds);

        // draw a CadetBlue rectangle
        Rectangle rectBounds = new Rectangle(10, 90, 50, 100);
        g.FillRectangle(beigeBrush, rectBounds);
    }
}
```

Listing 12.7

Window Controls

Controls are windows designed to gather input and display output. You have already been introduced to controls at the end of Chapter 8 when you created a Windows program to browse the Accounts Receivable file. The process for using any other control is the same. You drag the control from the Toolbox to the form and position it the way you want. Then you use the Properties Window to configure the design time properties of the control and add any event handlers that you need.

TextBoxes, Labels, and Buttons.

A TextBox is a control that allows the user to type string data into the program. The string contained inside the text box is exposed as the Text property. From within your code you can get or set the Text by accessing it through the variable referencing the Textbox. No screen scraping, messages, or Window handles are necessary.

```
string myText = txtMyTextBox.Text;
```

Figure 12.8 shows a simple input screen that contains a label, text box, and a button. The idea should hopefully be intuitive. The label should tell the user what kind of information they should type into the text box. The button is to trigger some kind of action. It is a way for the user to say, "Ok, I've typed your information. Now go do something with it."

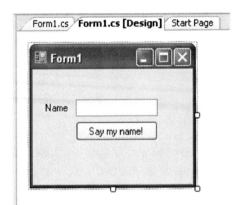

Figure 12.8

The click handler for the button is below. It simply reads the Text property of the text box and displays it in a message box.

```
private void sayButton_Click(object sender, EventArgs e)
{
    string name = nameTextbox.Text;
    MessageBox.Show(name);
}
```

Listing 12.8

Text boxes work great for entering string data, but certain kinds of data are more recognizable when formatted in a standard way. For instance, I could probably give you some data that looks like

(999) 555-5555

You would probably guess that the data stores a phone number. .NET provides a different kind of text box called a MaskedTextBox that provides the formatting as the user types. The next example demonstrates the MaskedTextBox by reading a name and phone number from an input screen and displaying them in a message box.

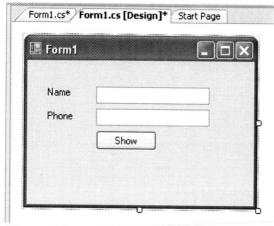

Figure 12.9

The form in Figure 12.9 contains two text boxes but the bottom one is really a MaskedTextBox. When you select the MaskedTextBox and go to the Properties Window you can click on the Mask property to display the Input Mask dialog. From there you can select an existing mask or create your own.

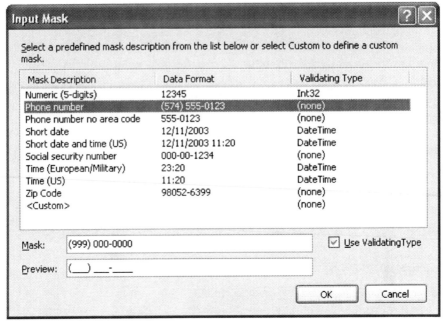

Figure 12.10

After selecting the Phone number format the mask is displayed in the MaskedTextBox. Any text that is entered will be formatted according to the phone number mask.

Setting the Tab Order

One of the great things about Windows programming is that a user can go directly to a field they want to use by clicking on it instead of tabbing through an entire screen. However users should still have the ability to tab from one field to the next without having to reach for the mouse. A good user interface will minimize the number of times the user has to move their hand back and forth between mouse and keyboard. So tabbing from field to field is an important feature of any windows application.

The order that your program tabs between the controls is defaulted to the order that you place the controls on the form. If you moved controls around during development or had to go back and add controls that you had forgotten then the tabbing order may be inconsistent. Your users will not be happy with you if the tab order has them bouncing all over the screen.

To set the tab order, select each control and set its TabIndex property to indicate its proper order in the tab sequence. If you do not want the control to be a tab stop then set its TabStop property to false. Static text controls cannot accept focus, so they cannot be tab stops.

CheckBoxes and RadioButtons

CheckBoxes and RadioButtons are similar in that they each have a label and a way to check or uncheck the control. Each stores a Boolean value of true or false indicating if the control is checked or not. The difference is that RadioButtons can be grouped so that only one RadioButton in the group can be checked at a time. Checking one RadioButton in the group unchecks all the others in the same group.

You group RadioButtons by placing them in the same container control, such as a GroupBox. The GroupBox is a rectangle with a label in its top left corner. You will find the GroupBox in the ToolBox under the Containers heading. You may have to click the Containers heading to expand the section to see the GroupBox.

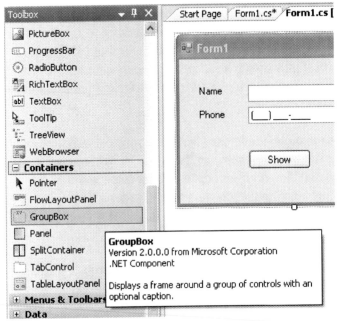

Figure 12.11

After placing a GroupBox on your form it will serve as a container for any controls that you place within it. If you click on the GroupBox and drag it around, you will notice that the controls that it contains get dragged around too. They also keep their relative positions within the GroupBox.

The next screen is designed for a fictional business named Bob's Dating Service. Bob is in the business of match making and he needs software that allows a user to enter her personal information so that she can be matched up with the love of her life. Version 1.0 of the screen is only useful for mate seekers who are not very picky about who they date because the only information it collects is the name, phone number, and gender.

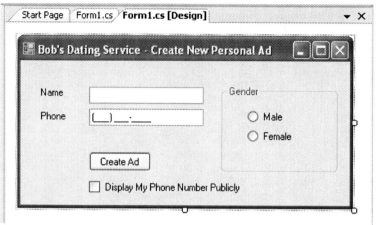

Figure 12.12

Obviously, this form does not really contain enough data about a user to effectively match her to the love of her life. However, it does show us RadioButtons and CheckBoxes. We will use it as a starting point and add to it later as we learn about more controls.

The Form contains the nameTextBox and maskedPhone controls that we had earlier. It also has a Button control that will be used to submit user information to the database, not that we have a database yet. The form also has a CheckBox, and a GroupBox containing two Radio Buttons. The CheckBox provides a way to the user to specify whether or not they want to display their phone number publicly on their ad. The title of the GroupBox is *Gender*, set by the GroupBox's Text property. The RadioButtons in the Gender GroupBox allow a user to indicate if they are male or female. In the Property Window you can set the *Checked* property to *true* for one of the RadioButtons, making that one checked by default when the program runs. Since we will not cover databases for a couple more chapters, the *Create Ad* button will create an XML string containing the data and display it in a message box.

```
private void createAd_Click(object sender, EventArgs e)
{
    StringBuilder builder = new StringBuilder();

    builder.Append("<PersonalAd>\n");
    builder.AppendFormat("\t<Name>{0}</Name>\n", nameTextBox.Text);
    builder.AppendFormat("\t<Phone>{0}</Phone>\n", maskedPhone.Text);

    if (maleRadio.Checked)
        builder.Append("\t<Gender>Male</Gender>\n");
    else
        builder.Append("\t<Gender>Female</Gender>\n");

    if (publicCheckBox.Checked)
    {
        builder.Append("\t<PublicDisplayPhone>true"
            + "</PublicDisplayPhone>\n");
    }
    else
    {
        builder.Append("\t<PublicDisplayPhone>false"
            + "</PublicDisplayPhone>\n");
    }
    builder.Append("<PersonalAd>");

    MessageBox.Show(builder.ToString());
}
```

Listing 12.9

After creating the user interface and implementing the createAd button's Click event as shown above, version 1.0 of Bob's Dating Service is ready for beta testing.

List Boxes and Combo Boxes

Bob called. He says that his users are not happy with the people that they have been dating through his service. He thinks that if we put more information in the personal ads then people will be able to make better choices. So for the next version of the product we are going provide a way for users to list hobbies. He also gave us a bit of information that he did not give use before (which happens a lot in this industry). Apparently Bob has locations in Chicago, New York, and San Francisco. We have to give the users a way to choose which locations they want to match against because the last thing we want is for someone to discover that their true love lives on the other side of the country.

The next version of the screen is shown below. We have added a ComboBox that will hold the office locations of the dating service so that the user can choose which location they want to be matched at. We also added a new GroupBox labeled *Hobbies*. The Hobbies GroupBox contains a set of controls that a user can use to add and remove hobbies from her personal ad.

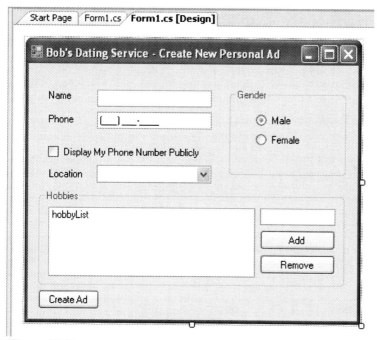

Figure 12.13

First we will implement the Location ComboBox. The ComboBox has an Items property, which stores a collection of objects to display. You can add those items at design time through the Properties

Window by clicking on the ComboBox and selecting its *Items* property.

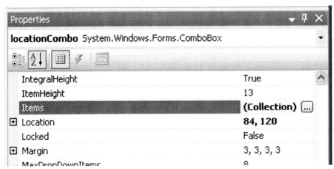

Figure 12.14

When you click on the ellipses in the value of Items you will see a multi-line text box that you can use to add items to the ComboBox's list. Each line of text will be a new item in the list. While this is easy and requires no code, it also makes the program less configurable because that list will be hard coded into the program. If Bob opens a location in Dallas we will have to add that location to this list and recompile the program. It would be better to load the location data at runtime because then we could easily change the code to read the data from a file or database, allowing Bob to update the location data himself.

To load the location ComboBox at runtime we add a Load event to the form and write the following code.

```
private void Form1_Load(object sender, EventArgs e)
{
    locationCombo.Items.Add("New York");
    locationCombo.Items.Add("Chicago");
    locationCombo.Items.Add("San Francisco");
}
```

Listing 12.10

Another interesting property of the ComboBox is the *DropDownStyle* property. This property is an enumeration that has three values;

Simple, *DropDown*, and *DropDownList*. By default the DropDown value is used. The DropDown style will cause a list to drop, from which a user can select an item. It also allows the user to edit the string in the text box. This is often a useful feature but in our case it is not what we want. We would not want Bob's users to think they can match against any city in the world just by typing it in. The DropDownList style will also drop a list of items that the user can choose from, but its text box is read only. That is the style we want.

Next we need to add the code behind the Click events to add and remove hobbies from the ListBox. Double click on the Add Button and the Remove Button in the Hobbies area to add the event handlers for both of those buttons. The following code segment implements the Load event for the Form as well as the Click events for the Add and Remove Buttons.

```
private void Form1_Load(object sender, EventArgs e)
{
    locationCombo.Items.Add("New York");
    locationCombo.Items.Add("Chicago");
    locationCombo.Items.Add("San Francisco");
}

private void addButton_Click(object sender, EventArgs e)
{
    if (newHobbyText.Text.Length > 0)
    {
        hobbyList.Items.Add(newHobbyText.Text);
    }
}

private void removeButton_Click(object sender, EventArgs e)
{
    // if there is an item selected in the list box then
    // delete it from the list
    if (hobbyList.SelectedIndex > -1)
    {
        hobbyList.Items.RemoveAt(hobbyList.SelectedIndex);
    }
}
```

Listing 12.11

In the event handler for the Add Button we only add the text if its length is greater than zero. We add the text through the *Items.Add* method. By default the items will be displayed in the order they are added. If you want them to be sorted then you need to set the ListBox's Sorted property to true. You can either set the Sorted property in code or in the Property Window when the ListBox is selected in design mode.

The ListBox knows which item is currently selected through its *SelectedIndex* property. The index of the first item in the list is 0. If no item is currently selected then SelectedIndex will be -1. In the removeButton_Click method we must make sure that SelectedIndex is greater than -1. Otherwise if the user clicks the removeButton when nothing is selected the program would crash for attempting to remove an item at an invalid index.

The last step to completing this version of the program is to make sure that we add the data for the location and hobbies into the database record. The createAd_Click handler needs to be modified so that the XML record gets a field for the Location and a field that will store a comma separated list of hobbies. The next listing shows the new version of the createAd_Click method.

```
private void createAd_Click(object sender, EventArgs e)
{
    StringBuilder builder = new StringBuilder();

    builder.Append("<PersonalAd>\n");
    builder.AppendFormat("\t<Name>{0}</Name>\n", nameTextBox.Text);
    builder.AppendFormat("\t<Phone>{0}</Phone>\n", maskedPhone.Text);

    if (maleRadio.Checked)
        builder.Append("\t<Gender>Male</Gender>\n");
    else
        builder.Append("\t<Gender>Female</Gender>\n");

    if (publicCheckBox.Checked)
    {
        builder.Append("\t<PublicDisplayPhone>true"
            + "</PublicDisplayPhone>\n");
```

```
    }
    else
    {
        builder.Append("\t<PublicDisplayPhone>false"
                + "</PublicDisplayPhone>\n");
    }
    builder.AppendFormat("\t<Location>{0}</Location>\n",
        locationCombo.SelectedText);

    string hobbiesString = "";
    foreach (string s in hobbyList.Items)
    {
        hobbiesString += s + ",";
    }

    builder.AppendFormat("\t<Hobbies>{0}</Hobbies>\n",
                        hobbiesString);

    builder.Append("<PersonalAd>");

    MessageBox.Show(builder.ToString());
}
```

Listing 12.12

The new version of createAd_Click adds a node for the location by taking the ComboBox's SelectedText property. The SelectedText property is the string that appears in the text area of the combo box. Whichever item the user selected in the list will appear in that area. To build the entry for the Hobbies we create a comma separated list of values by looping through the Items property in the hobbyList ListBox. Because the Items property is a collection we can use a foreach loop to iterate through the strings in the list. Figure 12.15 shows the use of this new version of Bob's Dating Service.

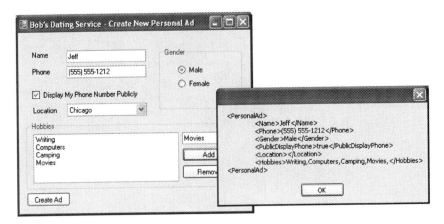

Figure 12.15

The TabControl

Bob called again. He is much happier with the latest version of his program. More of his customers have found true love without having to relocate to another city. Business is booming and wants to provide more features for his customers. The feature set includes a welcome message, storing a user's birth date, a list of dislikes, and the ability to upload a photo.

But our screen is already becoming cluttered and adding more controls to it would probably make it too difficult to use. We need to organize our user interface to add these new features without cluttering up the screen.

The TabControl is a stack of control containers with tabs sticking out so users can choose which tab they want to work with. The tabs are configurable in design mode. At design time you can add new tabs, set the text at the top of each tab, and place controls on the TabPages within the control. At runtime the user will click on the tab that they want to work with. You can use the TabControl to group user interface controls into related areas so that the program is easier to use.

The TabControl is located on the Toolbox under the Containers heading. To place a TabControl on a form, drag it from the ToolBox and drop it on the form. Then you can resize it and position it the way you want.

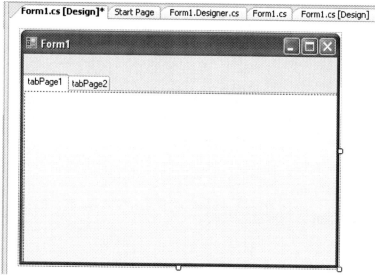

Figure 12.16

To add or remove tabs or to change the text on one of the tabs, just select the TabControl and look at the Property Window.

Figure 12.17

The TabPages Property is a collection of TabPage objects. By clicking on the ellipses you can display a dialog that allows you to edit properties for each individual TabPage.

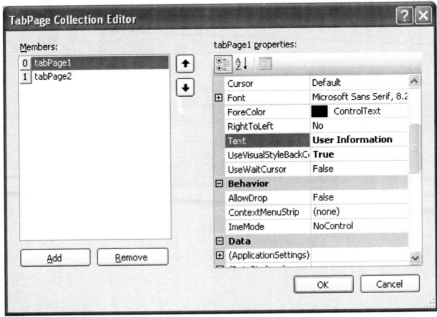

Figure 12.18

In Figure 12.18 you can see some of the properties of the TabPages. The property I am most interested in is the Text property, which holds the text that is displayed at the top of the tab. The first Tab in our program will hold user information and the second tab will hold information about the likes and dislikes of the user.

Our new requirements will require three tabs. To add these new tabs, click on the Add button. Then change the text property of all three tabs so that their values are "User Information", "Interests", and "Photo". Then go back to the form designer and place the controls on your tab. The first tab appears below.

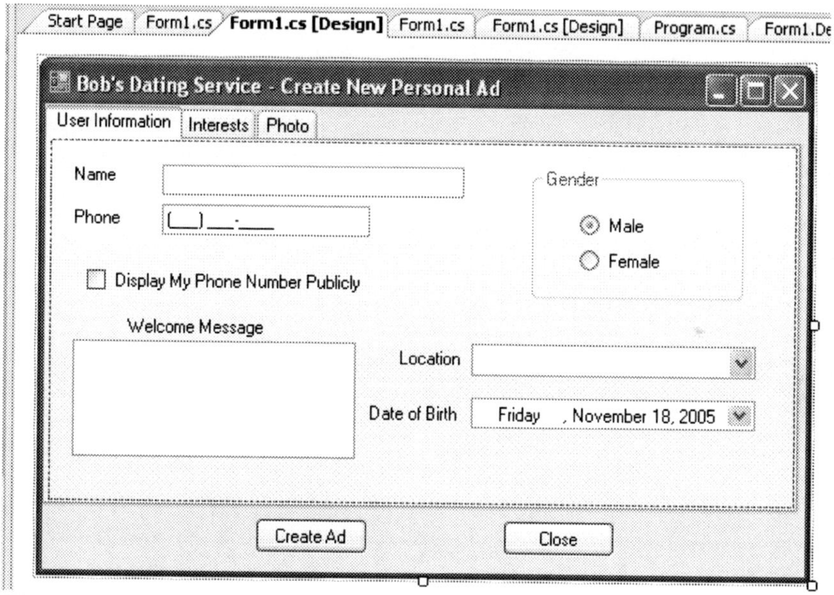

Figure 12.19

The Name, Phone, and Gender areas are the same as they were in the previous version. Now, we have added a second TextBox named welcomeMessage and set its *Multiline* property to true. A multiline TextBox can be resized vertically and its Text can contain line breaks. We have also added a DateTimePicker control to store the birthdate.

The DateTimePicker control will display a calendar when clicked and the user can browse to a date.

The second tab contains the user's hobbies and dislikes. The hobby GroupBox is as it was in the previous version. The Dislikes GroupBox is new here, but its functionality is the same as the hobbyList. The user can add and remove items from it using the Add and Remove buttons.

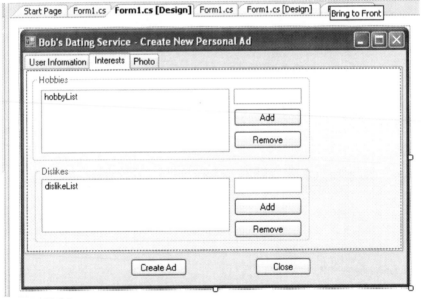

Figure 12.20

The third tab contains a PictureBox control with two buttons for loading an image file into the PictureBox and clearing the PictureBox. With the PictureBox control selected, go to the Property Window and choose *StretchImage* for the *SizeMode* property. Otherwise the PictureBox will not scale the image and it will not display well.

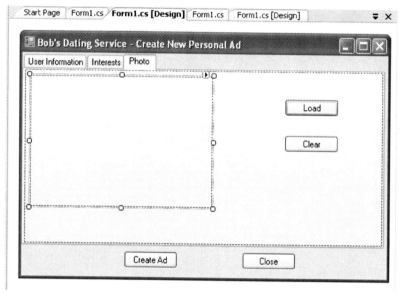

Figure 12.21

The other important property for the PictureBox is the ImageLocation property. The ImageLocation is a string value that stores the complete path to the image file being displayed. We want the user to be able to browse for an image on her computer and display it in the PictureBox. The Click event handler for the Load button will handle that for us. To clear the image we only need to set the ImageLocation property to an empty string, "".

Now that the user interface is completed you should add the necessary event handlers. Most will be the same as before. Below is the complete listing that implements all the event handlers for this program.

```
using System;
using System.Collections.Generic;
using System.ComponentModel;
using System.Data;
using System.Drawing;
using System.Text;
using System.Windows.Forms;

namespace Example12_7
{
    public partial class Form1 : Form{
        public Form1(){
            InitializeComponent();
        }

        private void createAd_Click(object sender, EventArgs e)
        {
            StringBuilder builder = new StringBuilder();

            builder.Append("<PersonalAd>\n");
            builder.AppendFormat("\t<Name>{0}</Name>\n",
                    nameTextBox.Text);
            builder.AppendFormat("\t<Phone>{0}</Phone>\n",
                    maskedPhone.Text);

            if (maleRadio.Checked)
                builder.Append("\t<Gender>Male</Gender>\n");
            else
                builder.Append("\t<Gender>Female</Gender>\n");

            if (publicCheckBox.Checked)
                builder.Append("\t<PublicDisplayPhone>true"
                    + "</PublicDisplayPhone>\n");
            else
                builder.Append("\t<PublicDisplayPhone>false"
                    + "</PublicDisplayPhone>\n");

            builder.AppendFormat("\t<Location>{0}</Location>\n",
                locationCombo.SelectedText);

            builder.AppendFormat("\t<Birthdate>{0}</BirthDate>\n",
                this.dateTimePicker1.Value.ToShortDateString());

            string hobbiesString = "";
            foreach (string s in hobbyList.Items)
            {
                hobbiesString += s + ",";
            }
            builder.AppendFormat("\t<Hobbies>{0}</Hobbies>\n",
                                        hobbiesString);

            string dislikesString = "";
            foreach (string s in hobbyList.Items)
            {
                dislikesString += s + ",";
            }
```

```csharp
    builder.AppendFormat("\t<Dislikes>{0}</Dislikes>\n",
                                    dislikesString);

    builder.AppendFormat(
        "\t<WelcomeMessage>{0}</WelcomeMessage>\n",
        welcomeMessage.Text);

    builder.Append("<PersonalAd>");

    MessageBox.Show(builder.ToString());
}

private void closeButton_Click(object sender, EventArgs e)
{
    Close();
}

private void Form1_Load(object sender, EventArgs e)
{
    locationCombo.Items.Add("New York");
    locationCombo.Items.Add("Chicago");
    locationCombo.Items.Add("San Francisco");
}

private void addButton_Click(object sender, EventArgs e)
{
    if (newHobbyText.Text.Length > 0)
    {
        hobbyList.Items.Add(newHobbyText.Text);
    }
}

private void removeButton_Click(object sender, EventArgs e)
{
    // if there is an item selected in the list box then
    // delete it from the list
    if (hobbyList.SelectedIndex > -1)
    {
        hobbyList.Items.RemoveAt(hobbyList.SelectedIndex);
    }

}

private void addDislikeButton_Click(object sender,
                                    EventArgs e)
{
    if (dislikeText.Text.Length > 0)
    {
        dislikeList.Items.Add(dislikeText.Text);
    }

}
```

```
private void removeDislikeButton_Click(object sender,
                                            EventArgs e)
{
    if (dislikeList.SelectedIndex > -1)
    {
        dislikeList.Items.RemoveAt(dislikeList.SelectedIndex);
    }
}


private void clearImageButton_Click(object sender,
                                        EventArgs e)
{
    pictureBox1.ImageLocation = "";
}

private void loadImageButton_Click(object sender,
                                        EventArgs e)
{
    OpenFileDialog dialog = new OpenFileDialog();
    if (dialog.ShowDialog() == DialogResult.OK)
    {
        // get the file name
        string imageFileName =
            dialog.FileName;

        // load the image
        pictureBox1.ImageLocation = imageFileName;
    }
}
}
```

Listing 12.13

The Click event handler for the loadImageButton uses a class we have
not used yet in this book. The OpenFileDialog class is one of a set of
standard dialog boxes that .NET provides for common tasks. In the
next chapter we will work more with dialogs boxes. We display the
file dialog with the ShowDialog method and if the user clicks the OK
button then ShowDialog will return the value DialogResult.OK. In
that case we use the dialog's FileName property as the string for the
ImageLocation property on the PictureBox. Setting the
ImageLocation will load the image file and display the image in the
Picture box.

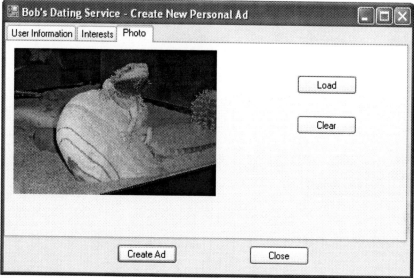

Figure 12.22

The TreeView

The TreeView is user interface control that you can use to display
data that is hierarchical in nature, such as the directories and files on
your computer. Figure 12.21 shows the TreeView used by Windows
Explorer to navigate the directory structure on your computer.

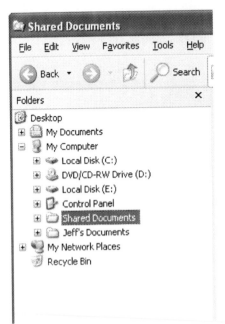

Figure 12.23

The TreeView class contains many useful properties that affect its appearance and behavior, such as the *ImageList* property, which contains a list of images that can be displayed in the nodes of the tree. An important property of the TreeView class is the *Dock* property. Using the Dock property you can bind one or all edges of a control to its container. Setting the Dock property to Fill will bind all edges, filling the container.

To add nodes to the tree you create instances of the *TreeNode* class and add them to the TreeView's *Nodes* collection. Each TreeNode has its own Nodes collection as well. You add generations to the tree by adding TreeNode objects to the Nodes collection of other TreeNodes that already exist in the tree.

```
TreeNode parent = new TreeNode("Parent Node");
parent.ImageIndex = 0;

TreeNode child = new TreeNode("Child Node");
child.ImageIndex = 1;

parent.Nodes.Add(child);
treeView1.Nodes.Add(parent);
```

The code segment above adds a parent node to a TreeView and then adds one child node. The Text is passed to the contructor of the TreeNode. The ImageIndex property is used by the TreeView containing the node to figure out which image to display for that node, if any. Figure 12.22 shows what the TreeView constructed with this code might look like.

Figure 12.24

There are several useful properties and methods in the TreeNode. We cannot cover them all, but some of the most common properties are listed in Table 12.2.

Table 12.2 – TreeNode Properties and Methods

Property	Type	Description
Text	string	The text displayed in the node
BackColor	Color	The background color of the node
ForeColor	Color	The foreground color
ImageIndex	int	Index of an image within an ImageList
Index	int	The position of the node in the collection
Nodes	TreeNodeCollection	Collection of TreeNodes
Parent	TreeNode	The parent node
SelectedImageIndex	int	Index of image to display when node is selected
Tag	object	An object associated with this node
Dock	DockStyle	Binds edges of control to container

The ListView

The ListView can display tabular data, such as rows of records from a database table. The ListView can display its items in rows, showing all the details of the items, or it can display its items as icons. Windows Explorer uses a ListView to display the files in the currently selected folder.

Figure 12.22 shows the ListView displayed in two different views.

Figure 12.25

The ListView contains a collection of ListViewItem objects that it displays in its window. The ListViewItem class has a collection of *ListViewItem.ListViewSubItem* instances. (The ListViewSubItem class is actually defined inside the ListViewItem class.)

The manner in which the items are displayed depends on the ListView's View property. If the View is set to *LargeIcons* then the columns will be hidden and instead, the ListView will display the image associated with each ListViewItem with the item's text below it. See the first image in Figure 12.25. Setting the value of the View property to *Details* causes the ListView to display its items as rows, with each of the item's SubItems displayed as columns, like in the second image of Figure 12.25.   Other View settings exist for you to experiment with.

To add items to the ListView you create ListViewItem instances and add them to the ListView's Items collection. The next code segment adds two ListViewItems to a ListView. Each ListViewItem is given SubItems to store a phone number and email address.

```
ListViewItem item = new ListViewItem("Bob");
item.SubItems.Add("555-123-4567");
item.SubItems.Add("bob@bobscompany.com");
listView1.Items.Add(item);

item = new ListViewItem("Fred");
item.SubItems.Add("555-123-7890");
item.SubItems.Add("fred@bobscompany.com");
listView1.Items.Add(item);
```

The code segment creates a ListViewItem, passing the string "Bob" to the constructor. It then adds two subitems, calling the SubItems.Add method. The Add method has several overloaded versions but the simplest version just accepts a string and internally creates a ListViewItem.ListViewSubItem object. Figure 12.26 displays what this ListView might look like.

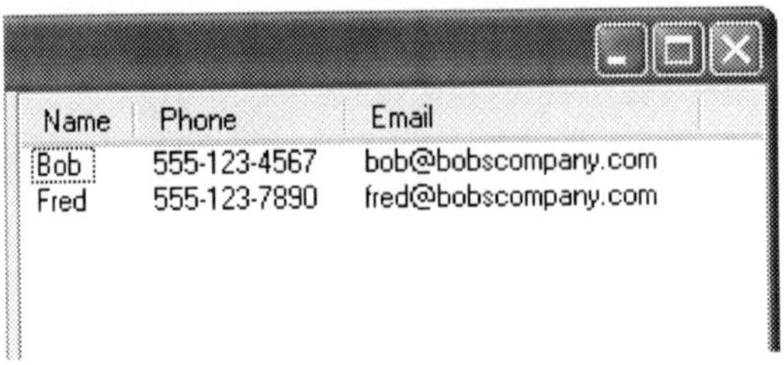

Figure 12.26

Using the TreeView and ListView is like using any other control. You place them on the form and use the Property Window to set properties and add event handlers. It is the structure of their data that add the complexity. However, with that complexity come flexibility and power. If your application needs to display a lot of data on the screen at the same time, then use of these controls will help you present information to your user in a more organized way.

Chapter 13 – The User Interface

There are certain user interface devices that Windows users have
grown accustom to over the years and using them will make your
applications seem more familiar to your users. These devices include
menus, toolbars, and status bars. In this chapter we will work with
these tools to learn how to create user interfaces that Windows users
will be familiar with. We will also create and use dialog boxes, which
provide a way to gather input from a user.

Creating Menus

Anyone familiar with Windows applications has worked with menus.
The menu provides a way for the user to send commands to the
application. A typical menu is a strip across the top of the main
window that contains the title text of drop-down menus. When the
user clicks on a menu's title text, that menu will be displayed.

It is common for many Windows applications to have a File menu, an Edit menu, and a Help menu along with other menus that are specific to the application.

To create a menu you drag a MenuStrip control from the Toolbox and drop it on to the Form while it is open in design mode. The MenuStrip can be found by expanding the *Menus and Toolbars* group on the Toolbox. When you drag a MenuStrip to your form you will see a MenuStrip component appear at the bottom of your design window. Clicking on the MenuStrip component will display its properties in the Property Window, allowing you to change properties such as the Name of the MenuStrip variable.

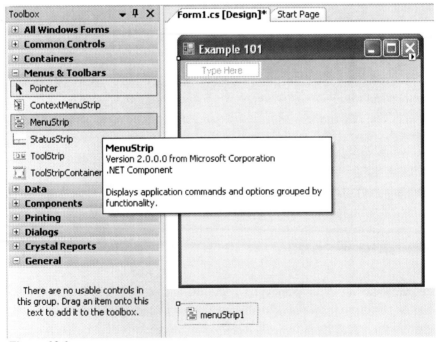

Figure 13.1

The MenuStrip will also appear at the top of the Form. You add items to the menu by clicking in the vacant menu item area and typing in the item's Text. When you add an item to the menu the designer adds an object of type ToolStripMenuItem to your Form. The ToolStripMenuItem contains several properties that you can configure in the Property Window. Among them are the Name, Text, BackColor, and BackgroundImage properties. It also has several events that you can handle, the most important event being the Click event.

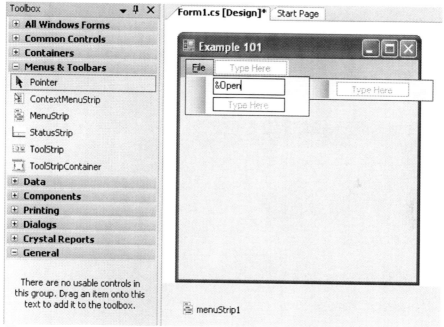

Figure 13.2

Each time you add an item to the MenuStrip the designer creates new vacant menu item spots. In Figure 13.2 you can see that after the File menu item was added, new item positions were created by the designer that we could use to create even more menu items. After creating the Open menu item we could add another menu item beneath it or we could add an item to the right of it to create a cascading affect. You can also click and drag menu items around the designer to change the order they are listed in the menu.

Access Keys

An Access Key is a key that can be used in combination with the Alt key to select a menu item just as if clicking it. You set the Access Key by placing an ampersand, '&' in the menu item's Text, immediately before the character that will be used as the Access Key. In Figure 13.2 you can see that the ampersand is located just before the 'O' character in Open. The menu shows that 'O' is the Access Key by underscoring the 'O' character.

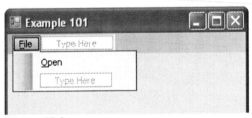

Figure 13.3

Shortcut Keys

Access Keys will only work when the menu item for that Access Key is visible. Another key combination called a Shortcut can also be assigned to a menu item. The Shortcut can be a key used in some combination of Control, Alt, and Shift. You can also use Function keys as shortcuts for your menu items. Shortcuts will work even when the menu item for the shortcut is not currently displayed.

To add a shortcut you need to set the ShortCutKeys property of the ToolStripMenuItem. You set the ShortCutKeys property by selecting the menu item that you want to create the shortcut for and then clicking on its ShortCutKeys property in the Property Window. The Shortcut designer window will appear as in Figure 13.4.

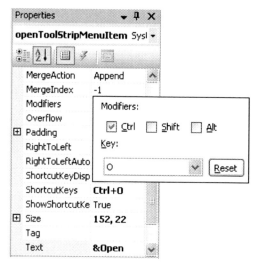

Figure 13.4

After setting the shortcut it will appear next to the text of the menu item.

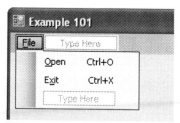

Figure 13.5

Menu Separators

A Menu Separator is a line between two menu items. Separators can be used to form visual groups within a menu to make them easier for the user to navigate. To create a separator you set the menu item's text to a single dash, '-'. After pressing enter the menu designer will convert the newly added menu item to a separator.

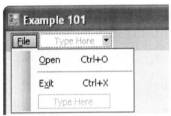

Figure 13.6

Implementing Menu Click Events

After you have the menu designed the way you want it you need to add the event method for the Click events for the menu items. You can add the Click event from the Property Window by selecting the menu item that you want to add the Click event for, selecting the events view in the Property Window, and double clicking on the Click event. Alternatively, you can double click the menu item in the menu designer.

The next example has three menu items. The File menu has the Open and Exit menu items. There is also a Help menu that has an About menu item. Double clicking the menu items creates empty event methods that you can implement to do whatever your application calls for.

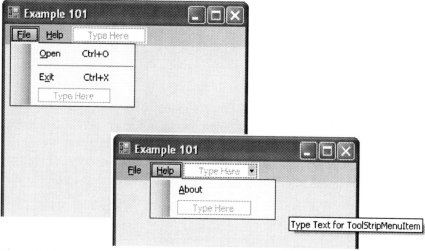

Figure 13.7

The event methods for the Click events of these menu items are listed below.

```
private void openToolStripMenuItem_Click(object sender,
                                                      EventArgs e)
{
    MessageBox.Show(this, "Not implemented yet");
}

private void exitToolStripMenuItem_Click(object sender,
                                                 EventArgs e)
{
    Close();
}

private void aboutToolStripMenuItem_Click(object sender,
                                                  EventArgs e)
{
    MessageBox.Show(this, "Not implemented yet");
}
```

Listing 13.1

Context Menus

Each control can have its own context menu listing a menu of commands specific to that control. If a control has a context menu it will be displayed whenever the user clicks the right mouse button over that control.

To create a Context Menu you drag a ContextMenuStrip component from the Toolbox and drop it on your Form in the designer. Selecting the ContextMenuStrip component at the bottom of the designer displays your context menu near the top of your window so you can edit the menu items just like you did with the MenuStrip earlier in this chapter.

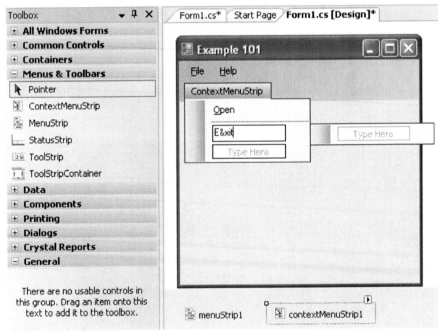

Figure 13.8

In Figure 13.8 you can see that a ContextMenuStrip object named contextMenuStrip1 has been placed at the bottom of the Form and has been selected for editing. Two ToolStripMenuItems have been added, labeled as Open and Exit. You can add Click event methods to the menu items of the ContextMenuStrip by double clicking on the menu items.

After designing the context menu you can assign it to a control by setting that control's ContextMenuStrip property to reference the appropriate ContextMenuStrip object. This can be done by assigning the reference in code or by selecting the control and clicking in the ContextMenuStrip property in the Property Window. Setting the Form's ContextMenuStrip property to contextMenuStrip1 from the application shown in Figure 13.8 will cause the context menu to be displayed whenever the user clicks the right mouse button over the Form.

Dialog Boxes

A Dialog Box is a Window that contains controls to either gather input from the user or display output. A dialog box is really just another Form object in your application. You can display a dialog box in two ways; Modal or Modeless.

A *modal dialog* is one that completely takes over the application. When you display a Modal dialog the rest of the application is effectively disabled until the user dismisses the dialog. You would use a modal dialog when you know that you cannot continue processing until the user provides the information requested in the dialog. For instance, you cannot load a file until you know the name of it. A modal dialog can be used to prompt for a file name. After the dialog is dismissed by the user the program can get the name of the file from the dialog and continue its processing.

A *modeless dialog* is one that is displayed without disabling the rest of the program. In the Windows' Wordpad program, the Find dialog, shown in Figure 13.9 is an example of a modeless dialog. You can continue editing files in wordpad, even while the Find dialog is visible.

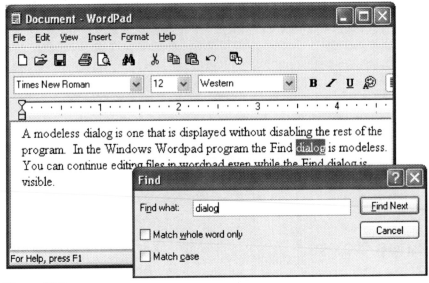

Figure 13.9

Creating a dialog is simply a matter of adding a new Form to your project. Whether it is modal or modeless depends on how you display it. If you display a Form by calling its ShowDialog method it will be displayed as a modal dialog. The ShowDialog method will not return until the user dismisses the dialog. The return value of ShowDialog will be a value from the DialogResult enumeration, such as DialogResult.OK or DialogResult.Cancel.

If you display a form using its Show method then that dialog will be modeless. The Show method has a void return value.

Creating a Dialog Box

In this section we will add a dialog box to a Windows Application and display it as a modal dialog. The dialog we will create will be an About box. An About box is normally displayed from the Help menu. It contains useful information about the product, such as the title, version, and information about the company that wrote the software.

First create a new Windows Application. When your project is open in Visual Studio .NET, right click on the project node of the Solution Explorer. Then click on Add, Windows Form.

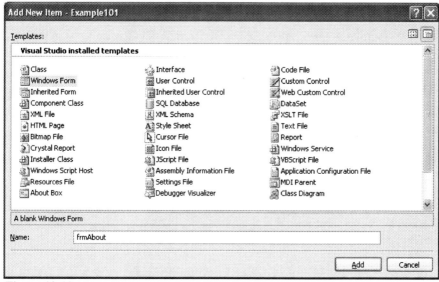

Figure 13.10

When the Add New Item box appears (which happens to be a modal dialog box) set the Name to frmAbout. Then click the Add button so that the Form opens in the designer. Drop some labels on the form and set their text to describe you, your organization, or something about the application. Also drop a button on the form with the text "OK".

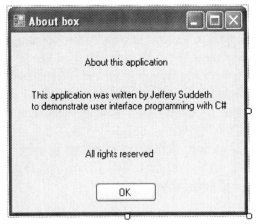

Figure 13.11

The OK button is the button that will dismiss the dialog box. Add a Click event method for the OK Button and within its event method, set the DialogResult property of the Form to DialogResult.OK. Setting the DialogResult of the form will close the form. The value of the DialogResult property will be returned from the ShowDialog method.

```
private void button1_Click(object sender, EventArgs e)
{
    DialogResult = DialogResult.OK;
}
```

Listing 13.2

After creating the About box and implementing the button's Click event, we need to provide a method to display the dialog. Typically the About box is displayed from the Help menu. So create a Help menu and add an item with the text, "About". Then add the following event method for its Click event.

```
private void aboutToolStripMenuItem_Click(object sender, EventArgs e)
{
    frmAbout aboutBox = new frmAbout();
    aboutBox.ShowDialog(this);  // don't care about return value
}
```

Listing 13.3

With a modal DialogBox you really want the user to dismiss the box by clicking on one of the buttons instead of clicking the close button in the control box. It would be a good idea to remove the control buttons in the upper right corner of the dialog. To remove the control buttons select the About box in the designer and set its ControlBox property to false in the Property Window. You will notice that the three control buttons will disappear.

Running the application, you should be able to click on the *About* menu item from the Help menu to display the About box. While the About box is on display the rest of the application will be disabled.

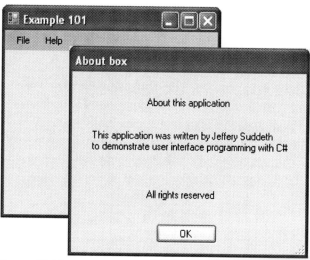

Figure 13.12

The Toolbar

The Toolbar is another user interface feature that you may want to include in your application. It creates a strip across the top of the window, usually just below the MenuStrip, where you can place controls for single-click access to common commands.

Visual Studio .NET 2005 ships with the ToolStrip class to implement Toolbar functionality. This class is a major update from the previous version of Visual Studio. Not only can you add buttons to the ToolStrip, but you can also add ComboBoxes, TextBoxes, Labels, Separators, and other controls to improve your user interface.

Adding a ToolStrip

To add a ToolStrip to your form you can add it directly to the Form, which will place it at the top of the Window, or you can first add a ToolStripContainer and then add one or more ToolStrips to the container. In this section we will add the ToolStrip directly to the Form.

You add the ToolStrip by dragging the ToolStrip control from the ToolBox and dropping it on to the Form. The designer will draw a bar across the top of the Form and will also display a ToolStrip component at the bottom of the designer window that you can select to bring its properties into the Property Window. You will find the ToolStrip control in the *Menus & Toolbars* group on the Toolbox.

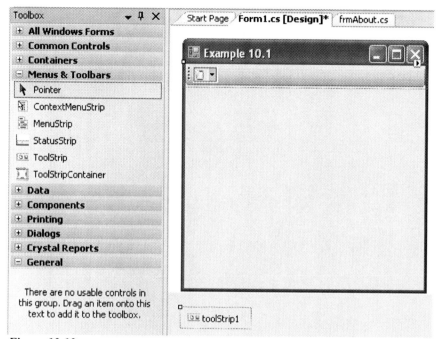

Figure 13.13

When the ToolStrip component is selected you will see a combo box appear on the ToolStrip, as shown in Figure 13.13. Clicking on the thumb of the combo will display the different controls that you can place on the ToolStrip. Clicking one of those controls will add it to the strip and advance the combo box to the next position. Clicking on the part of the combo box that does not drop will place the default control on the strip, which happens to be the ToolStripButton.

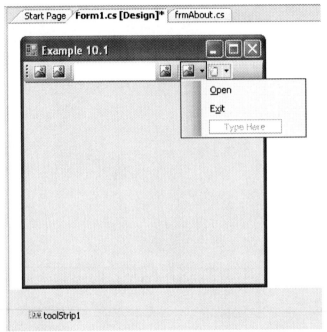

Figure 13.14

In Figure 13.14 we have added several controls to the ToolStrip. First we added two buttons, followed by a separator bar. Next we added a text box and a button, followed by another separator. Then we added a split button, which is really just a type of menu.

Selecting each of those controls allows us to edit their properties in the Properties Window. Some of the tool strip controls, like the buttons do not display their text on the control. Instead their text is displayed as a tool tip when the mouse hovers over the control, saving space on the tool strip. Also through the Property Window, you can add any event methods for each of the control's events. Because the Click event is the default event, you can quickly add Click events by double clicking the components in the ToolStrip.

The code below shows the event methods for the ToolStrip in Figure 13.14.

```
private void exitToolStripMenuItem_Click(object sender, EventArgs e)
{
    Close();
}


private void toolStripButton1_Click(object sender, EventArgs e)
{
    // exit the application
    Close();
}

private void toolStripFindButton_Click(object sender, EventArgs e)
{
    // find button
    string message = "Text not found: " +
        toolStripTextBox1.Text;

    MessageBox.Show(this, message, "Find Command",
        MessageBoxButtons.OK, MessageBoxIcon.Information);
}

private void openToolStripMenuItem_Click(object sender, EventArgs e)
{
    MessageBox.Show(this, "Not implemented yet");
}

private void toolStripButton2_Click(object sender, EventArgs e)
{
    // open a file
    MessageBox.Show("Open command is Not implemented yet");
}
```

Listing 13.4

The first event method is linked to one of the ToolStripMenuItems on the split button; the one with the "Exit" text. The second event method is linked to a tool strip button whose purpose is also to close the program. The third method is the most interesting for this example. It reads the text from the ToolStripTextBox and uses it to build a message. Then it displays that message with MessageBox.Show. This event method could be used to find text in a large, multiline text box or perhaps to send a search request on the Internet.

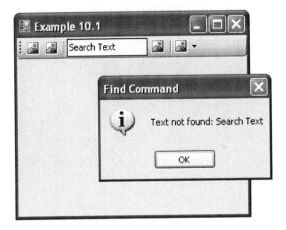

Figure 13.15

Setting the Toolbar Images

To set the image of a toolbar button you set its Image property. Select the toolbar button so that its properties appear in the Property Window. Then select the Image property. You will be prompted with a dialog box asking you to import an image file. Just click the Import button and browse to find an icon file that will be used as your buttons image. Depending on your installation, Visual Studio .NET may come with a library of bitmaps and icons that you can use in your programs. In Figure 13.16 we have loaded an icon of a red X to shutdown the program.

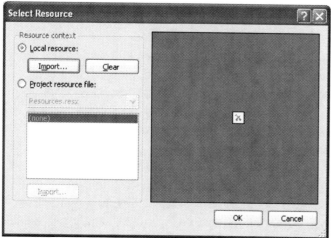

Figure 13.16

When you import an image file through the designer the image will be saved in a resource file. The resource file is an XML format file that is included in your project. Any resources, such as images, sounds, or animations that you import into your resource file are compiled into your program so you do not have to distribute the file you imported.

Figure 13.17 shows our tool strip with some stock icons in place of the default.

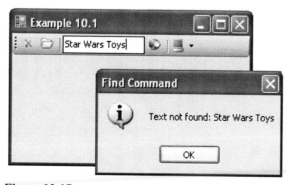

Figure 13.17

Using the ToolStripContainer

Modern applications often have more than one tool bar. In fact, there are often several tool bars that can be hidden, displayed, and even moved around within their container. Visual Studio .NET 2005 provides the ToolStripContainer control to support this advanced toolbar functionality. The ToolStripContainer can be found on the Toolbox in the *Menus & Toolbars* group.

In this section we create a program that searches the internet for keywords that the user types in into a TextBox. The key words that the user types in will be appended to a web request, which will be sent to the Google website to perform the search. The results of the search will be displayed in an embedded web browser window. The application will have a ToolStripContainer, containing a TextBox and a Button to submit the query.

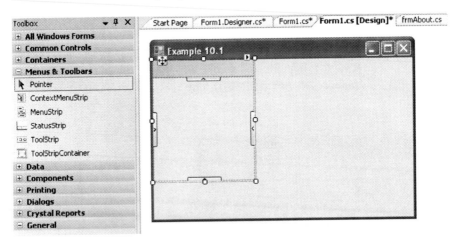

Figure 13.18

You can place the ToolStripContainer on the Form by double clicking the ToolStripContainer in the Toolbox or by dragging and dropping. You can then set its Docking property to *Fill* so that it fills the entire contents area of the form, docking against all four sides. Clicking on the small tab areas inside the container will expand a bar region where you can place tool strips. In Figure 13.19 the ToolStripContainer is docked to the entire content area of the form and two ToolStrips have been added to its upper region.

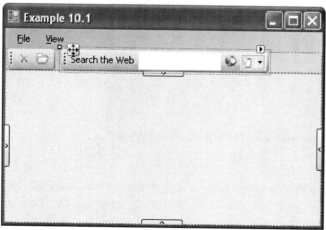

Figure 13.19

When the tool strip is selected within container the positioning icon, which looks like the cross hairs, will appear as shown in Figure 13.19. If you click and drag the positioning icon you can drag the tool strips to the position you want them in the container.

Also in Figure 13.19 we have added a menu strip. The File menu contains the Open and Exit menu items, which perform the same operation as the open and close tool strip buttons. The View menu has a cascaded menu for hiding and displaying the different tool strips.

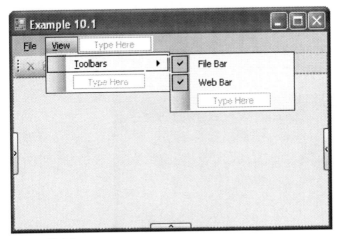

Figure 13.20

The menu items that cascade from the Toolbars menu are labeled "File Bar" and "Web Bar". For both of the menu items we set their *Checked* property to true in the Properties Window so that they display a check mark. We also set their *CheckOnClick* property to true so that the check mark will be toggled on or off whenever the menu item is clicked. The *File Bar* menu item will toggle the Visible property of the tool strip for file operations and the *Web Bar* menu item will toggle the Visible property of the tool strip holding the web searching controls.

The event handlers for all menu items and tool strip controls are below.

```
private void exitToolStripButton_Click(object sender, EventArgs e)
{
    CloseCommand();
}

private void openToolStripButton_Click(object sender, EventArgs e)
{
    OpenCommand();
}
```

```
private void fileBarToolStripMenuItem_Click(object sender,
EventArgs e)
{
    toolStrip1.Visible = !toolStrip1.Visible;
}

private void webBarToolStripMenuItem_Click(object sender,
                                    EventArgs e)
{
    toolStrip2.Visible = !toolStrip2.Visible;
}

private void webSearchButton_Click(object sender, EventArgs e)
{
    WebSearchCommand();
}

private void openToolStripMenuItem_Click(object sender,
                                                EventArgs e)
{
    OpenCommand();
}

private void exitToolStripMenuItem_Click(object sender,
                                                EventArgs e)
{
    CloseCommand();
}

private void CloseCommand()
{
    Close();
}

private void OpenCommand()
{
    MessageBox.Show("Open not implemented");
}

private void WebSearchCommand()
{
    string msgText = "Not Found: " + webSearchText.Text;
    MessageBox.Show(this, msgText, "Web Finder",
        MessageBoxButtons.OK, MessageBoxIcon.Information);

}
```

Listing 13.5

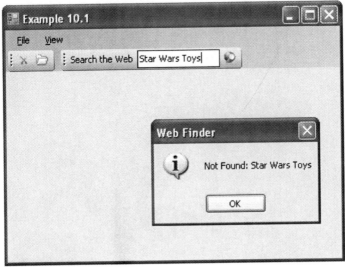

Figure 13.21

Searching the Web – For real this time!

In this section we will finally implement the web searching functionality. With the Form open in design mode double click on the WebControl component in the Toolbox. The WebControl will drop into the form and dock itself against all for sides of the content area.

You use the WebControl by setting its Url property, which is an object of type Uri. The constructor for the Uri takes a string that would normally be a web address. That string could also be a URL address for any type of file that the WebBrowser knows how to display, such as an image or text document.

After placing the WebBrowserControl on the form, go back to the WebSearchCommand method from the previous listing and replace it with the following implementation.

```
private void WebSearchCommand()
{
    string[] searchWords = webSearchText.Text.Split(' ');

    string googleSearch = "http://www.google.com/search?hl=en&q=";
    for(int i = 0; i < searchWords.Length; i++)
    {
        googleSearch += searchWords[i];
        if (i < searchWords.Length - 1)
        {
            googleSearch += "+";
        }
    }
    webBrowser1.Url = new Uri(googleSearch);
}
```

Listing 13.6

The Click event of the webSearchButton calls the
WebSearchCommand method. This version of the
WebSearchCommand method splits the text from the webSearchText
TextBox on the space character to get an array of strings for a web
query on Google's web server.

We initialize our googleSearch string with the web address for the
Google search program and a few default parameters. Then we
append our search words to the string. The result should be a valid
Google search string request, such as

http://www.google.com/search?hl=en&q=Star+Wars+toys

Then we pass that string to the Uri constructor and assign the object to
the web browser's Url property. If you are connected to the Internet
the browser control will automatically send the request to the Google
web server and display the results.

We have just made a custom web searching tool.

Figure 13.22

The Status Bar

Another popular user interface item is the status bar. The status bar displays information about the current status of your application. You may want to display information about the current record number, a message showing if your program is connected to a server, or the status of the Numlock or Capslock keys.

To add a status bar to your application drag a StatusStrip control from the Toolbox and drop it on to the Form. The StatusStrip will stretch along the bottom of the Form. You will also see the StatusStrip component at the bottom of the designer window.

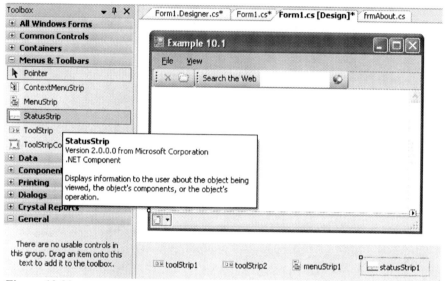

Figure 13.23

When the status strip is selected the designer will display a control combo box on the strip that you can use to place controls on the status bar. Clicking on the thumb will allow you to select one of the controls supported by the StatusStrip to place the control on the status bar. If you click on the other part of the combo box you will get the default control type for the StatusStrip, which is the ToolStripStatusLabel control.

Adding the ToolStripStatusLabel to the status bar creates a variable of that type on the Form. When selected, you can modify its properties in the Properties Window.

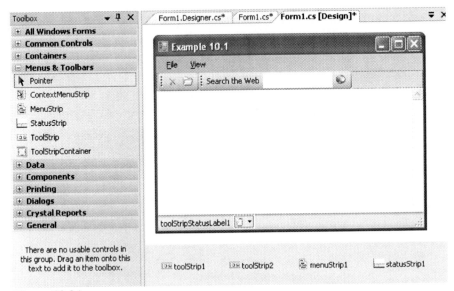

Figure 13.24

The status label has several properties that you can use to customize its appearance. The Text property contains the Text that is displayed in the label. If you set the BorderSides property to display some or all borders, you can change the look of the status label even further. By setting the BorderStyle to one of its enumeration values you can give your status label a 3D look.

Windows Common Dialogs

There are some operations that are common among most applications, such as opening and saving files or choosing fonts and colors. The Windows operating system provides a set of common dialogs for these activities to make them easier for users. If a user has experience using the Open File Dialog in one Windows application and your application uses the same Open File Dialog, the user will feel more at home learning to use your application.

Using the common dialogs is a lot like using dialogs that you created. All you have to do is instantiate the dialog class and invoke the object's ShowDialog method. To make it even easier, Visual Studio .NET's Toolbox has dialog box components that you can drop on your form. Dropping a common dialog component on your form adds a member variable of that dialog type to your Form's class.

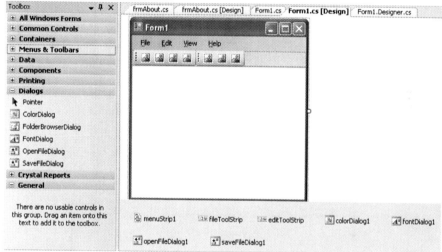

Figure 13.25

The Open File Dialog

Figure 13.25 shows a Form for a text editing application in design mode. The Form contains a menu strip and a tool strip container with two tool strips. There is also a TextBox with its Dock property set to *Fill* so that it fills the entire client area of the Form. It also contains several common dialog components, including an OpenFileDialog instance named *openFileDialog1*.

The File menu contains a ToolStripMenuItem variable named *openToolStripMenuItem*, which should allow the user to browse for a file and open it into the text editor when clicked. Figure 13.26 shows the Open File Dialog being used to browse for a file.

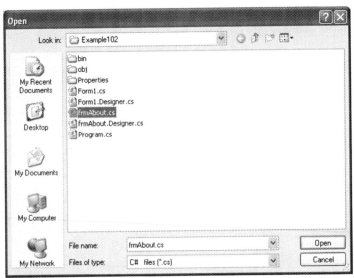

Figure 13.26

The following event method can be registered for the openToolStripMenuItem's Click event.

```
private void openToolStripMenuItem_Click(object sender, EventArgs e)
{
    // set the file extension filter
    openFileDialog1.Filter =
        "txt files (*.txt)|*.txt"
        + "|HTML files (*.html)|*.html"
        + "|C#   files (*.cs)|*.cs"
        + "|All files (*.*)|*.*";
```

```
if (openFileDialog1.ShowDialog() == DialogResult.OK)
{
    fileName = openFileDialog1.FileName;

    StreamReader reader = new StreamReader(fileName);
    textBox1.Text = reader.ReadToEnd();
    reader.Close();
}
}
```

Listing 13.7

The event method starts by setting the Filter property of the OpenFileDialog. Setting the filter allows the user to filter the file types that show up in the dialog to make it easier to find the types of files they want. In this example we filter on text files, HTML documents, and C# source code. The last filter is for *.* so that all files can be displayed.

Next the method calls the ShowDialog method. This method displays the dialog and allows the user to browse for a file. If the user dismisses the Open File Dialog by clicking the OK button then ShowDialog will return DialogResult.OK. Then we can get the complete path and name of the file they selected from the FileName property and use it to load the file into the Text property of the TextBox.

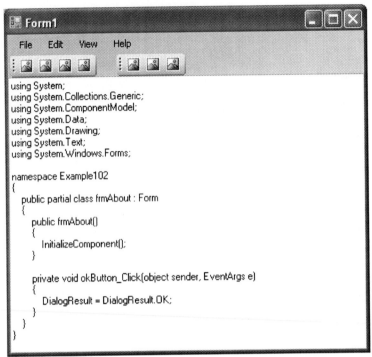

Figure 13.27

The Save File Dialog

The Save File Dialog works the same was as the Open File Dialog.
The following event handler uses the Save File Dialog to get the name
of the file the user wants to save. It then uses that file name to create a
StreamWriter and write the contents of the TextBox's Text to the
stream.

```
private void saveasToolStripMenuItem_Click(object sender,
                                            EventArgs e)
{
    // set the file extension filter
    saveFileDialog1.Filter =
        "txt files (*.txt)|*.txt"
        + "|HTML files (*.html)|*.html"
        + "|C#   files (*.cs)|*.cs"
        + "|All files (*.*)|*.*";
```

```
    if (saveFileDialog1.ShowDialog() == DialogResult.OK)
    {
        fileName = saveFileDialog1.FileName;

        StreamWriter writer = new StreamWriter(fileName);
        writer.Write(textBox1.Text);
        writer.Close();
    }
}
```

Listing 13.8

The Color Dialog

The color dialog is used to choose a color. What ever color the user selected on the dialog will be stored in the dialog's Color property, which is a Color enumeration type. Figure 13.28 shows the color dialog.

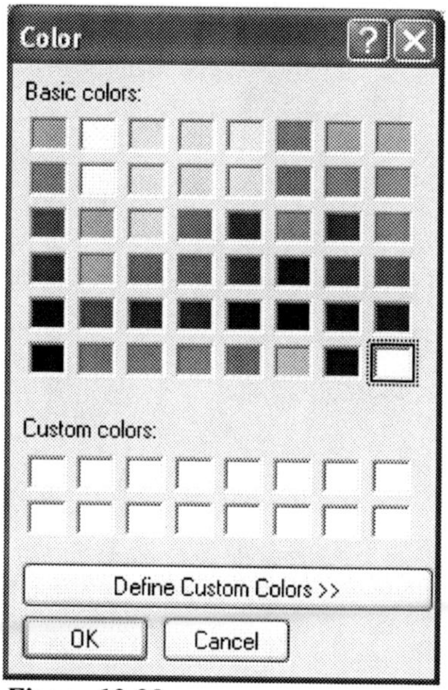

Figure 13.28

The text editor program's View menu has two ToolStripMenuItems that display the color dialog. The first will change the TextBox's background color. The other one will change the foreground color.

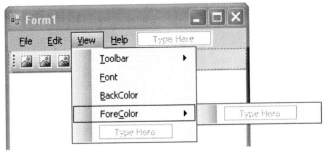

Figure 13.29

The following two event methods are invoked when the user clicks the BackColor and ForeColor menu items.

```
private void backColorToolStripMenuItem_Click(object sender,
                                              EventArgs e)
{
    colorDialog1.Color = textBox1.BackColor;
    if (colorDialog1.ShowDialog() == DialogResult.OK)
    {
        textBox1.BackColor = colorDialog1.Color;
    }
}

private void foreColorToolStripMenuItem_Click(object sender,
                                              EventArgs e)
{
    colorDialog1.Color = textBox1.ForeColor;
    if (colorDialog1.ShowDialog() == DialogResult.OK)
    {
        textBox1.ForeColor = colorDialog1.Color;
    }
}
```

Listing 13.9

The first event method is triggered when the user clicks the menu item to set the back color. The method sets the color dialog's Color property to match the current value of the TextBox's BackColor property. If the user clicks OK then whatever color was selected on the dialog will be used as the new BackColor property on the TextBox. The second method does the same for the TextBox's ForeColor property.

The Font Dialog

The Font dialog will allow the user to browse and select a font that has been installed on the system. The user can choose the font name, style, and size. They can also choose a strikethrough or underscore font. The dialog's Font property is an instance of the Font class that matches the font currently selected in the dialog.

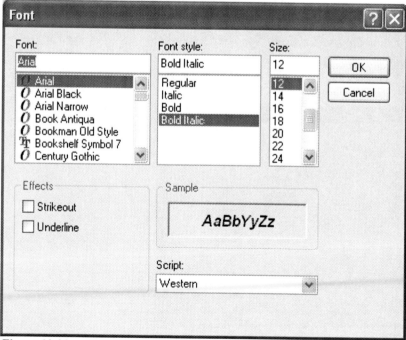

Figure 13.30

The View menu on the Text editor program has a ToolStripMenuItem labeled as "Font". When the user selects the Font menu we should display the Font dialog to allow the user to choose a font for the TextBox. The following event method will can be registered to the font menu's Click event.

```
private void fontToolStripMenuItem_Click(object sender,
                                         EventArgs e)
{
    fontDialog1.Font = textBox1.Font;
    if (fontDialog1.ShowDialog() == DialogResult.OK)
    {
        textBox1.Font = fontDialog1.Font;
    }
}
```

Listing 13.10

The method first sets the dialog's Font property to the current font of the TextBox. Then after the dialog is displayed and the user clicks the OK button, the method sets the TextBox's font to match the font of the dialog.

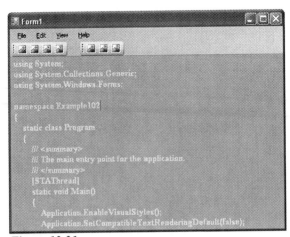

Figure 13.31

Chapter 14 – User Controls and ActiveX

Software is a lot easier to write if you do not have to reinvent the wheel for every program. That is what this chapter is really about. Here you will learn how to create and use UserControls, which are user interface components that can be reused by other .NET applications. You will also see how to work with COM objects and ActiveX controls.

User Controls

A user control is a user interface component can be embedded in an executable project or referenced from a DLL. In this section we will create a user control for entering customer information. We will store the control in its own DLL so that the same data entry screen can be shared between multiple Windows programs. We will also build a Windows application to test the control.

The process of creating and testing a user control is fairly straightforward. In fact, creating the user control is very much like creating a dialog box. The basic steps are to add the user control to the project, open it in design mode, and then place controls from the Toolbox onto the user control.

Creating and Testing a User Control

The following 9 steps will guide you through creating and testing the CustDataEntry control.

1. Create the Control Library Project

To create the project, start Visual Studio and create a Windows Control Library project.

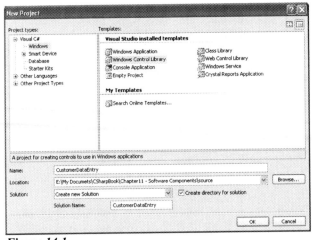

Figure 14.1

Name the project CustomerDataEntry and click the OK Button. Visual Studio will create the project and add a UserControl object named UserControl1. The UserControl will be opened in design mode.

After it is added to the project, the User Control will show up in the Solution Explorer as a child node of the project. Like the Form, the User Control consists of three files. The first is given the default name of UserControl1.cs. It is the file that you add your properties, methods, and event delegate methods to. If you expand the UserControl1.cs node in the Solution explorer then you will see the other two files used by the designer. The source file for designer generated code, called UserControl1.Designer.cs. The UserControl1.resx file is the resource file used by the designer to add images, sounds, and other resources to the control.

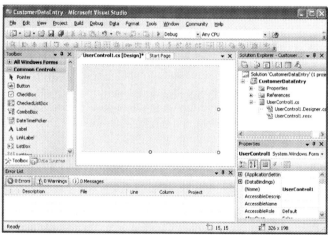

Figure 14.2

The UserControl is a type of control container that you can drop other controls on. You can also implement events such as Load, Paint, and KeyPress, just like a Form object.

2. Build the controls user interface in the designer.

For this example change the UserControl1 Name property to
CustDataEntry. Then drop five TextBoxes on the form and three
Labels having the Text *Name*, *Address*, and *City, State, Zip.* The text
boxes should be named *txtName*, *txtAddress*, *txtCity*, *txtState*, and
txtZip. For each of the TextBoxes, set their Modifiers property to
Public so that they will be accessible from outside of the class.

Also place two Buttons labeled as *OK* and *Cancel*. The result should
look something like Figure 14.3.

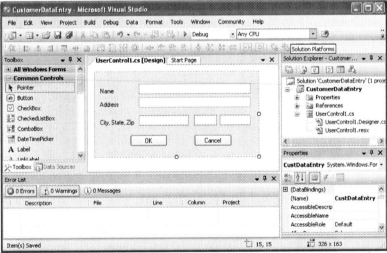

Figure 14.3

3. Add Events to notify the container of a button click

The control needs to be able to notify its container when the OK and
Cancel buttons have been clicked. To notify the container of these
Button clicks the control will fire events that we will define. Switch to
the code view and add the following event definitions.

```
// delegates and events defined
public delegate void OkButtonClick(object sender, EventArgs e);
public event OkButtonClick OkClickEvent;

public delegate void CancelButtonClick(object sender, EventArgs e);
public event CancelButtonClick CancelClickEvent;

// protected methods to fire the events
protected void OnOkButtonClick()
{
    if (OkClickEvent != null)
    {
        OkClickEvent(this, new EventArgs());
    }
}

protected void OnCancelButtonClick()
{
    if (CancelClickEvent != null)
    {
        CancelClickEvent(this, new EventArgs());
    }
}
```

Listing 14.1

The code defines two delegates and events for the OkClickEvent and the CancelClickEvent. It also defines protected methods to invoke the event delegates if they are not null.

4. Implement the Button Click events to invoke our own events

Next we need to implement the two Buttons' Click events to call the OnOkClick and OnCancelClick methods. Double click the OK and Cancel buttons in the designer to add the following Click event handlers.

```
private void okButton_Click(object sender, EventArgs e)
{
    OnOkButtonClick();
}

private void cancelButton_Click(object sender, EventArgs e)
{
    OnCancelButtonClick();
}
```

Listing 14.2

5. Build the Control

After you successfully build your control library, a new control group will appear in your Toolbox named Customer Data Entry Components. If you expand the group the CustDataEntry control will appear.

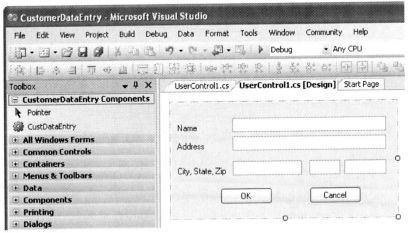

Figure 14.4

6. Create a Windows Application to test the control

Next we will create a project that uses our control. Right click on the solution in the solution explorer and select Add and New Project. Choose *Windows Application* in the *Add New Project* dialog and name the project *UserDataProgram*. Then click OK.

7. Add the Control to your Form

After the project is created and your form is open in design mode, double click the CustDataEntry control on the Toolbox to add one to your form. Then size and position the control to your own taste.

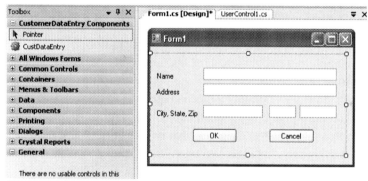

Figure 14.5

8. Register delegates for the CustDataEntry events

Now we need to add event handlers for the Ok and Cancel click events. With the CustDataEntry control selected go to the Property Window and click on the lightening bolt to see the available events for this control. You should see the OkClickEvent and CancelClickEvent events listed. Double click each of those events to

add event handlers for them. Then implement the event handlers with
the following code.

```
private void custDataEntry1_CancelClickEvent(object sender,
                                                    EventArgs e)
{
    MessageBox.Show("Cancel Clicked");
}

private void custDataEntry1_OkClickEvent(object sender,
                                                    EventArgs e)
{
    MessageBox.Show("Ok Clicked: " + custDataEntry1.txtName.Text);
}
```

Listing 14.3

9. Run the Test Application

We are finally ready to test out are application. Build the application
from the build menu or by right clicking the UserDataProgram project
node in the Solution Explorer and choosing *Build* from the Popup
menu. Make sure that UserDataProgram is selected as the startup
project by right clicking its project node and choosing
SetAsStartUpProject. Then run the program by pressing F5 or
clicking *Start Debugging* from the Debug menu.

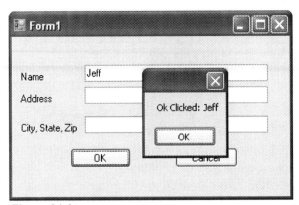

Figure 14.6

Adding Controls to the Toolbox

In the previous example we created a UserControl and a test program in the same solution. When we compiled the CustomerDataEntry project the control automatically showed up in the Toolbox. This is very convenient for creating a project to test the control but you may need to add a control to your Toolbox that you did not write. In that case you have to add the control by hand.

1. Begin a new Windows Application project

Close the solution containing the CustomerDataEntry project so that the CustDataEntry control is removed from your Toolbox. Then begin a new Windows Application Project.

2. Add the CustDataEntry control to the Toolbox

Right click on the Toolbox and click Choose Items. The Choose Toolbox Items dialog box will appear.

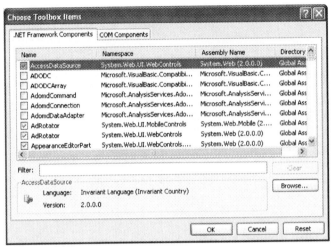

Figure 14.7

The Choose Toolbox Items dialog lists many .NET controls that you can add to your Toolbox. With this dialog you can customize your Toolbox, adding the controls you use and removing the controls that you do not.

Since our CustDataEntry control is not in the list of known controls we have to browse to find it. Click the Browse button to browse for the DLL file that we created in the last section.

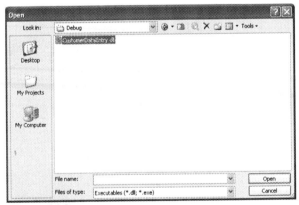

Figure 14.8

After selecting the file and clicking Open, the CustDataEntry control will be listed and selected in the Choose Toolbox Items dialog. Click the OK button to dismiss the dialog. The CustDataEntry control will then appear in the Toolbox.

Figure 14.9

3. Use the CustDataControl as any other control

Once the control is in your Toolbox you can use it as you would use any other control. Double click the CustDataEntry control in the Toolbox to add an instance to your Form. Then you can set its properties, handle its events, and call its methods from your Form class.

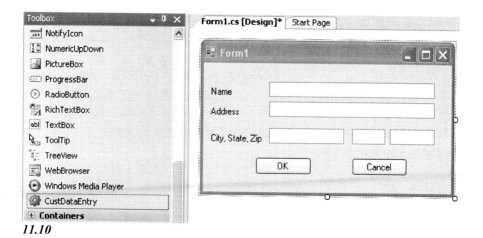

11.10

Now that we have packaged our user data entering functionality into a UserControl, we can create as many applications as we want that require a customer data entry screen and use this same control with very little coding. Customers will also find our applications easier to use because using a common component like the CustDataEntry control means that our applications will have a standard look and feel for screens requiring this functionality.

Creating .NET components that do not have a user interface is no different from creating a normal C# class. If the class is public and defined in a Class Library project then it is accessible by any .NET language. If you need to use a component that pre-dates .NET then you may need to use a COM component, the topic of the next section.

COM Components

Before .NET, there was COM, the Component Object Model. COM is a binary standard for software components so they can be used by applications written in different languages. At the time COM was developed it was a great stride forward in software component reuse. COM is the technology that made it possible to embed those Excel spreadsheets in your Word documents.

While COM allowed us to get more mileage out of our software components, it still required quite a bit of work by the programmer. Unlike .NET, COM does not provide a Common Type System so marshalling data between C++ and Visual Basic took some effort.

COM works by defining interfaces that provide certain types of functionality. Then one or more classes can implement the interfaces. The implementation classes are completely hidden from any client program, even the name of the implementation class is not known.

Hiding this information provides location transparency. The client program simply declares the interface pointer and asks the COM library to create the object. The implementation class could be in a DLL loaded in-process, an EXE file running in its own process, or even on a different machine.

The COM interfaces and classes are identified by unique 128 bit structures called Globally Unique Identifiers, *GUIDs*. Those GUIDs are listed in the system registry, along with information about the file that contains the implementation class. A COM client asks the COM API to create a component by specifying the GUID for the interface that it wants. Another ID for the component, called a progid, is a more readable string. For instance, the *SAPI.SpVoice* progid can be used to instantiate the object implementing the SpVoice interface.

With .NET around there is little need for creating new COM components these days. Even so, there is a lot of legacy code out there that is already built with the COM architecture and it is very likely that some of that functionality will be needed by your applications. The next example will create an application that allows the user to type any text they want into a multiline TextBox and then have the computer read that text back to them. That's right. Get some speakers or headphones for your computer if you need to because in this section, we will make your computer read to you using the Microsoft Speech API, a COM based technology.

Using a COM Component

Visual Studio makes using a COM component simple. To use a COM object you need to set a reference to it from your project. Then Visual Studio .NET will generate a managed class that encapsulates the COM component. Instead of using the COM component directly, you will use the wrapper class generated by the development environment.

To create the reading program, follow the next five steps.

1. Create a Windows Application project

To get the project started, create a Windows Application project. The only three controls required are a Label, a Button, and a TextBox.

Figure 14.11

Set the TextBox's Multiline property set to true. Then change the Label's Name property to *lblDescription* and set its BorderStyle property to *Fixed3D*.

2. Add a reference to the COM object

Add a reference to the Speech component library by right clicking the references node in the Solution explorer and clicking on *Add Reference*. Select the COM tab on the Add Reference dialog and scroll down to find the Microsoft Speech Object Library. Select it and click the Ok button.

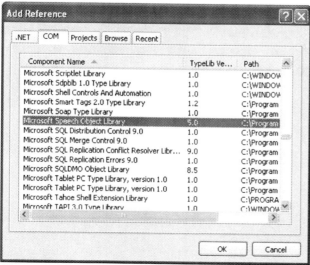

Figure 14.12

After Visual Studio adds the reference you will see the SpeechLib reference in the Solution Explorer under the References node.

3. Declare and instantiate the COM objects

Add member variables to your Form for the COM object references.

```
SpeechLib.SpVoiceClass voice;
SpeechLib.ISpeechObjectTokens voices;
```

The objects will be created in the Load event of the Form.

```
private void Form1_Load(object sender, EventArgs e)
{
    voice = new SpeechLib.SpVoiceClass();
    voices = voice.GetVoices("", "");
    lblDescription.Text = voices.Item(0).GetDescription(0);
}
```

Listing 14.4

The Form1_Load method also gets the description of the default voice and displays it in the lblDescription's Text property. The default voice is probably "Microsoft Sam". Depending on what software you have installed, you may have more than one voice.

4. Call the object's methods and properties

Next add event handlers for the Form's Load event and the button's Click event.

```
private void button1_Click(object sender, EventArgs e)
{
    voice.Speak(textBox1.Text,
        SpeechLib.SpeechVoiceSpeakFlags.SVSFDefault);
}
```

Listing 14.5

The voice.Speak method does the speaking. The button1_Click event handler passes the Text of the TextBox into the Speak method. The SpeechVoiceSpeakFlags enumeration can be used to specify options but we are using the default options.

5. Test the program.

After compiling the program, press F5 to run it. Type some text into the TextBox and click the Speak button.

Figure 14.13

ActiveX Controls

COM is an architecture that defines how a component is created and used. Some COM components are just objects and have no user interface, like the objects of the Speech API from the last example. Others have a user interface and can be hosted in container windows. COM components with user interfaces are more complicated because they need to communicate with the container control, paint themselves in the container control's drawing surface, and send events to the container.

At some point Microsoft decided to rename COM to ActiveX, but don't be confused. An ActiveX control is really just a COM component with a user interface. Using an ActiveX control is very similar to using a regular COM component. For the next example we will create a movie player using the Windows Media Player ActiveX control. The entire project will be completed in 5 steps.

1. Create a Windows Application

As always, the first thing you need to do is create a Windows Application that will host the ActiveX control. Name the application *activexdemo1*.

2. Add the ActiveX control to your Toolbox

To use the control we need to add it to the Toolbox. Right click anywhere on the Toolbox and click on the *Choose Items M*enuItem. When the Choose Toolbox Items dialog appears, click on the COM tab. The COM tab will list all ActiveX controls that are registered on your system. Find and select the Windows Media Player control. Then click the OK button.

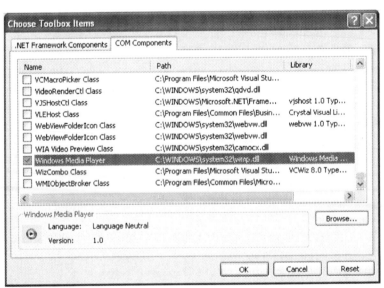

Figure 14.14

The Windows Media Player control will show up on your Toolbox.

Figure 14.15

3. Place the ActiveX Control on your Form

Place the control on the Form as you would any other control. Size and position control as you like. The default name of the control is axWindowsMediaPlayer1, which is fine for this example. We should anchor all four sides of the control so that if the user resizes the Form the control will resize with the form as well.

To Anchor the control make sure it is selected in the Property Window and click on the Anchor property. An anchor designer window will appear so that you can click on any of the sides that you want anchored. For this example select all four, as shown in Figure 14.16.

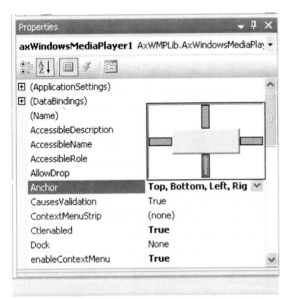

Figure 14.16

We should also place a button on the form to allow a user to browse for a media file. Place a Button near the bottom of the form and change its Name property to *browseButton*. The Form should look something like Figure 14.17.

Figure 14.17

4. Call the Methods and Properties of the Control

We need to implement the Click event of the browseButton to browse for a media file. Drop an OpenFileDialog on the form so that you can browse for the media file. Then double click the browseButton to add its Click event handler and write the following code that loads the file into the media player.

```
private void browseButton_Click(object sender, EventArgs e)
{
    if (openFileDialog1.ShowDialog() == DialogResult.OK)
    {
        // open the file
        string fileName = openFileDialog1.FileName;
        axWindowsMediaPlayer1.URL = fileName;
    }
}
```

Listing 14.6

The media player is designed load media files from the internet so the property you set when you want to load a file is named *URL*. Setting this property loads the file. Then the user can play the movie by clicking the Play button on the media player.

5. Run the program

The last step is to run the program. Make sure that your test program is set as the StartUpProgram in the Solution Explorer and press F5 to launch. Then click the Browse button to browse for a media file on your system. You can test this program with any file type supported by your version of the media player, which should include mp3 and wma music files.

Chapter 15 – Working With Data

Database access is the perfect example of source code reuse. The basic operations are always the same; add, retrieve, update, and delete records. The only thing different is the structure of the data. Yet each database system has its own native programming library that is not compatible with other databases, making it difficult to port applications to other database systems. So it is not surprising that numerous database libraries have been developed over the years to encapsulate the implementation details of database operations.

In this chapter we talk about how to access a database using ADO.NET, the set of classes that .NET provides for database access.

Databases

Most business applications need to access some kind of a database. That database could be a flat file, a directory of files, or it could be a server program that handles data requests from client programs. The later case is most common because database servers are optimized for managing large amounts of data and many concurrent connections. In the case of Microsoft Access, the tables are contained within a file with the MDB extension and the "server" is the JET database engine that your program communicates with using the classes that ADO.NET provides.

A database consists of a collection of tables. Each table is defined as a set of columns and a collection of rows. Each row has a field of data for each column in its table.

A *Relational Database* is a database that defines relationships between the tables. Consider the logical relationship between a Customer table and an Orders table. A customer can have many orders but each order can belong to only one customer. This type of relationship is called one-to-many.

The Customer record can be thought of as the parent record of each Order record belonging to that customer. If you delete the Customer record while it still has orders in the Orders table then those orders would be orphaned records. A relational database gives us the ability make that logical relationship a physical one by putting constraints or rules on the table, such as not allowing a Customer record to be deleted if it has any Order records, preserving the integrity of the database.

A database table usually defines a *primary key* to uniquely identify every record in the table. The primary key is normally a combination of one or more fields in the table. If a table contains child records that are linked back to a parent record then the value of that parent's primary key is usually stored in the child record. It is that field that provides the link to the parent record. When a table contains a field that stores a primary key from some other table, that field is called a *foreign key*.

Consider two tables that store Customers and Orders. The Customer table may be defined to hold customer information and a primary key. Table 15.1 shows what a Customer table might look like.

Table 15.1 – Definition of the Customer Table

Field Name	Data Type
CustomerID	int, auto counter, primary key
Name	string
Address	string
Phone	string

The Customer table is defined to store the Name, Address, and Phone of a Customer, as well as a CustomerID field that will uniquely identify a record in the table. The CustomerID field is the primary key.

The Customer and Orders table have a parent-child relationship, with Customers being the parent table. Each Customer can have one or more Orders, giving the tables a one-to-many relationship. The definition of the Orders table is below.

Table 15.2 – Definition of the Order Table

Field Name	Data Type
OrderID	int, auto increment, primary key
CustomerID	int, foreign key
OrderDate	DateTime
ShipDate	DateTime

The Orders table definition stores the OrderID as its primary key. It also stores the CustomerID as the foreign key to link it back to the customer record of the customer who placed the order.

The Northwind Trader Database

An example of a database is the Northwind Trader database, which you can install with Microsoft Access. The Northwind Trader database is a sample database that contains tables for Customers, Orders, Employees, and other data commonly used by businesses. We will use the Northwind Trader database in the examples that follow.

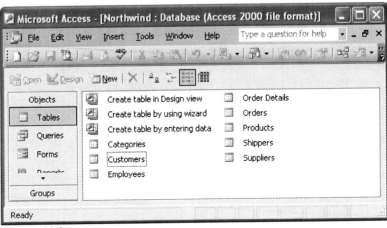

Figure 15.1

Introduction to SQL

Most databases use a language called SQL, Structured Query Language, to process their commands. While SQL (commonly pronounced "sequel") is a large topic, the basics are easily grasped by looking at a few statements. The basic operations for any database are to add, retrieve, update, and delete records. The SQL language supports these operations with the following four statements.

The Insert Statement

The insert statement will add new records to a table. To insert a record you must specify the name of the table and the values for the fields. The following statement inserts a new record into the Customers table of the Northwind Trader database.

INSERT INTO Customers (CustomerID, CompanyName)
VALUES ('SUD100', 'Jeff Suddeth')

The Insert statement takes the name of the table that you want to insert a record into. Then in parentheses you must specify the list of fields you are setting values to. After the *Values* keyword there is another set of parentheses that include the list of values to be assigned to the fields. The statement above creates a new Customers record and sets the *CustomerID* field to "SUD100" and the *CompanyName* field to "Jeff Suddeth". All other fields will be null unless the field has a default value defined.

The Select Statement

Use the Select statement to retrieve a set of records based on the criteria you specify. The select statement may return zero or more records depending on the conditions of your selection. The following statement does not specify any selection criteria. It will return the CustomerID and CompanyName fields from every row in the table.

SELECT CustomerID, CompanyName
FROM Customers

To add search criteria to the select statement you can use the where clause. The where clause takes a comma separated list of conditions. The following select statement will select the record we added above.

SELECT CustomerID, CompanyName
FROM Customers
WHERE CustomerID = 'SUD10';

The Update Statement

Use the update statement to modify existing records. To use the update statement you must specify the table you want to update, the fields that you want to change the values of, and the new values for those fields. The update statement uses a where clause to determine which records the update will apply to. The next statement updates the record we previously added by setting the Contact Name field.

UPDATE Customers SET ContactName='Jeffery'
WHERE CustomerID='SUD10'

You can update multiple fields in the same statement, separating the assignments by commas.

UPDATE Customers
SET ContactName='Jeffery', ContactTitle='Peon'
WHERE CustomerID='SUD10'

The Delete Statement

To delete a record you use the delete statement. The delete statement needs to know the name of the table you want to delete from and the criteria for the delete. The delete statement can remove zero or more records depending on the criteria of the where clause in your statement.

DELETE FROM Customers
WHERE CustomerID = 'SUD10'

There is a lot more that you can do with SQL, such as sorting selected records, grouping, and performing aggregate functions, but these basic four operations are enough to get us started using a database from C# code. Let us now examine the set of database classes collectively known as ADO.NET, which you will use to access the database.

The ADO.NET Classes

ADO.NET is the portion of the .NET library that deals with databases. Table 15.3 lists some of the common ADO.NET classes.

Table 15.3 – Classes of ADO.NET

Class	Description
DataSet	A set of database tables that can be filled from a database and used as a disconnected database
DataTable	A collection data rows and the columns that define their structure
DataRow	A Database Record
DataView	A view of the data. Can be filtered for search criteria and sorted
DataRowView	A single row from a DataView
DataRelation	A Parent-Child relationship between tables

The classes in Table 15.3 organize the data into table structures. They are declared within the *System.Data* namespace. The DataSet class is one of the most useful classes in .NET because it encapsulates a collection of tables and the relationships between those tables. It is essentially a mini database that you can use in memory. You can also fill the DataSet with tables and data from some other database, giving you a local cache of data.

Roll Your Own Database

In this section we use the ADO.NET classes from Table 15.3 to define a database of customer information. We will define the structure of the database by adding columns to a table named Customers. Then we will load some sample data into the table and persist the data to an XML file. When the program runs again we will load the database from the XML file and print the data that it contains. The complete listing is shown in Example15_1.cs.

```csharp
// Example15_1.cs
using System;
using System.Text;
using System.Data;
using System.IO;

namespace csbook.ch15
{
    class CustomerDatabase
    {
        public void MakeFile()
        {
            DataSet ds = new DataSet();
            ds.DataSetName = "CustomerDatabase";

            DataTable custTable = new DataTable();
            custTable.TableName = "Customers";

            // this will be the primary key
            DataColumn custId = new DataColumn("CustID",
                                        typeof(int));
```

```
    custId.AutoIncrement = true;
    custId.AutoIncrementSeed = 101;
    custId.AutoIncrementStep = 1;

    custTable.Columns.Add(custId);

    // make this the primary key
    custTable.PrimaryKey = new DataColumn[] { custId };

    // add some fields for customer data
    custTable.Columns.Add(new DataColumn("Name",
                            typeof(string)));

    custTable.Columns.Add(new DataColumn("Phone",
                            typeof(string)));

    custTable.Columns.Add(new DataColumn("Email",
                            typeof(string)));

    // add the table to the DataSet
    ds.Tables.Add(custTable);


    // add some records to the table
    DataRow row;
    row = custTable.NewRow();
    row["Name"] = "Evy";
    row["Phone"] = "123-555-9876";
    row["Email"] = "evy@evymail.com";
    custTable.Rows.Add(row);

    row = custTable.NewRow();
    row["Name"] = "Jon";
    row["Phone"] = "123-444-7384";
    row["Email"] = "jon@jonsmail.com";
    custTable.Rows.Add(row);

    row = custTable.NewRow();
    row["Name"] = "Eric";
    row["Phone"] = "123-666-7398";
    row["Email"] = "eric@ericsmail.com";
    custTable.Rows.Add(row);

    // dump to XML
    ds.WriteXml("customers.xml");

    Console.WriteLine("The file was created");
}

public void ReadFile()
{
    DataSet ds = new DataSet();
    ds.ReadXml("customers.xml");
```

```
        foreach (DataRow row in ds.Tables[0].Rows)
        {
            // get the data
            string name = (string)row["Name"];
            string phone = (string)row["Phone"];
            string email = (string)row["Email"];

            // build the string
            StringBuilder builder = new StringBuilder();
            builder.AppendFormat(
                "Name: {0}\t Phone: {1}\t Email: {2}",
                name, phone, email);

            // write the string
            Console.WriteLine(builder.ToString());
        }
    }

    public void Test(){
        if (File.Exists("customers.xml"))
        {
            ReadFile();
        }
        else
        {
            MakeFile();
        }
    }

    static void Main(string[] args){
        CustomerDatabase db = new CustomerDatabase();
        db.Test();
    }
  }
}
```

Listing 15.1

Listing 15.1 defines the Customers table to have the structure shown below.

Table 15.4 – The Customers Table

Field Name	Type
CustID	int, auto increment, primary key
Name	String
Phone	String
Email	String

To define the table we create a DataTable object and set its TableName property to "Customers". The DataTable has a property named Columns, which is a collection of DataColumn objects that define the columns of the table. Another important property of the DataTable is the PrimaryKey property. The PrimaryKey property is an array of DataColumn objects. You can set the primary key by creating an array of one or more DataColumns from the table and assigning a reference to that array in the PrimaryKey property.

The DataColumn class has many properties, many of which you won't care about for the examples here. However, two important properties are the *Name* and *DataType*.

The *Name* property is a string value that names the field. When you access a column of a DataRow you can use this name as an index instead of an integer so you don't have to remember the order of the columns.

The *DataType* property stores an instance of the Type class containing the type of data the column will store. The data are stored in the fields as object references so you can use any C# data type. If the DataType of a column is int then you can set the column's AutoIncrement property to true. If the AutoIncrement property is true then the column's value will be set automatically from a counter variable that is incremented every time a new row is created. This guarantees that the field will hold a unique value for each row in the table and makes the field a good candidate to use as a primary key.

Defining the Table Structure

The following code segment defines the Customer table structure. The CustID field is defined as an auto counter field and used as the primary key.

```
DataTable custTable = new DataTable();
custTable.TableName = "Customers";

// this will be the primary key
DataColumn custId = new DataColumn("CustID", typeof(int));
custId.AutoIncrement = true;
custId.AutoIncrementSeed = 101;
custId.AutoIncrementStep = 1;

custTable.Columns.Add(custId);

// make this the primary key
custTable.PrimaryKey = new DataColumn[] { custId };

// add some fields for customer data
custTable.Columns.Add(new DataColumn("Name", typeof(string)));
custTable.Columns.Add(new DataColumn("Phone", typeof(string)));
custTable.Columns.Add(new DataColumn("Email", typeof(string)));
```

Reading Rows of Data

The DataTable also has a property named Rows that stores the rows
of data. The rows are actually objects of the DataRow class. The
DataRow stores a collection of values that you can read or write to
using an index. You can either use an integer if you know the order of
the columns or you can use the name of the field. The following code
segment loops through the table's rows and obtains references to the
Name, Phone, and Email fields.

```
foreach (DataRow row in ds.Tables[0].Rows)
{
    // get the data
    string name = (string)row["Name"];
    string phone = (string)row["Phone"];
    string email = (string)row["Email"];

}
```

The DataRow stores the values as object references so the data must
be cast to the appropriate type before we can use it. In this case we
used strings.

Adding Rows of Data

We obviously need to add new rows to the table too. To create a DataRow object we call the Table's NewRow method. That method will instantiate a DataRow object and set its auto increment field for the primary key. Then we can set the other values of the record and add the row into the Table's Rows collection.

```
DataRow row = custTable.NewRow();
row["Name"] = "Evy";
row["Phone"] = "123-555-9876";
row["Email"] = "evy@evymail.com";
custTable.Rows.Add(row);
```

Storing the Data as XML

The DataSet stores a collection of DataTables in its Tables property. To dump the entire DataSet to an XML file we need to call the DataSet's WriteXml method, passing the name of the file as a string. Reading the file back in is just a matter of calling the ReadXml method.

```
// dump to XML
ds.WriteXml("customers.xml");
...

ds.ReadXml("customers.xml");
```

Filtering the Data with the DataView

The DataView class can be used to create a new view of the table that can be filtered or sorted without affecting the underlying table. The DataView is similar to a table in that it has a collection of rows but the objects in the DataView's Rows collection are of type

DataRowView. You use the DataRowView the same as you would use a DataRow. You use the name of the field as an index to get the value from the column. Once you have a DataView you can filter or sort the data without affecting the actual table.

You create a DataView by passing a DataTable to the DataView constructor.

```
// create a view that can be filtered and sorted
DataView view = new DataView(ds.Tables[0]);
foreach (DataRowView drv in view)
{
    Console.WriteLine(drv["Name"].ToString());
}

// find the record for Rick
view.RowFilter = "Name = 'Evy'";
foreach (DataRowView drv in view)
{
    Console.WriteLine(drv["Name"].ToString());
}
```

In the code segment we create a DataView for the first DataTable in the DataSet's Tables collection. Then we loop through the Rows collection, printing out the Name field as we go. Then we filter the view so that view only contains records where the Name field is "Evy". The foreach loop iterates through each row in the view of "Evy" records and prints out the Name field.

Loading the DataSet From A DataSource

DataSets scale well because they offload much of the work from the database server. They are also efficient because you do not have to keep an open database connection, making more database connections available for other programs that need to connect to the same database.

To load a DataSet from a database you need to establish a connection to the database and issue a command to select data into the DataSet. This process requires a connection class, a command class, and an adapter class. The connection, command, and adapter that you use may depend on the type of database. Microsoft Access, for instance has an OLE DB provider. The classes used to connect to an OLE DB database are shown in Table 15.5. They are defined in the *System.Data.OleDb* namespace. There is a similar set of classes used to connect to a SQL Server database shown in Table 15.5.

Table 15.5 – OLEDB Database Classes

Class	Description
OleDbConnection	The physical database connection
OleDbCommand	A command to execute on the database
OleDbDataAdapter	Moves data between the DataSet and the physical Database using a connection and a command
OleDbDataReader	Can iterate results returned from a command

Now that you have been introduced to the ADO.NET classes it is time to write some real code. The example in the next section connects to Microsoft Access' Northwind Traders database using the OleDb classes.

Connecting to Access using OLE DB

In this section we will use the Northwind Trader database that installs (optionally) with Microsoft Access. The program is a Console Application that simply loads a DataSet from the Customers table of the database. Then we loop through the records, printing the CustomerName field to the screen.

```csharp
// Example15_2.cs
using System;
using System.Data;
using System.Data.OleDb;

namespace csbook.ch15
{
    class Example15_2
    {
        static void Main(string[] args)
        {
            string conString =
                @"Provider=Microsoft.JET.OLEDB.4.0;"
                + @"data source=c:\data\Northwind.mdb";

            // create an open the connection
            OleDbConnection conn =
                new OleDbConnection(conString);
            conn.Open();

            // create the DataSet
            DataSet ds = new DataSet();

            // create the adapter and fill the DataSet
            OleDbDataAdapter adapter =
                new OleDbDataAdapter("Select * from Customers",
                                                    conn);
            adapter.Fill(ds);

            // close the connection
            conn.Close();

            DataTable dt = ds.Tables[0];
            foreach (DataRow dr in dt.Rows)
            {
                Console.WriteLine(dr["CompanyName"].ToString());
            }
        }
    }
}
```

Listing 15.2

The listing first creates a connection string that provides information to the OleDbConnection class. Specifically, the connection string contains the provider for the database engine that we want to connect to and the data source, which in this case is a Microsoft Access file. If the file were password protected we would also specify a User ID and Password in the connection string. After creating the connection string the program creates an OleDbConnection object, passing the connection string as the argument.

Next the listing opens the database connection by calling the connection's Open method. It also creates an empty DataSet that will later be filled from the database.

The OleDbAdapter class encapsulates the command to fill the DataSet. We create the adapter by passing a SQL query string and the database connection to its constructor. This query string will select all fields of all rows from the Customers table. The adapter's Fill method will execute the query through the connection and load the results into the DataSet that we pass to it. The results include the data from the query as well as the metadata, defining its structure. When the call is complete the DataSet will contain a table with all the Customer records from the database. At that point we can close the database connection so that it can be used by some other application.

The tables within the DataSet are represented by the DataTable class. Each DataTable has a collection of DataRow objects storing the rows from the query. The foreach loop iterates through the DataRows, displaying the CompanyName field. The DataRow object uses the string "CompanyName" as an index to find the field of that name and retrieve its value. The value is returned as an object type. Calling the virtual ToString method will result in displaying the string value of the field.

Connecting to a SQL Server Database

The SQL Server versions of the connection, command, and adapter classes are listed below in Table 15.6. They are defined in the *System.Data.SqlClient* namespace.

Table 15.6 – SQL Server Database Classes

Class	Description
SqlConnection	The physical database connection
SqlDataCommand	A command to execute on the database
SqlDataAdapter	Moves data between the DataSet and the physical Database using a connection and a command
SqlDataReader	Can iterate results returned from a command

SQL Server also installs a copy of the Northwind Trader database. The next example is similar to the previous except that it uses the SQL Server versions of the connection and adapter.

While the previous listing used an adapter to execute a command internally and fill a DataSet, this example uses the command object directly. The program calls the SqlCommand object's ExecuteReader method, which returns a SqlReader object. Then it uses the SqlReader to loop through the records that have been returned.

```
// Example15_3.cs
using System;
using System.Data;
using System.Data.SqlClient;

namespace csbook.ch15
{
    class Example15_3
    {
        static void Main(string[] args)
        {
            // create an open the connection
            SqlConnection conn =
                new SqlConnection("Data Source=DESKTOP;"
                    + "Initial Catalog=Northwind;"
                    + "Persist Security Info=True;"
                    + "User ID=jeff;Password=password");

            conn.Open();

            // create a SqlCommand object for this connection
            SqlCommand command = conn.CreateCommand();
            command.CommandText = "Select * from Customers";
            command.CommandType = CommandType.Text;

            // execute the command that returns a SqlDataReader
            SqlDataReader reader = command.ExecuteReader();

            // display the results
            while (reader.Read())
            {
                string output = reader["CompanyName"].ToString();
                Console.WriteLine(output);
            }

            // close the connection
            reader.Close();
            conn.Close();
        }
    }
}
```

Listing 15.3

Data Binding

Window controls have the ability to bind their properties to the properties of other objects. When two properties are bound, a change in one is reflected in the other.

For example, consider the following listing for the *Student* class. The Student has two properties; the string value *Name* and the double value *Gpa*.

```
class Student
{
    private string name;
    private double gpa;

    public string Name
    {
        get { return name; }
        set { name = value; }
    }

    public double Gpa
    {
        get { return gpa; }
        set { gpa = value; }
    }
}
```

If we declare an instance of the Student as a member of a Windows Form we can bind the Name and Gpa properties to the Text properties of a pair of TextBoxes.

```
// create the student
student = new Student();
student.Name = "Jeff";
student.Gpa = 4.0;

// bind the properties
textBox1.DataBindings.Add(new Binding("Text", student, "Name"));
textBox2.DataBindings.Add(new Binding("Text", student, "Gpa"));
```

We can also put a Button on the Form that displays the current values of the student's Name and Gpa. This allows us to view the changes made to the object after we change the text in the TextBox.

```
private void testButton_Click(object sender, EventArgs e)
{
    MessageBox.Show("Name: " + student.Name
        + " GPA: " + student.Gpa);
}
```

Running the example we can see that when the form first opens the initial values are displayed.

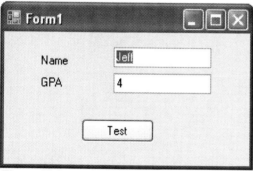

Figure 15.2

Then we can change the text in the text boxes and click the Test Button. The message box displays the values of the student object, which have been changed to the new values in the TextBoxes.

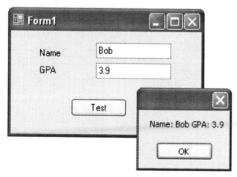

Figure 15.3

This type of data binding is called Simple Data Binding. We can also bind a ListBox control to an array or collection of data. Binding to a collection of data is called Complex Data Binding. To Bind the ListBox to a collection you set the ListBox's DataSource property. The ListBox will display the first public property of each item in the collection in its list. The next example binds an array of strings to a ListBox.

```
public partial class Form1 : Form
{
    string[] names =
        {
            "Jeff",
            "Rachel",
            "Katy",
            "Evy",
            "Ben"
        };

    public Form1()
    {
        InitializeComponent();
    }

    private void Form1_Load(object sender, EventArgs e)
    {
        listBox1.DataSource = names;
    }
}
```

When the form is displayed the names in the string array appear in the ListBox.

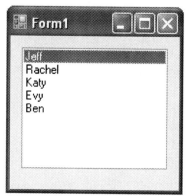

Figure 15.4

Using the DataGridView

The DataGridView is a control designed to be bound to database tables. You will find the DataGridView in the Data group on your Toolbox. In this section we will use the DataGridView to build a SQL interface for the Northwind Trader database. This application is surprisingly simple using the classes provided by ADO.NET.

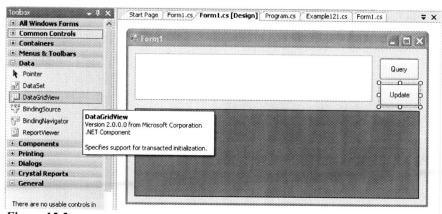

Figure 15.5

To create the user interface place a TextBox on the form and set its Multiline property to true. Then add two buttons, setting their Text properties to Query and Update. Finally, place a DataGridView component on the form. Your form might look something like the one in Figure 15.5.

Since we are going to connect to a Microsoft Access database we need to use the OleDb classes. At the top of the file you should add the following using statement to gain access to the System.Data.OleDb namespace.

```
using System.Data.OleDb;
```

The Form's Load event should create an OleDbConnection object, an OleDbCommand object, and a DataSet object. Each of these objects should be stored as members of your Form class.

```
private void Form1_Load(object sender, EventArgs e)
{
    // connect to the database
    string conString =
        @"Provider=Microsoft.JET.OLEDB.4.0;"
      + @"data source=c:\data\Northwind.mdb";

    // create an open the connection
    conn = new OleDbConnection(conString);

    command = conn.CreateCommand();

    // create the DataSet
    DataSet ds = new DataSet();
}
```

Next you need to implement the select button's Click handler. The method should start by clearing the DataSource property of the DataViewGrid and creating a fresh DataSet. Then it should reopen the connection. Set the Command object's CommandText property to the Text from the TextBox control. Then create an adapter with the command and fill the new DataSet. Finally, set the DataGridView's

DataSource property to the first table in the DataSet's Table collection.

```
private void button1_Click(object sender, EventArgs e)
{
    // clear the grids data source
    dataGridView1.DataSource = null;

    // create a new DataSet
    ds = new DataSet();

    // open the connection
    conn.Open();

    // run the query
    command.CommandText = textBox1.Text;
    adapter = new OleDbDataAdapter(command);
    adapter.Fill(ds);

    // close the connection
    conn.Close();

    // set the grid's data source
    dataGridView1.DataSource = ds.Tables[0];
}
```

The last step is to implement the Click event handler for the Update button.

```
private void button2_Click(object sender, EventArgs e)
{
    // clear the grids data source
    dataGridView1.DataSource = null;

    // open the connection
    conn.Open();

    // run the query
    command.CommandText = textBox1.Text;

    int affected = command.ExecuteNonQuery();
    MessageBox.Show("There were " + affected
            + " rows affected");

    // close the connection
    conn.Close();
}
```

The update button sets the DataGridView's DataSource property to null to clear the grid. Then it reopens the connection and sets the command object's CommandText property to whatever text is in the TextBox. This time the command is executed by the ExecuteNonQuery method. The ExecuteNonQuery method runs a command that updates or deletes records. It returns the number of rows affected by the command. Finally, the method displays a message box showing the number of rows affected and then closes the connection. Figure 15.6 shows a Select statement being executed on the database.

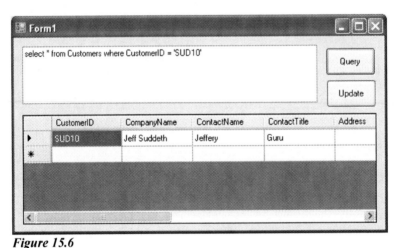

Figure 15.6

Figure 15.7 shows the update button being used to change the ContactTitle from Guru to Fool.

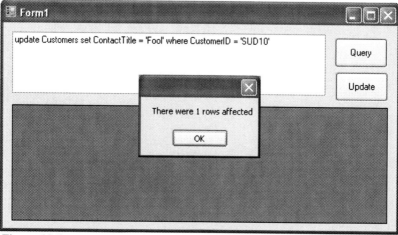

Figure 15.7

To verify that our update actually worked we can run the query again.

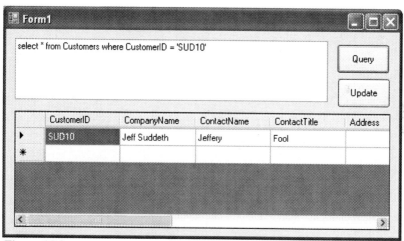

Figure 15.8

Chapter 16 – Using XML

XML stands for Extensible Markup Language. It is a self-describing data format that is useful in transferring data between systems. XML is especially useful with the Internet, where computers of many platforms exchange information.

.NET technology uses XML in many ways. If you happen to open your Visual Studio project files you will see that they are in XML format. The resource files used by the Visual Studio designer when you develop Windows programs are also XML files. And earlier in Chapter 15 you saw how the DataSet class uses XML files to persist the data from its tables.

There is a lot more to learn about XML than we can hope to cover in this chapter. In fact, there are complete books on the subject. In this section we will focus on simple XML documents and how to read and write them with C#. Standards for XML and related technologies have been developed by the World Wide Web Consortium, W3C. If you want to know more about these topics then you should begin with their website, http://www.w3.org/xml or purchase one of the many useful books covering the topic.

The Structure of XML Files

XML files are structured as a tree of XML *Elements*. There is one root element that contains child elements. Each of those child elements can contain child elements of its own, and so on. Each element begins and ends with a markup tag. The following statement is an example of an XML element named *Name* with the value "my name".

<Name> my name </Name>

An example of an XML file is the cust.xml file, shown below in Figure 16.1.

```
<?xml version="1.0" encoding="utf-8"?>
<CustomerRecord>
  <Name>Bob</Name>
  <Email>bob@bobsmail.com</Email>
</CustomerRecord>
```

Figure 16.1

The cust.xml file contains a root element named CustomerRecord which in turn, contains two child elements; *Name* and *Email*. The first line in cust.xml contains two important attributes. The version attribute tells the version of the XML rules that should be used to validate and parse the document. The encoding attribute tells which character set was used for generating the document. Both of those pieces of information can be used by XML parsers when loading the document.

Reading and Writing XML Documents

The industry standard interfaces for manipulating XML documents are the Document Object Model (DOM) and the Simple API for XML (SAX). Both of the technologies were developed by the W3C. The DOM is more flexible of the two, allowing you to move to different locations of the document to append, update, and remove elements. The SAX interface is for forward-only, sequential access of the elements.

.NET provides several classes for manipulating XML documents in the System.Xml namespace. The most common of them are listed below in Table 16.1.

Table 16.1 – XML Classes

Class Name	Description
XmlReader	Forward only, sequential iterator reading XML files, *abstract*
XmlWriter	Forward only, sequential writer to generate an XML document, *abstract*
XmlTextReader	Inherits XmlReader, reads XML document from a Text stream
XmlTextWriter	Inherits XmlWriter, streams XML to a text file
XmlDocument	Microsoft's implementation of the DOM
XmlNode	A single node from the XmlDocument
XmlNodeList	A list of nodes from the XmlDocument
XmlElement	A single element and its inner text

The XmlReader and XmlWriter are abstract classes so you cannot instantiate them directly. You will have to use their child classes for reading and writing XML as text files, such as the XmlTextReader and XmlTextWriter. The XmlDocument class is useful for loading XML from a file or for just parsing XML contained in a string variable. Once you load an XmlDocument you can select its XmlNodes individually or select an entire XmlNodeList. Later we will use the XmlElement class to create new nodes and append them into a document.

Using XmlTextReader and XmlTextWriter

The first XML example is Example16_1.cs. The Example contains two methods. The first is the WriteXml method, which generates an XML document. The second method is called ReadXml. The ReadXml method will load the document just created and iterate through the elements to find and print the Email field.

```
// Example16_1.cs
using System;
using System.Xml;
using System.IO;

namespace csbook.ch16
{
    class Example16_1
    {
        // create the file
        void WriteXml()
        {
            XmlTextWriter writer =
                    new XmlTextWriter("cust.xml",
                        System.Text.Encoding.UTF8);

            // set formatting to be indented
            writer.Formatting = Formatting.Indented;

            // start document and add root element
            writer.WriteStartDocument();

            // write the customer data
            writer.WriteStartElement("CustomerRecord");
            writer.WriteElementString("Name", "Bob");
            writer.WriteElementString("Email",
                                "bob@bobsmail.com");
            writer.WriteEndElement();  // end root element
            writer.WriteEndDocument(); // end document
            writer.Flush();
            writer.Close();
        }
```

```
        // read the file
        void ReadXml()
        {
            XmlTextReader reader =
                        new XmlTextReader("cust.xml");

            while (reader.Read())
            {
                // print only the email addresses
                if (reader.MoveToContent() ==
                            XmlNodeType.Element
                        && reader.Name == "Email")
                {
                    string email = reader.ReadElementString();
                    Console.WriteLine(email);
                }
            }
        }

        static void Main(string[] args)
        {
            // Test the methods
            Example16_1 ex = new Example16_1();
            ex.WriteXml();
            ex.ReadXml();
        }
    }
}
```

Listing 16.1

The XmlTextWriter class has several overloaded constructors. The version used by the WriteXml method takes a file name and an encoding parameter. We set the object's *Formatting* property to Formatting.Indented so that the resulting file is easier to read for us humans.

The WriteStartDocument method writes the top line of the document.

```
<?xml version="1.0" encoding="utf-8"?>
```

To create the CustomerRecord element we must begin and end with markup tags.

```
<CustomerRecord> ... </CustomerRecord>
```

Those tags are created by the WriteStartElement and WriteEndElement methods. In between we use WriteElementString to create the elements within the CustomerRecord. In the end we complete the document by calling WriteEndDocument, Flush, and Close.

The XmlTextReader class is an iterator that internally stores the current node. The reader's properties, such as Value and Name set their value from the current node. As the ReadXml method loops through the elements of the document it looks for the Email field. After each Read it calls MoveToContent and tests to see if the node's type is *Element* and if the node's Name is "Email". If so, it reads the value by calling GetElementString and prints it.

Using the XmlDocument Class

There are several ways to create XML documents. In the last section we created XML files with the XmlTextWriter class. Another way to create XML files is to use the XmlDocument class. The XmlDocument class stores the entire document in memory. Then you can use its WriteTo method to dump the document to a text file through an XmlTextWriter as the next example does.

```
// Example16_2.cs
using System;
using System.Text;
using System.Xml;
using System.IO;

namespace csbook.ch16
{
    class Example16_2
    {
        static void Main(string[] args)      .
        {
            // define an XML string
            string xml =
            "<CustomerRecord>"
                + "<Name>Katy</Name>"
                + "<Email>katy@katysmail.com</Email>"
        + "</CustomerRecord>";

            // load that string into an XmlDocument
            XmlDocument doc = new XmlDocument();
            doc.LoadXml(xml);

            // write it out to a file
            XmlTextWriter writer =
                    new XmlTextWriter("cust.xml",
                            System.Text.Encoding.UTF8);
            writer.Formatting = Formatting.Indented;

            writer.WriteStartDocument();
            doc.WriteTo(writer);
            writer.Close();
        }
    }
}
```

Listing 16.2

The Main method begins by creating an XML record in a string
variable. Then it uses the XmlDocument's LoadXml method to parse
that string into the XmlDocument. Once again the XmlTextWriter
class is used to write the document to file. However, this time we pass
the writer to the XmlDocument's WriteTo method and let it to the
work instead of us having to call all those WriteStart, WriteElement,
and WriteEnd methods ourselves. After all, the XmlDocument knows
what its nodes are. So why shouldn't it do the work?

Selecting Nodes from the XmlDocument

The next example loads an XML file into an XmlDocument object.
The document consists of a single element named CustomerRecord
that contains a Name and Balance. The program reads the Name and
Balance information and prints them to the screen.

```
// Example16_3.cs
using System;
using System.Xml;
using System.IO;

namespace csbook.ch16
{
    class Example16_3
    {
        static void Main(string[] args)
        {
            // load the document from file
            XmlDocument doc = new XmlDocument();
            doc.Load("cust.xml");

            // find the Name node
            XmlNode custNode =
                doc.SelectSingleNode("CustomerRecord");
            XmlNode nameNode = custNode.SelectSingleNode("Name");
            string name = nameNode.InnerText;

            XmlNode balanceNode =
                    custNode.SelectSingleNode("Balance");
            string balance = balanceNode.InnerText;

            Console.WriteLine("Name: {0}\t Balance: {1}",
                name, balance);
        }
    }
}
```

Listing 16.3

The cust.xml document is shown below for reference.

```
<?xml version="1.0" encoding="utf-8"?>
<CustomerRecord>
   <Name>Bob</Name>
   <Balance>125.00</Balance>
</CustomerRecord>
```

Figure 16.1

After the *doc* object parses the file, the document's FirstChild property will refer to the root element, the CustomerRecord node. From the FirstChild element we can then get to the *Name* element by calling the FirstChild's SelectSingleNode method and passing the string "Name" as the argument. The SelectSingleNode method will return an XmlNode object referring to the Name element. The InnerText property of the XmlNode holds the value that we want to display.

Fortunately XML documents can contain more than one record. Otherwise they would only be useful in single record transactions. We could change cust.xml to the following file in Figure 16.2.

```
<?xml version="1.0" encoding="utf-8"?>
<CustomerTable>
        <CustomerRecord>
                <CustID>101</CustID>
                <Name>Bob</Name>
                <Balance>125.00</Balance>
        </CustomerRecord>
        <CustomerRecord>
                <CustID>102</CustID>
                <Name>Steve</Name>
                <Balance>45.00</Balance>
        </CustomerRecord>
        <CustomerRecord>
                <CustID>103</CustID>
                <Name>Mike</Name>
                <Balance>9999.00</Balance>
        </CustomerRecord>
</CustomerTable>
```

Figure 16.2

The XmlDocument class has a method named
GetElementsByTagName that grabs elements whose name matches
the parameter you pass and returns them in an XmlNodeList object.
Then you can loop through the elements in that list and call
SelectSingleNode on each of them to get the specific fields from each
of the records.

```
XmlNodeList custNodes
    = doc.GetElementsByTagName("CustomerRecord");

foreach (XmlNode cust in custNodes)
{
    XmlNode custIDNode = cust.SelectSingleNode("CustID");
    string custId = custIDNode.InnerText;

    XmlNode nameNode = cust.SelectSingleNode("Name");
    string name = nameNode.InnerText;

    XmlNode balanceNode =
        cust.SelectSingleNode("Balance");
    string balance = balanceNode.InnerText;

    Console.WriteLine("ID: {0}\t Name: {1}\t Balance: {2}",
        custId, name, balance);
}
```

Adding Nodes to the Document

The last XML example that we will look at will add new nodes to an
existing document. The nodes are created as XmlElement objects by
the XmlDocument class' CreateElement method. The CreateElement
method takes a string parameter containing the name of the node.
Once a node is created you can set its InnerText property. You can
also append the node to its parent with the AppendChild method. See
listing 16.4 for an example.

```
// Example16_4.cs
using System;
using System.Xml;

namespace csbook.ch16
{
    class Example16_4
    {
        static void Main(string[] args)
        {
            // load the XML Document
            XmlDocument doc = new XmlDocument();
            doc.Load("cust.xml");

            // create a new customer node
            XmlElement newCustElement =
                    doc.CreateElement("CustomerRecord");

            // create the fields
            XmlElement custIdElement =
                    doc.CreateElement("CustID");
            XmlElement custNameElement =
                    doc.CreateElement("Name");
            XmlElement custBalanceElement =
                    doc.CreateElement("Balance");

            custIdElement.InnerText = "104";
            custNameElement.InnerText = "John";
            custBalanceElement.InnerText = "0.00";

            // add the fields to the new node
            newCustElement.AppendChild(custIdElement);
            newCustElement.AppendChild(custNameElement);
            newCustElement.AppendChild(custBalanceElement);

            // add the new customer to the document
            doc.DocumentElement.AppendChild(newCustElement);

            // persist the document
            XmlTextWriter writer = new XmlTextWriter("cust2.xml",
                            System.Text.Encoding.UTF8);
            writer.Formatting = Formatting.Indented;
            doc.WriteTo(writer);
            writer.Flush();
            writer.Close();
        }
    }
}
```

Listing 16.4

The program creates a node for the CustomerRecord and then creates three other nodes to store the CustID, Name, and Balance fields. The fields' values are set and then each field is appended to the new customer node through the call to its AppendChild method. Finally, the new customer node is itself appended into the document. The resulting output in Figure 16.3 shows that customer number 104 has been appended.

```xml
<?xml version="1.0" encoding="utf-8"?>
<CustomerTable>
     <CustomerRecord>
          <CustID>101</CustID>
          <Name>Bob</Name>
          <Balance>125.00</Balance>
     </CustomerRecord>
     <CustomerRecord>
          <CustID>102</CustID>
          <Name>Steve</Name>
          <Balance>45.00</Balance>
     </CustomerRecord>
     <CustomerRecord>
          <CustID>103</CustID>
          <Name>Mike</Name>
          <Balance>9999.00</Balance>
     </CustomerRecord>
     <CustomerRecord>
          <CustID>104</CustID>
          <Name>John</Name>
          <Balance>0.00</Balance>
     </CustomerRecord>
</CustomerTable>
```

Figure 16.3

Chapter 17 – Multithreaded Programming

The other day I saw an interesting display of multitasking. A man was drinking coffee, talking on his cell phone, and reading the newspaper while he was driving his car. Now *that* is multitasking! It is also something that I would not recommend for the risk of crashing your car. Fortunately, computers are much better at multitasking than humans are. However, while it is true that a computer does not have to worry about the risks of a physical crash, if we are not careful with our multitasking then our programs may still suffer a crash in another sense of the word.

Computers can perform multiple tasks at the same time by running each task in a separate thread. The CPU cycles through all running threads on the system, giving each a slice of time to do some work. Your programs can create new threads to perform multiple tasks concurrently. Your web browser for example, downloads several images and sound files (and ad banners and spyware) at the same time using multiple threads. You might also create a new thread to run a very time consuming report, handle a network request, or animate a sprite in your game, while your main thread is busily processing your program's message loop.

Creating Threads

You create a thread in C# by instantiating the Thread class. The Thread's constructor accepts a ThreadStart delegate as its parameter. The method that is encapsulated by the ThreadStart delegate is the method that the thread will call to do its work. Once the thread is created you begin its execution by calling its Start method.

The following example creates a thread that prints a line of text to the console window every second for five seconds.

```
// Example17_1.cs
using System;
using System.Threading;

namespace csbook.ch17
{
    class Example17_1
    {
        static void TimerMethod()
        {
            for (int i = 1; i < 6; i++)
            {
                Console.WriteLine(i);
                Thread.Sleep(1000);
            }
        }

        static void Main(string[] args)
        {
            // launch a thread that prints a line each second
            Thread t = new Thread(new ThreadStart(TimerMethod));
            t.Start();
            Console.WriteLine("Done");
        }
    }
}
```

Listing 17.1

Listing 17.1 includes the *System.Threading* namespace because that is where the Thread class and its ThreadStart delegate are defined. The Main method creates the thread by instantiating the Thread class with a new instance of the ThreadStart delegate that will call the TimerMethod method.

```
Thread t = new Thread(new ThreadStart(TimerMethod));
```

The call to the Thread object's Start method will begin execution of TimerMethod in the new thread. Immediately after starting the Thread the Main method prints the "Done" message to the console. The program's output, shown in Figure 17.1 shows that the "Done" message appears while the new thread is still executing.

The TimerMethod loops five times, printing its counter variable to the console. With each pass through the loop the method calls the static Thread.Sleep method to force the current thread to pause its execution for a thousand milliseconds.

```
1
Done
2
3
4
5
```

Figure 17.1

Background Threads and Program Termination

Normally a program ends when its Main method returns. With multithreaded programs there is more to the story. You may have noticed that with Example17_1.cs the Main method completed execution in less than a second but the program did not terminate until the TimerMethod was finished executing, about five seconds later.

.NET programs will not terminate until all *non-background* threads have terminated. Background threads are typically used for maintenance tasks. The .NET garbage collector for instance, runs in a background thread. By default when you create a thread it is *not* a background thread. To make it a background thread you must set the Thread object's *IsBackground* property to true. Changing the Main method to include the statement

```
t.IsBackground = true;
```

after creating the Thread will cause the program to terminate immediately after the Main method is finished executing, giving the output of Figure 17.2.

```
1
Done
```

Figure 17.2

Creating a Thread with Arguments

Requiring a ThreadStart method to take no arguments seems too limiting. After all, there are many tasks that would be executed in their own threads that might require parameters. You might, for instance need to start a thread that searches a file for information. Such a thread would certainly need to know the name of the file to search, as well as a string to search for.

One way to pass that information to a thread is to encapsulate the thread's method in a class with fields that store any parameters the thread might need. Listing 17.2 does just that.

```
// Example17_2.cs
using System;
using System.Threading;

namespace csbook.ch17
{
    class Example17_2
    {
        class TestThread
        {
            private string fileName;
            private string custRecord;

            public TestThread(string fn, string cr)
            {
                fileName = fn;
                custRecord = cr;
            }

            public void Test()
            {
                string output =
                    string.Format("Searching file {0} for"
                        + " Customer {1}",
                        fileName, custRecord);

                Console.WriteLine(output);

                // search the file ...
            }
        }

        static void Main(string[] args)
        {
            // create the TestThread object
            TestThread test = new TestThread("customers.dat",
                                             "Barney");

            // use the object's Test method as the ThreadStart
            Thread t = new Thread(new ThreadStart(test.Test));
            t.Start();
        }
    }
}
```

Listing 17.2

The constructor for the TestThread class accepts two parameters and stores them as members for the names of a file and a customer record. The Main method creates a TestThread object, setting the filename to "customers.dat" and the custRecord to "Barney". When the Thread is instantiated, the TestThread object's Test method is used as the starting point for execution. The Test method has access to the file name and customer record variables because they belong to the same object. By adding fields to the class, we can add any type of parameters that the thread's method would need.

A second way to pass parameters to a thread is by using a different type of delegate for the Thread constructor, one whose method signature expects a parameter of type object. The ThreadStartWithParameters delegate is new with .NET 2.0. Its signature is to return a void and accepted a single parameter of type object. Since any variable can be implicitly cast to an object type, such a method signature can accept any type of variable as its parameter.

When you create the thread with a ThreadStartWithParameters delegate then you must start the thread by calling the overloaded Start method that takes an object parameter. The object passed to the Start method will be passed as the parameter to the thread's method. Listing 17.3 uses the ThreadStartWithParameters delegate.

```
// Example17_3.cs
using System;
using System.Text;
using System.Threading;

namespace csbook.ch17
{
    struct Customer
    {
        public int recNo;
        public string custName;
```

```
        public void PrintRecord()
        {
            StringBuilder sb = new StringBuilder();
            sb.Append("<Customer>\n");
            sb.AppendFormat("\t<RecNo>{0}</RecNo>\n", recNo);
            sb.AppendFormat("\t<CustName>{0}</CustName>\n",
                                          custName);
            sb.Append("</Customer>");

            Console.WriteLine(sb.ToString());
        }
    }

    class Example17_3
    {
        static void PrintCustomer(object threadArg)
        {
            Customer cust = (Customer)threadArg;
            cust.PrintRecord();
        }

        static void Main(string[] args)
        {
            Customer cust;
            cust.recNo = 1;
            cust.custName = "Jeff";

            Thread t
                = new Thread(new
                ParameterizedThreadStart(PrintCustomer));
            t.Start(cust);
        }
    }
}
```

Listing 17.3

The Example17_3 class defines a method named PrintCustomer, which returns void and accepts an object type as parameter. The method assumes that the runtime type of the object passed to it will be an instance of Customer, a struct defined near the top of the listing. The Customer struct contains record number and a customer name fields.

The Main method first declares a variable of the Customer type and initializes its recNo and custName members to 1 and "Jeff". Then Main creates the Thread object, this time using a ParameterizedThreadStart delegate. The method used for the starting point of the thread is the PrintCustomer method, described earlier. Finally, the Main method calls the Thread's Start method. The output of the program is shown in Figure 17.3.

```
<Customer>
        <RecNo>1</RecNo>
        <CustName>Jeff</CustName>
</Customer>
```

Figure 17.3

Thread Synchronization

Threads often need to access the same data and resources, a situation which can give rise to synchronization problems. Consider the following code segment.

```
static string data = null;

static void ThreadMethod()
{
    while (true)
    {
        // do some work...

        if (data != null && data.ToUpper() == "QUIT")
        {
            Console.WriteLine("Exiting Thread");
            break;
        }
    }
}
```

In the code segment ThreadMethod uses a string variable named data to determine when to break from the loop. The if condition appears to do the responsible thing, checking that the variable is not null before invoking its ToUpper method.

The problem is that in a multithreaded program you never know when the CPU will switch from one thread to another. It is possible that the thread running this code segment could lose the CPU just after the data != null condition evaluates to true. Then some other thread might set the data variable to null before control of the CPU returns to this thread. Unfortunately for this thread, it already determined that data is *not* null. So it thinks it is safe to call data.ToUpper() when it is not. The thread invokes the ToUpper method on a null object, resulting in a thrown exception.

This type of problem, where data is getting changed by other threads when this thread is out of context, is called a *Race Condition*. The Race Condition is one of the most common types of bugs in multithreaded applications. By synchronizing the threads, we can guarantee that only one thread has access to the shared variable at a time and avoid the race conditions. The next few sections describe some of the synchronization objects provided by .NET.

The Monitor Class

One synchronization class provided by .NET is the Monitor class. A Thread can acquire a lock on an object by passing it to the Monitor's static Enter method. When the thread is finished with its shared data it can release the lock by passing the same object to the Monitor's static Exit method. If a thread calls Monitor.Enter with an object that another thread has already obtained a lock on then the thread will block until the lock is released through the Monitor.Exit call.

```
Object myLock = new myLock();
Monitor.Enter(myLock);
intList.Add(100);
Monitor.Exit(myLock);
```

The segment above acquires a lock an object named myLock and then adds the value 100 to a list of integers. Then the segment releases the lock through the call to Monitor.Exit. It is guaranteed that only one thread can use intList at a time provided that each thread first acquires the lock.

Since calling Monitor.Enter will block other threads until Monitor.Exit is called, it is very important to make sure that Monitor.Exit is called after each call to Monitor.Enter. One way to make this guarantee is to use a try-finally block.

```
try
{
    Monitor.Enter(myLock);
    intList.Add(100);
}
finally
{
    Monitor.Exit(myLock);
}
```

In the code segment above it is guaranteed that the finally block will execute, even if an exception is thrown by the intList.Add method. So the lock on myLock will always be released.

The lock statement

Another way to acquire a lock on an object is to use the lock statement. The lock statement will make the Monitor calls for us in an exception-safe manner.

```
// shared object used as a lock
object myLock = new object();

lock(myLock)
{
    // using a shared object
    intList.Add(100);
}
```

The lock statement accepts a reference type as its argument. When another thread calls lock on the same object, that thread will be blocked until this one exits the locked block of code.

The next example uses the lock statement to synchronize two threads. The threads are the producer and consumer of integers. The Producer thread creates random integers and puts them on a Queue<int>. The Consumer thread dequeues the integers and consumes them. Each thread method prints a message to the console to log its activity.

```
// Example17_4.cs
using System;
using System.Threading;
using System.Collections;
using System.Collections.Generic;

namespace csbook.ch17
{
    class ProducerConsumer
    {
        Random r;
        Queue<int> q;

        public ProducerConsumer()
        {
            q = new Queue<int>();
            r = new Random();
        }

        public void Producer()
        {
            int num = 0;
            int sleepTime = 0;

            while (true)
            {
                // get random values to produce and sleep
                lock(this)
                {
                    num = r.Next();
                    sleepTime = r.Next() % 20;
                    q.Enqueue(num);

                    // log activity
                    Console.WriteLine("Producer produced: {0}",
                        num);
                }
```

```
                    // go to sleep for a while
                    Thread.Sleep(sleepTime);
            }

        }

    public void Consumer()
    {
        int num = 0;
        int sleepTime = 0;

        Thread.CurrentThread.Name = "Consumer";
        while(true)
        {

            lock(this)
            {
                sleepTime = r.Next() % 10;

                try{
                    num = q.Dequeue();
                }
                catch(InvalidOperationException ex)
                {
                    // queue is empty
                    Console.WriteLine("Consumer: {0}",
                            ex.Message);
                }

                Console.WriteLine("Consumer consumed: {0}",
                        num);

            }
            Thread.Sleep(sleepTime);
        }
    }
}

class Example17_4
{
    static void Main(string[] args)
    {
        ProducerConsumer pc = new ProducerConsumer();

        // producer thread
        Thread producer =
            new Thread(new ThreadStart(pc.Producer));

        // consumer thread
        Thread consumer =
            new Thread(new ThreadStart(pc.Consumer));
```

```
        // start producing and consuming
        producer.Start();
        consumer.Start();

        // stop threads when user hits enter
        Console.ReadLine();
        try
        {
            producer.Abort();
            consumer.Abort();
        }
        catch (Exception)
        { }
        }
    }
}
```

Listing 17.4

The ProducerConsumer class of Listing17.4 contains two fields; a
queue of integers and a random number generator. The Produer thread
uses the random number generator to produce integers. Both threads
use the random number generator to sleep for a random duration of
time.

Both thread methods belong to the same object, which is the object
used as the lock. Each thread obtains a lock on the object through the
lock statement. When the producer has the lock it generates a random
number and adds it to the Queue. When the consumer has the lock it
attempts to dequeue an integer for consumption. If the queue is empty
when Dequeue is called then an InvalidOperationException is thrown.

The Main method of the program instantiates the ProducerConsumer
object and launches each thread. Then it waits for the user to press
enter while the other two threads produce and consume integers. After
the user presses enter the Main method uses the Abort method to
terminate both threads.

Deadlocks

When designing your multithreaded programs it is important to watch for deadlock situations. A deadlock can occur when two threads are trying to lock the same two objects and in turn block each other. The first thread may lock lock1 and then attempt to lock lock2. The second thread first locks lock2, which causes thread1 to block when it tries to lock that object. Then before thread2 releases lock2 it tries to lock lock1, which is already locked by thread1 causing thread2 to block.

The following two thread methods demonstrate a potential deadlock situation.

```
public void Thread1()
{
    while (true)
    {
        lock (lock1)
        {
            Console.WriteLine("Thread1 has lock1");
            lock (lock2)
            {
                Console.WriteLine("Thread1 has lock2");

            }
        }
    }
}

public void Thread2()
{
    while (true)
    {
        lock (lock2)
        {
            Console.WriteLine("Thread2 has lock2");
            lock (lock1)
            {
                Console.WriteLine("Thread2 has lock1");
            }
        }
    }
}
```

In the previous code segment, the Thread1 method locks *lock1* and then *lock2*. Simultaneously, Thread2 locks *lock2* and then *lock1*. It is likely that by the time Thread1 tries to lock lock2 it will already be locked by the Thread2 method, blocking Thread1. Likewise, by the time Thread2 tries to lock lock1, that lock will already have been obtained by Thread1, blocking Thread2. Both threads will be blocked, waiting for the other to release its lock.

The situation is similar to when four cars stop at an intersection and each waits for another to go first. The result is a deadlock where no one goes.

AutoResetEvents

In Listing 17.4, the consumer thread used a polling mechanism to consume integers from the queue. It executed a block of code every so often attempting to Dequeue an integer, hoping for the best. A more scalable solution is for the consumer thread to just block itself from execution until we know that there is work for it to do.

The AutoResetEvent is a synchronization object that two threads can use to coordinate their activities. The consumer thread can block itself while it waits for the event to be triggered. After the producer thread has created work for the consumer thread to do, the producer can trigger the event. The consumer will become unblocked, perform its work, and then wait for the event to trigger again.

The next example is a typical scenario in client-server programming. The server process will read a request from a client and then handle that request in a separate thread. In this example the client is the Console.ReadLine statement. A Reader thread reads commands from the keyboard and adds them to a queue. Then it triggers an AutoResetEvent to alert the worker thread that there is a message for it to process.

The Worker thread is a member of the same class as the Reader thread. The worker thread waits for the AutoResetEvent to trigger. When the event triggers, the worker thread is unblocked. It reads a message from the queue, processes the message, and then waits for the event to trigger again.

```csharp
// Example17_5.cs
using System;
using System.Collections.Generic;
using System.Threading;

namespace Example17_5
{
    class Program
    {
        class RequestHandler
        {
            Queue<string> messages;
            AutoResetEvent dataEvent;

            public RequestHandler()
            {
                messages = new Queue<string>();
                dataEvent = new AutoResetEvent(false);
            }

            public void Worker()
            {
                while (true)
                {
                    dataEvent.WaitOne();
                    lock (this)
                    {
                        try
                        {
                            string s = messages.Dequeue();
                            Console.WriteLine("Worker: {0}", s);
                        }
                        catch (InvalidOperationException)
                        { }
                    }
                }
            }
```

```
    public void Reader()
    {
        string data = "";
        do
        {
            // read data
            data = Console.ReadLine();
            lock (this)
            {
                messages.Enqueue(data);
            }
            dataEvent.Set();
        } while (data.ToUpper() != "QUIT");
    }
}

static void Main(string[] args)
{
    RequestHandler rh = new RequestHandler();

    Thread readerThread =
        new Thread(new ThreadStart(rh.Reader));

    Thread workerThread =
        new Thread(new ThreadStart(rh.Worker));

    readerThread.Start();
    workerThread.Start();

    workerThread.IsBackground = true;

}
}
}
```

Listing 17.5

The Mutex Class

The Mutex is another synchronization object that you can use in your programs. Like the Monitor class, you request to obtain a lock on the Mutex. If the Mutex is locked by another thread then the current thread blocks until the Mutex is available. The difference is that the Mutex is owned by the kernel of the operating system and can be shared by threads running in other programs. This allows you to synchronize threads running in different processes.

The disadvantage is that using a Mutex requires more processing and can affect the performance of your application. If your threads only need to be synchronized with other threads in the same process then the Monitor or Lock statement should be used instead.

The Mutex has 5 overloaded constructors. The one we will discuss here uses 2 arguments. The first is a bool parameter that indicates whether or not you want ownership of the Mutex when it is created. The second parameter is a string specifying the name of the Mutex. If a Mutex with that same name exists on the system then you will obtain a reference to the existing Mutex. If it does not exist then the Mutex will be freshly created.

To request ownership of the Mutex, you call its WaitOne method. It is possible to for the same thread to call WaitOne repeatedly, without blocking itself. However, when the method is finished with the thread-safe code it must call ReleaseMutex the same number of times it called WaitOne, otherwise other threads may still be blocked.

The following code segment uses a Mutex in a thread method named Thread1. The method performs some work that requires thread-safe access to system resources.

```
class MutexExample
{
    Mutex mtx;

    public MutexExample()
    {
        mtx = new Mutex(false, "MyMutex");
    }

    public void Thread1()
    {
        mtx.WaitOne();

        // do thread safe work

        mtx.ReleaseMutex();
    }
}
```

Thread Pools

The ThreadPool class is provided by .NET to make multithreaded programs more efficient. There is a significant amount of time involved in creating and starting a new thread. The ThreadPool circumvents this startup time by creating the threads ahead of time. Consider the following program, which is a basic server program that reads requests from a TCP socket.

```
// Example17_6.cs
using System;
using System.Net;
using System.Net.Sockets;
using System.Threading;

namespace csbook.ch17
{
    class Example17_6
    {
        static void Main(string[] args)
        {
            IPAddress [] addresses =
                    Dns.GetHostAddresses("localhost");

            TcpListener listener =
                    new TcpListener(addresses[0], 9956);

            listener.Start();
            while (true)
            {
                // get the next connection
                TcpClient client = listener.AcceptTcpClient();

                // create the session object
                ClientSession sess =
                    new ClientSession(client);

                // handle the request in a seperate thread
                Thread t =
                new Thread(new ThreadStart(sess.HandleRequest));
                    t.Start();
            }
        }
    }
}
```

Listing 17.6

Network programming is not covered until Chapter 18 so we will side step the few lines of network code at the top of the Main method and focus on the performance issue with this application. The problem is inside the while loop.

With each pass through the loop the program calls the TcpListener's AcceptTcpClient method. That method will block until there is a client connection and then return that connection as a TcpClient object. TcpClient is a class provided by .NET to encapsulate a network connection. Through a TcpClient object we can exchange requests and replies with other processes that may be running on the same computer or across the network.

For this example we created a class named ClientSession to handle each new client connection. Its implementation is not shown in the listing so that we can focus on the Main method but the class could look something like the following.

```
class ClientSession
{
    TcpClient client;

    public ClientSession(TcpClient tcpClnt)
    {
        client = tcpClnt;
    }

    public void HandleRequest()
    {
        // handle request ...
    }
}
```

The ClientSession class encapsulates a TcpClient, which it receives through its constructor. The HandleRequest method would read and process the request from the client.

After the Main method creates the ClientSession it launches a new thread to call the HandleRequest method. This way the main thread can listen for the next connection while the existing connections are serviced in their own threads.

```
// handle the request in a seperate thread
Thread t = new Thread(new ThreadStart(sess.HandleRequest));
t.Start();
```

For many server applications this design will be sufficient. However, for very busy or time-critical servers you may want to avoid the time it takes to start a new thread. Consider server that sends an order to the stock market. If your order goes into the market's queue even a nanosecond before the other guy, you win. Every CPU cycle counts.

The server from Listing 17.7 can be optimized by using the ThreadPool class instead of creating a new thread for each connection. The ThreadPool will execute a task in its own thread by running the method from an existing thread. When the method call is finished the thread will stick around so that it can be reused.

To use the ThreadPool you call its QueueUserWorkItem method, which takes 2 parameters. The first is a WaitCallback delegate, which will be used to invoke the thread method. Its method signature is to return void and accept a single parameter of the object type. The second parameter to QueueUserWorkItem is an object reference that the ThreadPool will pass to the method that it invokes through the WaitCallback delegate. You can use this second parameter to pass an object as a parameter to the thread method.

The following code segment could be used as a thread startup method when using the ThreadPool.

```
static void ThreadMethod(object arg)
{
    ClientSession sess = (ClientSession)arg;
    sess.HandleRequest();
}
```

The ThreadMethod accepts an object reference as its argument. It expects that reference to be an instance of ClientSession and casts the argument to that type. Then it calls the HandleRequest method.

We can now change the implementation of our server so that it uses the ThreadPool to handle client requests.

```
// Example17_7.cs
using System;
using System.Net;
using System.Net.Sockets;
using System.Threading;

namespace csbook.ch17
{
    class ClientSession
    {
        TcpClient client;

        public ClientSession(TcpClient tcpClnt)
        {
            client = tcpClnt;
        }

        public void HandleRequest()
        {
            // handle request ...
        }
    }

    class Example17_7
    {
        static void Main(string[] args)
        {

            IPAddress[] addresses =
                Dns.GetHostAddresses("localhost");

            TcpListener listener =
                new TcpListener(addresses[0], 9956);

            listener.Start();
```

```
while (true)
{
    // get the next connection
    TcpClient client = listener.AcceptTcpClient();

    // create the session object
    ClientSession sess = new ClientSession(client);

    // The ThreadPool will execute the method on a
    // separate thread as soon as one is available.
    ThreadPool.QueueUserWorkItem(
        new WaitCallback(ThreadMethod), sess);

}
}

static void ThreadMethod(object arg)
{
    // The ClientSession object was passed to
    // the QueueUserWorkItem method so we get it
    // hear and tell it to do its thing.
    ClientSession sess = (ClientSession)arg;
    sess.HandleRequest();
}
}
}
```

Listing 17.7

Now each time a new connection arrives, the while loop will create a new ClientSession object and pass it along with the WaitCallback delegate to the ThreadPool through the QueueUserWorkItem method. Each ClientSession will be handled in its own thread and the overall application performance will be greatly improved since most of the thread creation work will be done ahead of time.

Chapter 18 – Network Programming

Software is typically written in layers, called tiers. In a 2-Tier system the first tier provides the user interface. The second tier is usually some kind of database server. In an N-Tier system the responsibilities of user interface, business logic, network messaging, security, and database access have all been divided up into different objects that may be executing on different machines. Using an N-Tier architecture makes your applications more scalable because the workload is divided up more efficiently.

In this chapter we will be developing a client-server system to demonstrate network programming with .NET. The Framework Class Library provides classes to handle many of the network programming issues. In fact, simple client and server programs can be created with surprisingly few lines of code. However, we will at least need a brief introduction to network programming concepts to get started.

A Network Programming Overview

Programs that communicate over a network are the coolest to write. There is just something about doing something on one computer that has an affect on another.

In this section there will be a brief and very practical introduction to network programming. The topic itself is vast and could fill several books. Thanks to .NET we only need a bit of background information and then we can let the .NET classes do the real work for us. However, before we can use those .NET classes we must know what to use them for. Let's begin by looking at the protocols that make it possible for one computer to find another on the network.

Network Protocols

Before a program can talk to another on the network there are a set of protocols that both programs must follow. These protocols exist in independent layers so you can swap out one protocol without affecting the other layers. Most of these protocols are implemented inside the .NET library and you really only need to understand them if you are doing something more advanced than what we are showing here. However, I want to mention a couple of the most important ones.

Before you connect to a program across the network you must know the address of that computer. The most common protocol for identifying computers on a network is *IP* or *Internet Protocol*. An IP address is a set of 4 numbers separated by dots, such as 172.16.1.135. This address is kind of like a phone number for a computer. You may have more than one IP address because your computer can be connected to more than one network at the same time. You can find out which addresses your computer is using by going to a DOS window and typing the *ipconfig* command.

The other protocol you should be aware of is *TCP* or *Transmission Control Protocol*. TCP is the protocol that defines how the data is packaged up and sent from one computer to another.

So IP is used to identify a computer on the network and TCP is used to send data back and forth. As a .NET network programmer you typically don't need to worry about the implementations of those protocols. Instead, to send a message from a client program to a server your client will create a socket and connect it to the server. Once the connection is established you can call a method to send the request and then, if needed, you can read a reply. To connect to a server you need to know its address and port, which are covered in the next section.

Host Names, Addresses, and Ports

Computers are usually given names to make them easier to find on a network. A name is much easier to remember than an IP address because the names can describe the primary purpose of the computer, such as "JeffsLaptop" or "SQLServer1" but if you prefer, you could name them after the planets of the solar system, your favorite Star Wars characters, or whatever floats your boat. The names themselves are aliases for the IP address.

One name that exists on every computer is "localhost". The name localhost refers to the loopback interface on your computer. It allows your computer to talk to itself even if it is not currently connected to a network. The loopback address is always 127.0.0.1. For our application the client and server will both be running on the same machine so we will be using the loopback interface.

Your computer may have another name and IP address that you or your network administrator has set up. If you don't know the name of your computer you can get it by going to a DOS window and typing the *hostname* command.

Since a computer can run more than one server at a time, you need to know more than just the address of the computer where the server is running before you can talk to it. Each server listens for knew connections on its own port, identified by an integer. The server can use any available port as long as the client and server both know which port to use. However, there are some special ports that you should avoid because they are used for common applications like email and web servers. If you choose a port number that is over 6000 then you should be safe.

So for a client program to connect to a server it needs to know the server's IP address and port. If you don't want to have to remember the server's IP address then you can use the hostname instead. If you understand that then you are ready to create your first network program.

Creating a Simple Network Application

Here is a quick summary of creating a network application. You need to create two programs; the client and the server. The server will listen on a port for a new connection, which will be initiated by the client. The client will then send a request to the server. The server will handle the request and send a reply. Then both parties can close the connection and the transaction is complete. If this sounds like a lot to learn, don't worry. .NET provides classes to make this extremely simple.

In this section we will create a simple network application. The client will connect to the server and send a message containing a string. The server will send a reply back to the client. The reply will contain the original string sent by the client as well as its own string and an error code.

The SimpleMessage Library

To make our client and server understand each other they both need to know the format of the message. For our simple message we will use a class named SimpleMessage, containing a string for the request and an enumeration value for an error code. There will also be a string for the reply that will be filled in by the server. Since the client and server projects will both need access to the SimpleMessage class it is best to create a Class Library project for the SimpleMessage and set references to it from the client and server projects.

To begin, start Visual Studio .NET or whatever editor you are using and create a Class Library project named SimpleMessage. Rename the source file to SimpleMessage.cs and write the following code.

```
// SimpleMessage.cs
using System;

namespace csbook.ch18{
    [Serializable]
    public enum SimpleMessageError
    {
        ERROR_SUCCESS,
        ERROR_FAILED,
    }

    [Serializable]
    public class SimpleMessage
    {
        public string request;
        public string reply;
        public SimpleMessageError error;

        public SimpleMessage(){
            request = "";
            reply = "";
            error = SimpleMessageError.ERROR_SUCCESS;
        }
    }
}
```

Listing 18.1

Listing 18.1 defines the SimpleMessageError enumeration, which stores an error code for our simple server. Because it is so simple, the ERROR_SUCCESS and ERROR_FAILED values will be sufficient.

The SimpleMessage class contains two strings to hold the request and the reply. The request will be the text sent by the client to the server. The server will reply by creating a new SimpleMessage containing the original request. Then it will set the reply string and the error code. For our example the returned error code will always be success unless the client sends the "TEST ERROR" request.

The SimpleMessage and the SimpleMessageError are both defined with the Serializable attribute. This is necessary because the message object is going to be serialized to a network stream. To *serialize* an object is to write its contents to a stream such as a NetworkStream or a FileStream in a way that the object can be recreated from the stream later. This is how we will pass messages between the client and server. We will serialize them and deserialize them through the Network Stream.

Before continuing, make sure your SimpleMessage project compiles. If you are using Visual Studio .NET then just right click the project in the Solution Explorer and choose *Build*. If you are compiling the file by hand then remember to compile it as a library with the following command.

```
csc /out:SimpleMessage.dll /target:library SimpleMessage.cs
```

Figure 18.1

A Simple TCP Server

Now we will create the server. If you are using Visual Studio .NET, right click the solution in the Solution Explorer and click on *Add* and *New Project*. Choose the *Console Application* as the project type and name it *SimpleServer*.

Add a reference in the project to the SimpleMessage project that you created in the last section by right clicking *References* in the Solution Explorer and choosing *Add Reference*. When the Add Reference dialog appears, click on the *Projects* tab and then double click the SimpleMessage project.

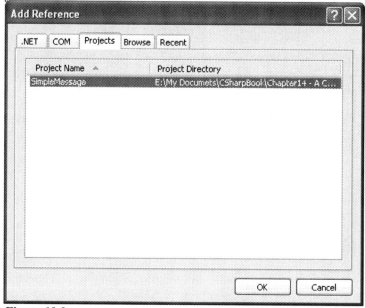

Figure 18.2

The SimpleMessage reference should appear in your list of references in the Solution Explorer. Now you are ready to write the code for the server.

Rename the Program.cs file to SimpleServer.cs by right clicking it in the Solution Explorer and choosing *Rename* from the context menu. Then write the following code in the SimpleServer.cs file.

```
// SimpleServer.cs
using System;
using System.Net;
using System.Net.Sockets;
using System.Threading;
using System.Runtime.Serialization.Formatters.Binary;

namespace csbook.ch18
{
    class SimpleServer
    {
        static void Main(string[] args)
        {
            // get an array of IP addresses localhost
            IPAddress[] addressList =
                Dns.GetHostAddresses("localhost");

            // create the TcpListener
            TcpListener listener =
                    new TcpListener(addressList[0], 9954);

            // start listening
            listener.Start();

            // go into a loop, waiting for new connections
            while (true)
            {
                TcpClient client = listener.AcceptTcpClient();

                // assign a thread to handle this request
                ThreadPool.QueueUserWorkItem(
                        new WaitCallback(RequestThread), client);
            }
        }
```

```
static void RequestThread(object arg)
{
    // cast the argument to the TcpClient
    TcpClient client = (TcpClient)arg;

    // create a BinaryFormatter to
    // serialize and deserialize the objects
    BinaryFormatter formatter = new BinaryFormatter();

    // get the NetworkStream
    NetworkStream stream = client.GetStream();

    // read the request
    SimpleMessage req =
        (SimpleMessage)formatter.Deserialize(stream);

    // handle the request and send back a reply
    Console.WriteLine("the request was {0}",
        req.request);

    SimpleMessage reply = new SimpleMessage();
    reply.request = req.request;
    reply.reply = "Thank you";
    if (req.request.ToUpper() == "TEST ERROR")
    {
        reply.error = SimpleMessageError.ERROR_FAILED;
    }

    formatter.Serialize(stream, reply);

    stream.Close();
    }
}
```

Listing 18.2

The Main method is short. It obtains a list of IP addresses for the "localhost" machine and uses the first address to listen for incoming requests. The TcpListener class is used to listen for incoming requests. Its constructor takes the IPAddress and port that client programs will connect to.

The TcpListener's Start method is called to put the listener in listening mode. Then the method goes into a loop listening for new connections. Inside the body of the loop the code will block on the AcceptTcpClient method until there is a new connection. When the connection is received it is passed to the ThreadPool so that it can be handled in a separate thread. The Main method then loops around and waits for the next connection.

The RequestThread method reads a request from the TcpClient socket and sends a reply. The method uses a BinaryFormatter object to deserialize the SimpleMessage object from the network stream. The Deserialize method returns an object type so we have to cast it to the type of object that this server is expecting. In this case the server is expecting a SimpleMessage object.

After the RequestThread method processes the request it creates a new SimpleMessage object to send as the reply. The BinaryFormatter's Serialize method will write the reply object to the stream so that it can be read back by the client program. Finally, we close the stream and the transaction is complete.

Compile the SimpleServer project, either from within Visual Studio .NET or by hand to be sure that there are no errors. If you compile by hand then remember to add the reference to the SimpleMessage.dll using the command shown in Figure 18.3.

```
csc /out:SimpleServer.exe /reference:SimpleMessage.dll SimpleServer.cs
```

Figure 18.3

If all goes well then you have a TCP Server program. If not then you have some errors to correct. Check your source code for differences from the listing and make sure you added the reference to the SimpleMessage project. If you are compiling from the command line then check your compiler command.

You can run the server now if you want to but it won't do anything until a client connects to it. So let's create the client program next.

A Simple TCP Client

Add a new Console Application to your solution and name it SimpleClient. Rename the Program.cs file to SimpleClient.cs and write the following code.

```
// SimpleClient.cs
using System;
using System.Net;
using System.Net.Sockets;
using System.Runtime.Serialization.Formatters.Binary;

namespace csbook.ch18
{
    class SimpleClient
    {
        static void Main(string[] args)
        {
            // create a TcpClient
            TcpClient client = new TcpClient();

            // connect to the server using the
            // correct hostname and port number
            client.Connect("localhost", 9954);
            if (client.Connected == false)
            {
                Console.WriteLine("Failed to connect");
                return;
            }

            // send a request
            SimpleMessage msg = new SimpleMessage();
            msg.request = "Cool Beans!";

            BinaryFormatter formatter = new BinaryFormatter();
            NetworkStream stream = client.GetStream();
            formatter.Serialize(stream, msg);

            // read the reply
            SimpleMessage reply =
                (SimpleMessage)formatter.Deserialize(stream);
```

```
        if (reply.error == SimpleMessageError.ERROR_SUCCESS)
        {
            Console.WriteLine("Success: {0}", reply.reply);
        }
        else
        {
            Console.WriteLine("Failed: {0}", reply.reply);
        }

        client.Close();
    }
  }
}
```

Listing 18.3

Listing 18.3 creates a TcpClient object and connects it to "localhost" using port 9954, which should match the same port number that the server is listening to.

The listing creates a SimpleMessage object and sets the request string to "Cool Beans!". The program creates a BinaryFormatter object to handle the serialization of the SimpleMessage objects. It also obtains the NetworkStream from the connected TcpClient. Then the program calls the BinaryFormatter's Serialize method to send the request to the server. Finally, the Deserialize method is called to read the reply.

Testing the Application

The best way to test the client and server programs is to run them both through the debugger. If you right click on the solution in the Solution Explorer you can click on *Set Startup Projects* from the context menu that appears. The dialog box shown in Figure 18.4 will appear, allowing you to choose which programs execute when you press F5.

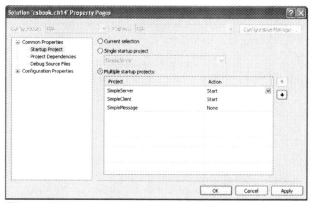

Figure 18.4

Click on the *Multiple startup projects* radio button. Then click in the combo box in the *Action* column to choose *Start* for the SimpleServer and SimpleClient projects. You can also specify the order of startup by selecting a row in the projects list and clicking the up and down arrows to the right. Make sure that SimpleServer is started before the client by selecting its row and clicking the up arrow until SimpleServer is on top. Then click the OK button.

With the SimpleClient.cs file open in Visual Studio .NET, set a breakpoint on the last line of the Main method. Otherwise the program's console window will disappear before you have a chance to see its output. When you press F5 the server will start, followed by the client. The server output is shown in Figure 18.5.

the request was Cool Beans!

Figure 18.5

The output from the SimpleClient program is shown in Figure 18.6.

Success: Thank you

Figure 18.6

Index

About the Author

Jeff Suddeth first learned to program when he was 12 years old on a Texas Intstruments TI-99 4A by typing in the source code of games from the backs of computer magazines. As a consultant or fulltime employee, he has written software for the Insurance and Financial industries using several languages and platforms. At this time he lives in the Chicago suburbs with his wife and 3 children.

Lightning Source UK Ltd.
Milton Keynes UK
14 August 2009

142688UK00001B/305/A